THE POLITICS OF CLIMATE CHANGE AND UNCERTAINTY IN INDIA

This book brings together diverse perspectives concerning uncertainty and climate change in India. Uncertainty is a key factor shaping climate and environmental policy at international, national and local levels. Climate change and events such as cyclones, floods, droughts and changing rainfall patterns create uncertainties that planners, resource managers and local populations are regularly confronted with. In this context, uncertainty has emerged as a "wicked problem" for scientists and policymakers, resulting in highly debated and disputed decision-making.

The book focuses on India, one of the most climatically vulnerable countries in the world, where there are stark socio-economic inequalities in addition to diverse geographic and climatic settings. Based on empirical research, it covers case studies from coastal Mumbai to dryland Kutch and the Sundarbans delta in West Bengal. These localities offer ecological contrasts, rural–urban diversity, varied exposure to different climate events, and diverse state and official responses. The book unpacks the diverse discourses, practices and politics of uncertainty and demonstrates profound differences through which the "above", "middle" and "below" understand and experience climate change and uncertainty. It also makes a case for bringing together diverse knowledges and approaches to understand and embrace climate-related uncertainties in order to facilitate transformative change.

Appealing to a broad professional and student audience, the book draws on wide-ranging theoretical and conceptual approaches from climate science, historical analysis, science, technology and society studies, development studies and environmental studies. By looking at the intersection between local and diverse understandings of climate change and uncertainty with politics, culture, history and ecology, the book argues for plural and socially just ways to tackle climate change in India and beyond.

Lyla Mehta is a Professorial Fellow at the Institute of Development Studies at the University of Sussex, UK, and a Visiting Professor at the Norwegian University of Life Sciences.

Hans Nicolai Adam is a Research Scientist at the Section for Water and Society at the Norwegian Institute for Water Research (NIVA) in Oslo, Norway.

Shilpi Srivastava is a Research Fellow at the Institute of Development Studies, University of Sussex, UK.

"From climate change to Covid 19, we are living in a highly uncertain world – yet also one of intense politics of life, knowledge and policy around what uncertainty means and for whom. Unpacking these politics in relation to some of India's most dynamic yet vulnerable places, this volume combines sophisticated conceptual analysis with new empirical insights aimed at charting transformative future pathways. Compelling reading for scholars and practitioners alike."

– Melissa Leach, Director, Institute of
Development Studies, UK

"This volume deepens our understanding of the tremendous uncertainties that climate change is introducing in different ecologies in India. The authors also highlight how affected communities are dealing with the impacts of these uncertainties on their livelihoods. It is this micro-level perspective that gives the book its distinctive value."

– Jairam Ramesh, Member of Parliament and
former Minister of Environment and Forests, India

"Addressing the existential challenge of climate change is compounded by the contested nature of knowledge on climate change impacts and solutions. By interrogating how experts, knowledge intermediaries and everyday people address uncertainties about climate change, this book provides a framework for how we know, and therefore, communicate, about climate change. Building on empirical cases from India, but with implications for wider geographies, the authors powerfully argue for appreciation of diverse ways of knowing and plural rather than unitary solutions, thereby contributing both to conceptual literature and climate practice."

– Navroz K. Dubash, Centre for Policy Research, India

"Climate change is rife with uncertainties, starting from what will change, how much and when to how it will affect our day-to-day lives and what can we do to adapt to these changes. As an atmospheric scientist, I have always focused on minimizing the uncertainty in climate projections with the expectation that it will lead to better adaptation strategies. But this book shows us that uncertainty is so deeply ingrained in the whole process that is may be better to 'embrace rather than eliminate uncertainty.' I particularly liked the case study approach that allowed me to understand how climate risk is perceived at grassroots level. Overall, I strongly recommend this book for climate scientists interested in expanding their understanding of uncertainty in climate change."

– Somnath Baidya Roy, Centre for Atmospheric Sciences,
Indian Institute of Technology Delhi, India

Pathways to Sustainability Series
Series Editors:
Ian Scoones and Andy Stirling
STEPS Centre at the University of Sussex

Editorial Advisory Board:
Steve Bass, Wiebe E. Bijker, Victor Galaz, Wenzel Geissler, Katherine Homewood, Sheila Jasanoff, Melissa Leach, Colin McInnes, Suman Sahai, Andrew Scott

This book series addresses core challenges around linking science and technology and environmental sustainability with poverty reduction and social justice. It is based on the work of the Social, Technological and Environmental Pathways to Sustainability (STEPS) Centre, a major investment of the UK Economic and Social Research Council (ESRC). The STEPS Centre brings together researchers at the Institute of Development Studies (IDS) and SPRU (Science Policy Research Unit) at the University of Sussex with a set of partner institutions in Africa, Asia and Latin America.

Titles in this series include:

The Politics of Uncertainty
Challenges of Transformation
Edited by Ian Scoones and Andy Stirling

Transformative Pathways to Sustainability
Learning Across Disciplines, Cultures and Contexts
The Pathways Network

The Politics of Knowledge in Inclusive Development and Innovation
Edited by David Ludwig, Birgit Boogaard, Phil Macnaghten and Cees Leeuwis

Building Innovation Capabilities for Sustainable Industrialisation
Renewable Electrification in Developing Economies
Edited by Rasmus Lema, Margrethe Holm Andersen, Rebecca Hanlin and Charles Nzila

The Politics of Climate Change and Uncertainty in India
Edited by Lyla Mehta, Hans Nicolai Adam and Shilpi Srivastava

For more information about this series, please visit: *www.routledge.com/Pathways-to-Sustainability/book-series/ECPSS*

THE POLITICS OF CLIMATE CHANGE AND UNCERTAINTY IN INDIA

Edited by
Lyla Mehta, Hans Nicolai Adam and
Shilpi Srivastava

Cover image: © Participant, Patharpratima photovoice group

First published 2022
by Routledge
4 Park Square, Milton Park, Abingdon, Oxon OX14 4RN

and by Routledge
605 Third Avenue, New York, NY 10158

Routledge is an imprint of the Taylor & Francis Group, an informa business

© 2022 selection and editorial matter, Lyla Mehta, Hans Nicolai Adam and Shilpi Srivastava; individual chapters, the contributors

The right of Lyla Mehta, Hans Nicolai Adam and Shilpi Srivastava to be identified as the authors of the editorial material, and of the authors for their individual chapters, has been asserted in accordance with sections 77 and 78 of the Copyright, Designs and Patents Act 1988.

The Open Access version of this book, available at www.taylorfrancis.com, has been made available under a Creative Commons Attribution-Non Commercial-No Derivatives 4.0 license

Trademark notice: Product or corporate names may be trademarks or registered trademarks, and are used only for identification and explanation without intent to infringe.

British Library Cataloguing-in-Publication Data
A catalogue record for this book is available from the British Library

Library of Congress Cataloging-in-Publication Data
Names: Mehta, Lyla, editor. | Adam, Hans Nicolai, editor. | Srivastava, Shilpi, editor.
Title: The politics of climate change and uncertainty in India / edited by Lyla Mehta, Hans Nicolai Adam and Shilpi Srivastava.
Description: New York, NY : Routledge, 2022. | Series: Pathways to sustainability | Includes bibliographical references and index.
Subjects: LCSH: Economic development—Environmental aspects—India. | Climatic changes—Government policy—India. | Environmental policy—India.
Classification: LCC HC440.E5 P65 2022 (print) | LCC HC440.E5 (ebook) | DDC 338.954—dc23/eng/20211006
LC record available at https://lccn.loc.gov/2021039123
LC ebook record available at https://lccn.loc.gov/2021039124

ISBN: 978-1-032-19079-2 (hbk)
ISBN: 978-1-032-19078-5 (pbk)
ISBN: 978-1-003-25758-5 (ebk)

DOI: 10.4324/9781003257585

Typeset in Bembo
by codeMantra

CONTENTS

Lists of illustrations ix
Notes on contributors xi
List of acronyms xv
Preface and acknowledgements xvii

1 Climate change and uncertainty: politics and perspectives 1
  Shilpi Srivastava, Lyla Mehta and Hans Nicolai Adam

2 Uncertainty from "above": diverse understandings, politics and implications 27
  Lyla Mehta, Hans Nicolai Adam, Mihir R. Bhatt, Synne Movik, Lars Otto Naess and Shilpi Srivastava

3 Uncertainty and environmental change: Kutch and the Sundarbans as environmental histories of climate change 55
  Vinita Damodaran, Rohan D'Souza and Subir Dey

4 Between the market and climate change: uncertainty and transformation in Kutch 83
  Shilpi Srivastava, Lyla Mehta, Lars Otto Naess, Mihir R. Bhatt and V. Vijay Kumar

5 The certainty of uncertainty: climate change realities of the Indian Sundarbans 107
  Upasona Ghosh, Darley Jose Kjosavik and Shibaji Bose

6 **Climate change and uncertainty in India's maximum city, Mumbai** 134
Hans Nicolai Adam, Synne Movik, D. Parthasarathy, Alankar, N.C. Narayanan and Lyla Mehta

7 **Bridging gaps in understandings of climate change and uncertainty** 161
Synne Movik, Mihir R. Bhatt, Lyla Mehta, Hans Nicolai Adam, Shilpi Srivastava, D. Parthasarathy, Espen Sjaastad, Shibaji Bose, Upasona Ghosh and Lars Otto Naess

8 **Conclusion** 186
Hans Nicolai Adam, Lyla Mehta and Shilpi Srivastava

Index *191*

ILLUSTRATIONS

Figures

1.1	A dwelling on the verge of being washed away in Ghoramara Island, Sundarbans, India	1
1.2	Photovoice engagement with women in a pastoral community in Kutch	8
2.1	Flooding in Mumbai during the monsoon	27
3.1	A sketch of the history of Cutch	58
3.2	Early survey and mapping of Sundarbans 1794	66
4.1	Coastal infrastructure projects undermine pastoralism in Kutch	83
5.1	Precarious fishing in the Indian Sundarbans	107
6.1	Koli fishers and urban expansion in Mumbai	135
7.1	Roundtable engagement in Gujarat, 2018	161
8.1	Recognising the multiple values of mangroves is important to sustain lives, livelihoods and adaptation pathways	186

Tables

3.1	Table showing climate-related events in 19th century Kutch	63
5.1	The climate shock history of Ghoramara Island. Compiled from the Participatory Hazard Ranking exercise in Ghoramara, 2016, by the authors	115

CONTRIBUTORS

Alankar is a Researcher with the SARAI Programme at the Centre for the Study of Developing Societies (CSDS), Delhi, and an Assistant Professor in the Department of Political Science, Ram Lal Anand College, University of Delhi, India. He received his doctoral degree from the Centre for the Study of Law & Governance, Jawaharlal Nehru University (India). His areas of interest include politics of water management, climate change impacts on marginalised communities and contested urbanisation.

Hans Nicolai Adam is a Research Scientist at the Section for Water and Society at the Norwegian Institute for Water Research (NIVA) in Oslo, Norway. He has a background in economics and completed a PhD in Development and Environment Studies from the Norwegian University of Life Sciences, Ås Norway. His research interests encompass interdisciplinary themes that concern climate change adaptation, science–policy interphase, knowledge politics, urban governance, and rural and indigenous people's rights and livelihoods. He is also actively engaged in different capacity-building projects against marine litter in South and South-East Asia.

Mihir R. Bhatt is currently working on uncertainty, transformation, cascading risks and co-location of hazards with All India Disaster Mitigation Institute (AIDMI) across 80 districts and 60 cities in India and in the five neighbouring countries through policy shaping, pilot projects, and co-learning. He is a Founder Member of Sphere India network of practitioner; Duryog Nivaran network on alternative thinking on disaster risk reduction; on the board of International Humanitarian Studies Association. He was Russel E. Train Fellow 1997; Eisenhower Fellow 2000; Ashoka Fellow 2004; and a Fellow at FXB Center for Health and Human Rights, Harvard School of Public Health.

Shibaji Bose is an independent consultant whose work draws on long-term visual ethnography and participatory visual action research in remote and climatically fragile zones in South Asia to help mediate between dominant and implicit narrative spaces.

Vinita Damodaran is a Professor of South Asian History and the director of the Centre for World Environmental History at the University of Sussex. Her work ranges from the social and political history of Bihar to the environmental history of South Asia, including using historical records to understand climate change in the Indian Ocean World. Her publications include *The British Empire and the Natural World: Environmental Encounters in South Asia* (2010) and *The East India Company and the Natural World* (2014).

Subir Dey is an Assistant Professor in the School of Arts and Sciences at Azim Premji University, Bangalore, India. Subir has taught history at Delhi University for three years. He is also a research associate with the Centre for World Environmental History, University of Sussex. He received his doctoral degree from the Centre for Historical Studies, Jawaharlal Nehru University, New Delhi. He has worked on unearthing histories of rural migration, social mobility and land use policy changes in colonial Assam. His broad research interests include exploring linkages between modern migration, resource politics and climate change in South Asia.

Rohan D'Souza is a Professor in the Graduate School of Asian and African Area Studies, Kyoto University. His PhD was awarded from the Centre for Historical Studies (Jawaharlal Nehru University, India). He was elected General Secretary of the Jawaharlal Nehru University Students Union (1989–1990) on the political platform of the All India Students Federation. An environmental historian by training, his current research interests and publications cover themes in political ecology, sustainable development and modern technology.

Upasona Ghosh is a Senior Lecturer at the Indian Institute of Public Health, Bhubaneswar, India. She has a PhD in Anthropology and MPhil in Women Studies (West Bengal State University, Kolkata). In her decade-long ethnographic research, she has focused on the linkage between climate, society and well-being in environmentally marginal environments. Her research further explores the history of marginalisation and political ecology to unearth experiential voices of actors and their actions towards sustainable pathways.

Darley Jose Kjosavik is a Professor of International Development Studies in the Department of International Environment and Development Studies, Norwegian University of Life Sciences (NMBU). She has an interdisciplinary academic background with a PhD in Development Studies. Her research interests include political economy of environment and development with special reference to marginalised social groups; gender and development; conflict, peacebuilding and development; sustainable development and climate change. Her research spans South Asia (particularly India) and Africa. She has published widely and her publications include *Political Economy of Development in India: Indigeneity in Transition in the State of Kerala* (with Nadarajah Shanmugaratnam), published by Routledge, 2015.

D. Parthasarathy is a Professor at the Department of Humanities and Social Sciences, IIT Bombay and Associate Faculty at the Centre for Policy Studies, and the Interdisciplinary Programme in Climate Studies at IIT Bombay. His specialisations and areas of interest include disaster governance, climate change vulnerability and transformation, coastal transformation and conflicts, legal pluralism and resource governance and urban studies. He is a social scientist who has worked with multi-disciplinary teams on issues related to urban flooding, coastal vulnerability, fisher well-being, climate change-related uncertainties and transformation, rural development, and gender inequalities.

Lyla Mehta is a Professor at the Institute of Development Studies and a Visiting Professor at the Norwegian University of Life Sciences. She uses the case of water and sanitation to focus on the politics of gender, scarcity, rights and access to resources, resource grabbing, and power and policy processes. Her work also focuses on climate change and uncertainty and forced displacement and resistance. She has extensive research and field experience in India and southern Africa, and is co-editor of *Environment and Planning E*. Her most recent book is *Water for Food Security Nutrition and Social Justice*, published by Routledge.

Synne Movik is an Associate Professor at the Department of Urban and Regional Planning, Norwegian University of Life Sciences, Ås, Norway. She is an environmental scientist focusing on the politics of environmental governance. Her research centres on understanding how certain ideas and "ways of doing" gain traction in environmental policy and planning and linkages with particular knowledge and power relations. She has worked in India, South Africa and Tanzania on environmental governance, livelihoods and the politics of access to water, energy and forests.

Lars Otto Naess is a Research Fellow and co-leader of the Resource Politics and Environmental Change Cluster, Institute of Development Studies, UK. He is a social scientist with 25 years of experience in work on climate change, development and agriculture. His research centres on the social and institutional dimensions of tackling climate change in a multi-risk context and the political economy of policy processes on climate change at the national and sub-national levels. His work has a strong focus on the social differentiation of climate change, including justice and equity.

N.C. Narayanan is a Professor at the Centre for Technology Alternatives for Rural Areas (CTARA), Associate Faculty of Centre for Policy Studies and Interdepartmental Programme on Climate Change of Indian Institute of Technology (IIT), Bombay. He works in the area of water policy and governance with normative concerns of sustainability and equity as pointers.

Espen Sjaastad is a Professor in the Department of International Environment and Development Studies (Noragric) at the Norwegian University of Life Sciences, with training in natural resource economics and institutional economics. His research interests include poverty, rural livelihoods and the environment, and economic and social analysis of land rights. His geographical emphasis has mainly been on Southern Africa and East Africa but also on India, West Africa and Norway.

Shilpi Srivastava is a Research Fellow at the Institute of Development Studies, UK. A political sociologist with interdisciplinary training in political science, law and governance and development studies, she has worked extensively on issues of water politics, regulation and rights. Her current research explores the cross-sectoral linkages between water and climate change. She draws on qualitative and participatory methods to explore the everyday encounters of marginalised communities with the changing climate as they intersect with wider issues in political economy and institutional politics. She is also the series co-editor for the Palgrave Pivot series on *Global Challenges in Water Governance*.

V. Vijay Kumar is the Director of Gujarat Institute of Desert Ecology, Bhuj, Gujarat. He has a PhD in Biosciences from Saurashtra University, Rajkot and 30 years of experience in the field of wetland ecology, herpetology, wildlife conservation and management, climate change, and grassland and saline land restoration/reclamation.

ACRONYMS

AWS	Automatic Weather Stations
BMC	Brihanmumbai Municipal Corporation
BRIMSTOWAD	Brihanmumbai Storm Water Drain System
BSF	Border Security Force
CBOs	Community-Based Organisations
CCD	Climate Change Department
CIDO	City and Industrial Development Corporation
CSOs	Civil Society Organisations
CSR	Corporate Social Responsibility
CPWD	Central Public Works Department
EIAs	Environmental Impact Assessments
EIC	British East India Company
GBM	Ganga–Brahmaputra–Meghna
GCMs	General Circulation Models
GHG's	Green House Gases
GUIDE	Gujarat Institute of Desert Ecology
HYV	High-Yielding Varieties
IK	Indigenous Knowledge
IMD	Indian Meteorological Department
INDCs	Intended Nationally Determined Contributions
IPCC	Intergovernmental Panel on Climate Change
MMRDA	Metropolitan Region Development Authority
MoES	Ministry of Earth Sciences
MRDPA	Mithi River Development and Protection Authority
MSPCB	Maharashtra Pollution Control Board
NAPCC	National Action Plan on Climate Change
NCMRF	National Centre for Medium Range Forecast

NDRF	National Disaster Response Force
NEERI	National Environmental Engineering Research Institute
NGOs	Non-Governmental Organisations
ORF	Observer Research Foundation
RCMs	Regional Climate Models
RCPs	Representative Concentration Pathways
SAPCC	State Action Plans on Climate Change
SEZs	Special Economic Zones
SHGs	Self-Help Groups
SIAs	Social Impact Assessments
SLR	Sea-Level Rise
STS	Science and Technology Studies
TISS	Tata Institute of Social Sciences

PREFACE AND ACKNOWLEDGEMENTS

As we finalise this volume during the COVID-19 pandemic, extreme weather events such as cyclones, floods and heatwaves have had devastating impacts on countries in the global North and South. Clearly, we are living in an uncertain world with a lot of politics concerning the causes and impacts of extreme events, alongside what uncertainties mean for different people in different places.

Uncertainty is a key factor shaping climate and environmental policy at international, national and sub-national levels. This book examines the concept of uncertainty in relation to climate change and unpacks the diverse discourses, practices and politics of uncertainty. The starting premise is that scientific projections of uncertainty (the "above") often overlook the lived realities of people who deal and live with this uncertainty on a daily basis ("below"). The book demonstrates deep differences in ways by which different actors from the "above", "middle" and "below" understand and experience climate change and uncertainty. It argues that diverse knowledges and approaches need to be deployed to understand and embrace climate-related uncertainties in order to facilitate transformative and socially just adaptation. It also stresses the need to promote transformative strategies that take the perspectives and interests of vulnerable communities who are at the forefront of climate change seriously.

The focus of the book is on India, one of the most climatically vulnerable countries in the world, which is also characterised by high levels of socio-economic diversity and inequality, as well as a range of geographical and climatic settings. The book captures this diversity through original empirical research from an urban environment (Mumbai, Maharashtra), dryland (Kutch, Gujarat) and a deltaic ecosystem (the Sundarbans, West Bengal). The localities offer ecological contrasts, rural–urban/peri-urban diversity, varied exposure to different climate shocks and diverse state and official responses. The chapters are authored by an interdisciplinary team of leading researchers from anthropology, sociology, economics, history, political science and the natural sciences.

This book presents findings of the Research Council of Norway-funded project "Climate change, Uncertainty and Transformation" (Project number 235449). We are grateful to the Research Council of Norway for their generous financial support and thank in particular Eivind Hoff-Elimari and Carina Leander of the Klimaforsk programme. The project was led by the Department of International Environment and Development Studies (Noragric) at the Norwegian University of Life Science (NMBU), and we are grateful to Noragric colleagues, in particular, the then Head of Department Poul Wisborg for his support and encouragement. We also thank Susan Brosstad, Anna Holm, Sidsel Gulbrandsen, Geir Jaegersen, Ingunn Andersen and Jayne Lambrou for their crucial support around the finance and administration over the life of the project. From IDS, Sarah Ollerenshaw offered efficient budget support to the project. Lyla Mehta was the Project Leader and worked closely with Hans Nicolai Adam and Shilpi Srivastava who were then postdoctoral researchers at Noragric (Norway) and the Institute of Development Studies (UK), respectively.

It has been a pleasure to work and interact with the project members and contributing authors Alankar, Mihir R. Bhatt, Shibaji Bose, Vinita Damodaran, Subir Dey, Rohan D'Souza, Upasona Ghosh, Darley Jose Kjosavik, Manasee Mishra, Lars Otto Naess, N.C. Narayanan, D. Parthasarathy, Espen Sjaastad, Synne Movik and V. Vijay Kumar during the research and publication process. We thank them all for investing so much energy, enthusiasm and passion in this project and have fond memories of the great project meetings and field trips we had together in Kutch, the Sundarbans and Mumbai. We owe a huge debt of gratitude to all the countless local people in the three research areas in Kutch, Mumbai and the Sundarbans whom we interviewed. We are extremely grateful to them for taking us into their homes, generously offering us their time and hospitality, and sharing their knowledge and experiences with us. We also thank the many others we interviewed in India, the United Kingdom and Norway and those who participated in the roundtables and project workshops in Delhi, Gandhinagar, Mumbai, Kolkata and Oslo.

We acknowledge several institutions that provided crucial support around administration and also facilitated fieldwork and workshops. We thank the Institute of Development Studies (IDS), UK, Norwegian Institute for Water Research (NIVA), Oslo, All India Disaster Mitigation Institute (AIDMI), Ahmedabad, Gujarat Institute of Desert Ecology (GUIDE), Bhuj, Indian Institute of Health Management Research (IIHMR), Kolkata, Indian Institute of Technology Bombay (IIT-B), Centre for the Study of Developing Societies (CSDS – Sarai), New Delhi and the STEPS Centre, UK.

Some chapters in this book also draw on ongoing research for the Tapestry project which is financially supported by the Belmont Forum and NORFACE Joint Research Programme on Transformations to Sustainability, which is co-funded by ESRC, ISC, JST, RCN and the European Commission through Horizon 2020 under grant agreement no. 730211.

The book is part of the ESRC STEPS Centre series on Pathways to Sustainability. We thank the STEPS Centre for supporting a small earlier project that helped develop initial ideas around uncertainty and climate change and also thank Ian Scoones for his constant interest and support. At Routledge, we thank Grace Harrison and Rosie Anderson for so enthusiastically embracing this project and efficiently facilitating its swift publication. We are grateful to Ruby Utting for her excellent support in finalising the volume and Shibaji Bose for his generous support with the artwork and photos. All responsibility for errors and omissions in the book rest with us, the editors of the volume. We dedicate this book to poor and marginalised people at the frontline of climate change whose voices, perspectives and experiences are too often missed in official climate change policies and discourses.

Lyla Mehta, Hans Nicolai Adam and Shilpi Srivastava
July 2021

1
CLIMATE CHANGE AND UNCERTAINTY

Politics and perspectives

Shilpi Srivastava, Lyla Mehta and Hans Nicolai Adam

FIGURE 1.1 A dwelling on the verge of being washed away in Ghoramara Island, Sundarbans, India (Photo credit: Shibaji Bose).

Introduction

Climate change is one of the most critical development challenges of our times. Across the globe, a range of climatic shocks and stressors, often framed as

DOI: 10.4324/9781003257585-1

"extreme" or "freak events", in the form of floods, droughts, heatwaves and cyclones are intensifying and slowly becoming the new normal (IPCC 2018). Research over the past few decades has demonstrated clearly the links between anthropogenically induced emissions and climate change (IPCC 2014, 2018). Through modelling and analysis, a range of projections for the future have been presented and contested, triggering a new kind of regulatory politics on scenarios and pathways (Beck and Mahony 2017). However, despite these scientific advancements, uncertainties in climate change projections remain particularly high with respect to the scale, intensity and impact of climate change (Curry and Webster 2011). These uncertainties, combined with economic and political drivers of change, make local-level effects difficult to predict (IPCC-SREX 2012) and can also lead to challenges in climate change-related decision-making (Wilby and Dessai 2010)

Uncertainty is characterised by indeterminacies where not enough is known about the probabilities of a particular set of outcomes and where they cannot be calculated (Knight 1921). Unlike risk, where probabilities of both outcomes and likelihoods are known (Wynne 1992; Stirling 1999), uncertainty is a situation where one does not know the odds and the probabilities cannot be calculated (Scoones and Stirling 2020). Walker *et al.* (2003: 5) define uncertainty as "any deviation from the unachievable ideal of completely deterministic knowledge of the relevant system" and highlight the importance of understanding the various dimensions of uncertainty for response and action. Within climate change debates, uncertainty is often referred to as a "super wicked problem" or a "monster" (van der Sluijs 2005; Levin *et al.* 2012) and scientists are increasingly acknowledging that uncertainty is here to stay and it may not be entirely possible to reduce or control (IPCC 2014).

However, there are deep differences in the ways uncertainty is understood, communicated and configured in policy- and decision-making around climate change (see Chapter 2). More fundamentally, significant gaps remain between how uncertainty is dealt within climate science and policy (characterised as the "above" in this volume), how it is experienced by people in their everyday lives (characterised as the "below" in this volume;) and how it is mediated and translated by the "middle" (i.e. the knowledge brokers and intermediaries between the two). These issues are the core focus of the book. Introducing the heuristics of the "above", "middle" and "below", we argue that theorising about climate-related uncertainty by experts, modellers and policymakers may have very little to do with how local people (men, women, third gender who are, in turn, differentiated by age, ableism, class, caste, location and ethnicity) make sense of climate change and live with climate-related uncertainties in everyday settings (see Figure 1.1). We demonstrate in different empirical settings that the reaction from "above" has often been to minimise and control uncertainty and capture it through quantitative assessments and modelling exercises. However, global and regional climate models are less predictable at the local level, especially because climate change often interacts with wider socio-economic drivers of change, increasing local-level uncertainties. For example, as discussed in Chapter 2, climate change models are associated with a "cascade of uncertainties" that increase with downscaling. These relate to uncertainties in projections, response to changes at global and national scales and the spatial and temporal distribution of impacts, thus creating an "envelope of uncertainty" (Wilby and Dessai 2010). The empirical chapters on Kutch, the Sundarbans and Mumbai demonstrate this cascading view of uncertainty in this volume.

A growing number of authors have discussed key differences between how experts (be they policymakers or scientists) and local people view and experience climate change (e.g. Hastrup and Skrydrstup 2013; Rudiak-Gould 2013; Hulme 2015; Conway et al. 2019). These authors have attempted to validate the place-based knowledge and agency of local expertise vis-à-vis climate and its changes underlining the epistemic contrasts (see García-del-Amo et al. 2020 for Spain; Das 2021 for India). This book builds on this scholarship and demonstrates deep differences in the ways different actors understand and experience climate change and uncertainty. It argues that diverse knowledges and plural approaches need to be deployed to understand and embrace climate-related uncertainties to facilitate transformative and socially just adaptation. The voices and experiences from "below" matter because it is these vulnerable groups living on the frontline – and the least responsible for creating climate change – who bear the brunt of anthropogenic climate change. Thus, their knowledges, experiences and responses must inform and feed into wider climate debates and strategies. Our research from India's drylands, wetlands and coast reveals that, neglecting locally relevant and bottom-up perspectives can lead to interventions that exacerbate uncertainties and vulnerabilities of poor and marginalised social groups.

The book demonstrates that it is important to capture a range of perceptions, experiences and responses to climate change and uncertainty (cf. Crate and Nuttall 2009; Jasanoff 2010; Wynne 2010) to appreciate the diverse dimensions of climate and address appropriate strategies regarding both adaptation and mitigation that go beyond short-term incremental impacts and address structural change. For many vulnerable groups at the forefront of climate change, adapting through incremental changes is clearly not sufficient, both because of their limited adaptive capacity and the neglect of wider structural conditions of inequity, powerlessness and marginalisation which can enable maladaptation and intensify structural inequalities and local vulnerabilities (Eriksen et al. 2021). These call for deep-rooted structural transformations (O'Brien 2012).

This volume addresses these challenges and epistemological tensions by examining the concept of uncertainty in relation to climate change from various vantage points of the "above", "middle" and "below", with specific reference to India. It also explores to what extent and how these divides can be bridged so that new hybrid perspectives can facilitate more transformative pathways to adapt to climate change. Our core proposition is that investigating and unpacking the gaps in diverse conceptions of uncertainty can facilitate processes that embrace rather than eliminate uncertainty. This is because subjective judgements, multiple knowledges and interpretations around uncertainty tend to be the best way forward instead of a singular value or recommendation (Stirling *et al.* 2007; Leach *et al.* 2010; Eriksen *et al.* 2015; Nightingale *et al.* 2020). These can ultimately help promote adaptation and mitigation processes that are both socially just and responsive to the socio-ecological diversity of contexts.

Climate change and uncertainty in the Indian context

India is not only a global hotspot for climate change impacts (Mani *et al.* 2018) but also has large population sections that are highly vulnerable to the impacts from climate variability and change (IPCC 2014). The causes for this social vulnerability are manifold. The majority of India's population remains dependent on climate-sensitive livelihoods such as agriculture, fisheries, forestry and allied activities. Besides, widespread poverty and growing social, economic and political inequalities in both rural and urban areas adversely affect adaptive capacities of local populations. A recent IPCC report (2018) warns that if global temperatures were to rise beyond 1.5 °C, India faces the prospect of being hit by unprecedented climate extremes and a sharp rise in extreme vulnerabilities of its population by 2050, with some areas potentially becoming uninhabitable. In 2020, 75% of districts suffer from climate extremes, with interchanging floods and droughts causing most damages and a spike in such events specifically from 2005 onwards (Mohanty 2020). While extreme events are not new to India (see the historical analysis in Chapter 3), their frequency and severity have increased in recent years. India's pastoralists, farmers and fishers are severely affected because their traditional ways of living and coping with climate uncertainties are being tested as new uncertainties – which we term radical uncertainty – are threatening their livelihoods further (see Chapters 4–6). When new patterns (such as increased frequency or severity of floods) are witnessed in areas that are historically, for the most part, exposed to droughts (e.g. Kutch; Chapter 4), knowledge uncertainties abound as there is little or no prior experience or data to fall back on, giving rise to radical uncertainty. How should India prepare for climate action in the context of this radical uncertainty?

As an emerging economy, India is the third largest contributor to Green House Gases (GHGs) emissions globally, while also having one of the lowest GHG emissions per capita (Dubash 2019). Development inequalities are, however, not limited to differences between the global North and global South. As a recent study highlights in the Indian context (Lee *et al.* 2021), vast disparities exist between a growing middle- and upper-middle class and poorer communities in India,[1] the former having an up to seven times higher carbon footprint than the latter. How India will deal with climate change has consequently profound ramifications for its population and its social, environmental and economic policies as well as global climate action. Hence, it is important that development-focused interventions are implicitly intertwined with climate policy and their impacts on the ground (Dubash 2019).

At the national level, India's key strategy papers on climate change are the National Action Plan on Climate Change (NAPCC) (Government of India 2008), the State Action Plans on Climate Change (SAPCC) and, more recently, the Intended Nationally Determined Contributions (INDCs) (see MOEFCC 2015). These documents acknowledge the impacts of climate change on natural resources and people's livelihoods. As we also found in our research in particular contexts in Gujarat, Maharashtra and West Bengal, the official plans continue to place disproportionate emphasis on mitigation and issues of international equity and redistribution, while questions of adaptation, domestic equity and access to natural resources remain side-lined (Bidwai 2012; Venkatesh 2018). The NAPCC has also been criticised for being ill-suited to the Indian context, doing little to balance climate and development concerns and inter-state differences (Bidwai 2012; Dubash et al. 2018). The SAPCCs have seen poor implementation and limited participation by key stakeholders and practitioners in designing strategies and do not acknowledge variations in the ways climate change will play out across regions (see also Chapters 4–6) and the relative capacities of different states to respond to climate change (Dubash and Jogesh 2014; Kumar and Naik 2019). This is despite the initial and cautious optimism that SAPCCs could be a base for mainstreamed climate concerns into development planning (Dubash and Jogesh 2014).

While officials discuss adaptation and climate-friendly initiatives, often there is insufficient actionable planning and dedicated financial allocation for adaptation. The MGNREGA (the largest rural public works programme in the world) has, for instance, been mainstreamed to include climate adaptation concerns (Adam 2015). However, the "retrofitted" scheme is not tailored for taking on a dedicated climate adaptation role, lacking integration of participatory vulnerability assessments, planning or addressing of structural power imbalances (Eriksen et al. 2021). India's cities have also been found to sorely lack strategic integration of climate risks that are informed by principles of sustainable adaptation (Singh et al. 2021), as we also examine in Chapter 6 for Mumbai. This reflects a national trend wherein adaptation funds remain underutilised or diverted for different purposes (Venkatesh 2018). While India is on track to achieve – or even surpass – its ambitious INDCs, which is a positive signal, questions remain on the fundamental premise of being closely linked to a green economy discourse that is associated with business and market-friendly principles, technological optimism and neglect of issues concerning power inequity, marginalisation and resource distribution (Unmüßig et al. 2012).

Srivastava et al. (Chapter 4) discuss how recent mitigation efforts around renewable energy parks can contribute to spatial injustice by leading to further dispossession of pastoralists in Kutch and elsewhere (also see Yenneti et al. 2016). Similarly, Adam et al. (Chapter 6) argue that prioritising mitigation in state-led discourses on climate change within cities has led to the dominance of market-driven agendas and business ventures, often in the name of energy efficiency and the green economy (e.g. Government of India 2008; MoEFCC 2015). Overall,

India's climate policy framework is "fragmented and lacks clarity" (Kumar and Naik 2019: 1), displaying the urgent need for a broad-based, inclusive and dedicated climate action for the next decade and beyond. These tensions and trade-offs in the "above" need careful analysis and unpacking, as these top-down interventions often have dramatic impacts on local livelihoods, people's agency, identity and well-being and, more broadly, on the sustainability of India's development trajectory.

Wider relevance

This volume advances critical social science scholarship on climate change by addressing these challenges and tensions in a lower-middle-income country. Our focus is on marginal environments in India which, despite being ecologically dynamic and climatically vulnerable, suffer from historical neglect. We focus on an urban environment (Mumbai, Maharashtra), dryland (Kutch, Gujarat) and a deltaic ecosystem (Sundarbans, West Bengal) and also analyse their challenges from a historical perspective. These localities offer ecological contrasts, rural–urban/peri-urban diversity, varied exposure to different climate shocks and diverse state and official responses to climate change and its associated uncertainties. Drawing on diverse theoretical and conceptual approaches (see below) and methodologies, the book investigates the intersection between local understandings of climate change uncertainty with science, politics, culture, history, livelihoods, ecology and a wider political economy in India.

In the past decade, scholarship on climate change in India has increased significantly, indicating the growing interest and importance of climate change in its wider development politics and practice. Several authors have provided a rich account of the national policymaking context in India, locating it within the broader climate and development politics (Dubash 2012, 2018; Taylor, 2014), or within a particular sector or across sectors (Mahdi 2018; Dubash 2019). Other volumes focus on India's climate diplomacy (Saran and Jones 2016) and impacts of adaptation policy (Chattopadhyaya 2014). This is in addition to the vast literature, journal articles, assessment studies (Government of India 2020) and newspaper articles (online and print) that continue to explore the local manifestation of climate change in different state contexts and methodological advancements involving vulnerability assessments that move beyond single values or indicator-based assessments (Singh *et al.* 2017; Das 2021). Our book builds on this scholarship but takes climate-related uncertainty as its starting point as it connects the global, national and local scales to locate the diverse politics and practice(s) around uncertainty. Further scholarly and practical contributions are as follows:

First, this volume is a significant contribution to understanding how climate-related uncertainty is understood, experienced, leveraged, lived and embodied by scientists, policymakers and lay people who are socially differentiated due to gender, class, caste, ethnicity and so on. We respond to Jasanoff's call to synchronise scientific framings of climate change with "the mundane rhythms of lived lives and specificities of human experience" (2010: 238). In doing so, we introduce the heuristic of "above" and "below" and the "middle" to examine differences in understandings, discourses and practices around uncertainty and climate change and explore the knowledge politics and socio-economic dynamics that shape and alter responses to uncertainty.

Second, climate-related uncertainty has predominantly been characterised as a challenge or a problem that needs resolution. Despite the opening up of approaches to uncertainty and a greater acceptance of the need to embrace it, official responses to dealing with climate-related uncertainty continue to be predominantly driven by top-down, technical and managerial solutions (Beck and Mahony 2017; Mehta *et al*. 2019) which, as the book will demonstrate, often falter in the face of complex local realities and can create new vulnerabilities (also see Eriksen *et al*. 2021). Despite a significant emphasis on integrating local knowledge in climate adaptation and decision-making in recent years, much of the scholarship continues to operate within the domain of climate risk (Conway *et al*. 2019; Conway and Vincent 2021; Singh *et al*. 2021). Within Indian scholarship, there is limited engagement with the issue of uncertainty barring the work of climate scientists on hydrological resource assessments and planning (Bhave *et al*. 2018; Joseph *et al*. 2018; Singh and AchutaRao 2019). This book is, to our knowledge, the first attempt at providing a collection of rich empirical insights on diverse perceptions and experiences of climate-related uncertainties in an Indian context, bringing together macro, meso and micro perspectives. It also stresses the need to prioritise transformative strategies that seriously take on board the perspectives and interests of vulnerable people who bear the brunt of climate change.

Third, we build on growing calls that focus on the need for decision-making under uncertainty (Dessai *et al*. 2003). In other words, rather than approaches that look at climate science alone in guiding policy responses, there is now a growing body of work that focuses on bringing together top-down and bottom-up climate knowledge and assessments (Conway *et al*. 2019). In line with these shifts, new concepts and practices such as adaptive management practices have emerged that also embrace uncertainty through scenario planning and social learning (Pahl-Wostl *et al*. 2007; Brugnach *et al*. 2008; Totin *et al*. 2018; Kale and D'Souza 2018), creating a citizen science of climate change (Panda 2016), or through assessing the impacts on decision-making and adaptation behaviours (Singh *et al*. 2016). However, this approach of bridging has found very little salience in the Indian policy context (see Chapters 2 and 7). Both conceptually and empirically, very limited work exists in this domain in the Indian context (Panda 2016). Various chapters in this volume show how uncertainty is viewed by many actors from the "above" as a form of policy paralysis. We explore these various stereotypes and tropes attached to uncertainty while seeking out positive ways in which uncertainty can open up pathways to transformative change. For example, the practices associated with pastoralism are geared to deal with uncertain dynamics in ecologically dynamic spaces such as drylands, but these have tended to be ignored in mainstream policymaking. Chapter 4 explores instead how these can be built on to create potentials for transformative action to deal with growing radical uncertainties associated with climate change in drylands (Figure 1.2).

Fourth, the volume contributes to methodological expansion and innovation through its creative application of different disciplinary approaches and methods to study impacts and experiences of, and responses to, climate change and uncertainty across different temporal and spatial scales. It draws on a wide range of epistemic frames, with chapters authored by an interdisciplinary team of leading researchers from anthropology, sociology, economics, history, political science and the natural sciences. The volume draws on original empirical insights from the Indian Sundarbans, Mumbai and Kutch, based on mixed methods (e.g. ethnographic research, visual methodologies, participatory mapping and hazard ranking, semi-structured interviews, participant observation, and quantitative surveys) informed by empirically rich, multi-disciplinary and longue durée research in three distinct socio-ecological settings. Policy analysis and key informant interviews were used to engage with perspectives from "above", and natural science expertise was used to understand climate change trends over time. The book also draws on expertise from the arts and humanities. For example,

FIGURE 1.2 Photovoice engagement with women in a pastoral community in Kutch (Photo credit: Shibaji Bose).

Chapter 3 is based on original archival work to analyse colonial understandings of uncertainty in marginal environments, their impacts then and now, and how these inform contemporary climate change debates. In all the research sites, researchers used photovoice to allow hidden and marginalised perspectives to come to the fore through storytelling and visual images. Finally, we also convened roundtables to bridge divides across different disciplinary perspectives and institutional siloes (see Chapters 2 and 7). While unable to get rid of unequal power relations and biases, they at least revealed how these continue to shape and perpetuate dominant paradigms and perspectives.

In the remainder of the introduction, we develop the conceptual framework for this volume, setting the chapters in their context and highlighting the links across various themes.

Heuristics of uncertainty

As discussed, conceptualisations of uncertainties are varied and are embedded in different realms of knowledge and disciplinary traditions. The largely northern focused literature of Science and Technology Studies (STS) has been critical in elucidating the narrow ways in which uncertainty is often conceptualised by modellers, scientists and planners (e.g. Wynne 1992; Stirling *et al.* 2007). Other literatures from an anthropological and sociological tradition, and from the perspective of complex ecologies, have demonstrated how local people live with uncertainty and how practices have evolved to deal with it (e.g. Scoones 1994; Vasavi 1999; Adger *et al.* 2001; Mehta 2005; Marschke and Berkes 2006; Berkes and Berkes 2009). A growing literature in the Indian context and beyond has highlighted the importance of local perceptions about climate variability (Vedwan and Rhoades 2001; Panda 2016; Conway *et al.* 2019) and resource scarcity (Mehta 2005), and their impact on coping and adaptation behaviours; the importance of local knowledge in adapting to climate change (e.g. Naess 2013); and the wider intersections with local power and social dynamics (Coulthard 2008; Taylor 2014; Adam *et al.* 2018). While some gaps are being bridged through citizen science of climate change (Panda 2016) and transformative scenario planning (Kale and D'Souza 2018; Totin *et al.* 2018), largely these different analytical traditions have not spoken to each other. We seek to bridge these literatures through the following heuristics on uncertainty with the caveat that neither of these three categories is homogenous and there is a lot of fluidity across these categories (e.g. scientists can be experts from "above", take on advocacy roles as the "middle" and also experience climate change impacts from "below").

Uncertainty from "above"

Uncertainty from "above" is represented by climate scientists, policy elites and decision-makers. This is usually linked to powerful agencies, although we concede that there will be hierarchies within these and they are not homogeneous categories (Mehta *et al.* 2019). Uncertainty and climate change from "above" tend to draw on singular rationalities and may seek out singular ways to understand causality (Hulme 2017). At the larger/global scale, the climate is usually seen as abstract and invisible (Rudiak-Gould 2013). The standard approach for conceptualising uncertainty is to quantify it in terms of probabilities (e.g. Sigel *et al.* 2010) and statistical models that accommodate sophisticated data with multiple variables across a range of spatial and temporal scales. Of course, as Mehta *et al.* (Chapter 2) show, many modellers acknowledge the limits to models and their predictions due to limited understandings of the climate system and challenges with attribution and downscaling (Shackley and Wynne 1996; Kandlikar *et al.* 2005; Stainforth *et al.* 2007; Curry and Webster 2011; Hulme 2013). Moreover, models often become "fluid objects" (Hastrup 2013: 13) where scientific uncertainties are used as a rhetorical device for strategic ends or to negotiate authority in a disputed domain (Campbell 1985).

Representations of uncertainty are not *a priori*; they are constructed and rationalised through processes. Therefore, different understandings from "above" are linked to particular institutions, positions and contextual factors. As is evident during the COVID-19 pandemic, scientists also struggle with communicating uncertainty effectively to politicians and the public who crave certainty while wanting their research to be policy relevant. For this purpose, boundary ordering devices such as "people [the middle], texts, maps and ideas" play a strong role in science–policy communications as they facilitate the movement of ideas across different social worlds (Star and Griesemer 1989; Shackley and Wynne 1996). Mehta *et al.* (Chapter 2) explore some of these challenges at the science–policy interface, where uncertainty is often truncated into risks, producing calculative actions and controlling visions that end up closing down possibilities for collaboration, mediation and plural framings. Both Mehta *et al.* (Chapter 2) and Movik *et al.* (Chapter 7) discuss the role of bridging devices and hybrid knowledges in bringing the perspectives of the "above" and "below" together, alongside their challenges. Largely, our research has demonstrated that, most often, many of the livelihood practices that intersect with climate change remain unrepresented in the language, representations and imaginaries of the "above", at least in the Indian context. Thus, the narrow frame of uncertainty needs to be broadened and diversified to encompass varieties of uncertainties as understood, experienced and embodied by the "below".

Uncertainty from "below"

Climate change narratives and perceptions pervade the everyday realities of local people whom we call the "below", especially those who live at the interface of climate stressors, risks and shocks. These constitute people living in the squatter settlements of megacities such as Mumbai, who are exposed to chronic flooding during monsoons or displacements for urban development, or the fisher folks in Mumbai, Kutch and the Sundarbans whose livelihoods are threatened due to changes in climate, commercialisation processes and aggressive patterns of industrialisation (Srivastava and Mehta 2017).

A rich body of literature has elucidated how people attach meaning and significance to the world they inhabit and, in turn, gain meanings from the natural world to understand and live with change (cf. Rudiak-Gould 2009; Hastrup and Skydrstrup 2013). Urban studies have also highlighted how uncertainty is an essential dimension of urban life itself and has been a focal theme of those engaged in planning, building and governing cities (Zeiderman *et al.* 2015). Thus, many indigenous knowledge (IK) systems evolve through adaptive learning based on developing a complex knowledge base of the environment and lessons from past mistakes – a version of "post-normal" science (cf. Funtowicz and Ravetz 1993). While the repertoire of local people is rich and diverse concerning ecological uncertainties which are also experienced in cultural terms (e.g. Bon Bibi in the Sundarbans; Chapter 5), this is also being challenged in multiple ways as we show in the subsequent chapters.

As discussed, climate change and its intersection with other drivers of change present a radical uncertainty that can push local people to the limits of coping or trigger maladaptation. This can lead to a sense of powerlessness for those whose lives and survival are at the frontline of climate change and uncertainty (Hulme, personal communication, 2014) and trigger distress diversification, as we show in the empirical chapters. For example, in all three sites, marginalised people are confronted with climate-related uncertainties and the threat of displacement (Mumbai and the Sundarbans), difficulties in sustaining livelihoods (Kutch, Mumbai and the Sundarbans) and the impacts of neoliberal and unequal growth patterns. In urban Mumbai (Chapter 6), poor people living in flood-prone areas, whose lives and livelihoods are entrenched in informality, lack rights to housing and basic services. This has increased their vulnerability to climatic events. At the same time, they are blamed as "encroachers" that cause flood-related uncertainties for the city in the first place. In Kutch (Chapter 4), pastoralists need to deal with changes in rainfall and a declining grass cover alongside hostile government policies and rapid industrialisation that is leading to dispossession from the commons. Thus, for the "below" in Kutch, Mumbai and the Sundarbans, climate change as a cause for change is often used to signify concerns around shifts in their cultural, physical, social and economic worlds (cf. Hulme 2017). The climate signals are not abstract and distanced but deeply embedded with their livelihoods, migration, mobility and everyday decision-making.

Thus, uncertainty from "below" concerns the framings of lay and local people as differentiated by gender, age, sexuality, class, ethnicity, race and caste. It is "experiential", non-official knowledge, not necessarily played out at the verbal or articulated level but instead is a more "practical" or tacit form of knowledge (cf. Bourdieu 1977). While our concern is largely with marginalised groups and perspectives, this can also be a very heterogeneous group consisting of both rich and poor, powerful and powerless people (Mehta *et al.* 2019).

There are, of course, gendered dimensions of climate change and uncertainty as experienced by the "below" and these are highlighted across various chapters. For example, in the Sundarbans (Chapter 5), the growing precarity and livelihood insecurity, due to the loss of land because of erosion and sea-level rise, have led to women needing to move to less profitable, more fragile, risky and marginal activities such as crab catching. This is risky and physically stressful. While both men and women are affected, the intensity is felt more by female-headed households, not least due to massive male out-migration. Also, for many women who are responsible for the health and sustenance of their families, climate change is not something in the future but very much experienced in the here and now, in terms of the impacts of extreme events and stressors on access to safe drinking water, fodder for their animals, availability of fish in the sea and so on. Chapter 4 also elucidates, through the photovoice engagement, many of these gendered, socially and culturally embedded experiences of uncertainty, which are revealed through the powerful images of the "invisible" care economy in Kutch.

Uncertainty and the "middle"

While there are clear power differentials between "above" and "below", with the "above" tending to be more powerful, we contend that there is potential for collaboration and bridging, usually facilitated by what we have called the actors and spaces in the "middle". The "middle" often plays a critical role in bridging gaps between "place-based" experiences and expertise on climate change and the most detached expert assessments and solutions (cf. Rudiak-Gould 2013; see Chapter 7).

The "middle" is not a scalar category, but a functional one (Srivastava, unpublished). It is constituted by actors who attempt to facilitate convergence across diverse interests through mediation and brokerage. However, they can also use their agency to block particular pathways of change or maintain the *status quo*. In this vein, it is important to identify these boundary actors and unpack their politics of bridging (Chapter 7). Across various chapters, the "middle" is constituted through its functional attributes, and it is embedded in diverse formal and informal networks (as civil society actors, politicians, street-level bureaucrats) and engages in practices of policy translation, mediation, alliance-building and gatekeeping, thereby blocking, shaping and encouraging processes of change (Srivastava, unpublished). As intermediaries, they bridge or create epistemic and institutional divides across the "above" and "below" and facilitate or hinder transformative pathways (cf. Stein *et al.* 2018). Most often, the "middle" struggles to translate messages from "below" to the "above" (see Chapter 4). But it can also play a key role in reframing and shifting dominant discourses, for example, around the so-called unproductive nature of the drylands in Kutch (see Chapter 4). At times, actors in the "middle" can resort to politicising uncertainty for their own ends (see Chapter 5). The "middle" thus performs a variety of functions including translation, bridging and co-production, the latter being significantly crucial for facilitating small but emerging alternatives to deal with uncertainties that can enable locally led and appropriate adaptation processes.

In response to possible caveats from careful readers, we acknowledge that climate change and uncertainty from "above", "middle" and "below" have different relative strengths, epistemological entry points and potential for complementarity (Berkes and Berkes 2009; Mehta et al. 2019), and some actors operate across all three levels. For example, a scientist can be an expert representing the "above", try to mediate between local communities and the state as the "middle" and also experience the changing rhythms of climate change as the "below".

Dimensions of uncertainty

In this book, we focus on three types of uncertainties: (1) *aleatoric or ecological uncertainties*, namely, ecological systems characterised by a high degree of variability and disequilibrium dynamics, thus having unknown effects; (2) *knowledge or epistemic uncertainties*, which refer to indeterminate knowledge about changes and their impacts; and (3) *uncertainties linked to larger political economy conditions*, which are unanticipated outcomes due to socio-political interventions and intersections and how they are experienced by diverse groups (Wynne 1992; Mehta et al. 1999; Walker et al. 2003; Mehta et al. 2019). All these uncertainties are experienced, framed and interpreted differently by diverse actors and are linked to relations of power that justify different institutional practices and responses (Rein and Schön 1993; Mehta et al. 2019). Historical understandings of both macro- and micro-level changes are also critical to conceptualising and experiencing uncertainty (see Chapter 3). Uncertainty can also be politicised and manipulated by powerful actors or used as an excuse to do nothing (Mehta et al. 1999; Dessai and van der Sluijs 2007). Configurations and experiences of uncertainty are also affected by location-specific contexts. For example, urban residents and institutions in Mumbai may experience and relate to weather-related uncertainties in a different way compared to rural and natural resource-dependent communities (Kutch or the Sundarbans), where extreme variability has a direct impact on their resource access and livelihoods. We now focus in detail on these three dimensions which we discuss below.

Aleatoric uncertainty

The ontological roots of uncertainty lie in several disciplines. These perspectives recognise the inherent variability of a system, for example, Heisenberg's Uncertainty Principle (Heisenberg 1958), which states that there is a limit to what we can know about any given particle at any given point in time. The fact that there is ontological uncertainty in physics is sufficient for a scientist to conclude that uncertainty is a real phenomenon and not just a deficiency in our ability to observe or know, that is, epistemological uncertainty (see below). In relation to ecological systems, uncertainty refers to the unpredictable, variable and volatile nature of the natural systems in which humans interact (Mehta *et al.* 1999). Ecological systems are dynamic, non-equilibrium systems that are characterised by a high degree of variability and volatility (e.g. in the case of extreme weather events). Chaos, randomness and stochastic processes are the order of the day (Scoones 2004). Modellers and climate scientists refer to this as aleatory uncertainty – the natural fluctuations, a high degree of variability and disequilibrium dynamics having unknown effects (AchutaRao 2016; see Chapter 2). All three sites discussed in this book are highly dynamic and uncertainty is writ large in their landscapes. For example, ecological uncertainty is manifested in the ever-changing rhythms of the river that gobbles up and creates new islands in the Sundarbans; the erratic rainfall in Kutch; and the impacts of extreme rainfall events, sea-level rise and flooding on marginal, low-lying lands in Mumbai.

However, often such endemic uncertainties get framed as risks rather than being acknowledged as a fundamental property of the system. Damodaran *et al.* (Chapter 3) map this friction by analysing the colonial interventions in marginal environments of Kutch and the Sundarbans. They argue that owing to the stabilising and normalising instinct pursued by the rulers, these environments were often framed as environmental extremes which needed to be normalised and tamed. For instance, in Kutch, the colonial administration linked migration not to pastoral rhythms and coping strategies but exclusively to rainfall deficit and weather uncertainty. Well irrigation, consequently, became the widely accepted official response.

Knowledge politics and uncertainty

A post-structural understanding of knowledge is essentially grounded in the belief that knowledge is socially constructed and inherently plural and partial (Haraway 1988). Thus, different actors frame uncertainty differently, and this is primarily guided by the knowledge systems in which they are embedded and these, in turn, result in knowledge-based uncertainties. This may be due to different interpretations and different normative judgements about a certain event or a long-drawn-out process spread across a particular time scale (Weick 1995; Klinke and Renn 2002). For example, flooding can be viewed as a climate event or a failure of governance in Mumbai (Chapter 6) and villagers have diverse interpretations of the cyclical nature of droughts in Kutch (Chapter 4). These interpretations can be shaped by certain assumptions, value judgements about particular resources (e.g. the coastline as a resource frontier for estate and industrial development in Kutch and Mumbai vs. a rich ecosystem sustaining livelihoods), biases and political commitments as in the sedentary bias associated with pastoralism (see Chapter 4).

These framings highlight how climate realities and futures are socially and politically constructed by different social groups, communities and institutions, and how these constructions often get fed into specific types of – and often contrasting – responses. Thus, framing uncertainty as a "monster" would entail a different set of responses (e.g. taming, controlling and reducing it through better scientific modelling; see Chapter 2) as opposed to framings that call for "living with uncertainty" and should lead to policies and programmes which are more locally grounded with possible socially just outcomes. For example, when policymakers in Gujarat often refer to "reducing" uncertainty, they are largely referring to the gaps in information, that is, epistemological uncertainty (Chapter 4). However, as we show, these notions are also mediated by certain knowledge frames and institutional dynamics that eventually shape responses to climate-induced uncertainty.

Several chapters in this book highlight this contrast in different sites and spaces. For example, Mehta *et al.* (Chapter 2) and Movik *et al.* (Chapter 7) highlight this divergence at the interface of science and policy, while the ethnographic insights from Srivastava *et al.* on Kutch (Chapter 4), Ghosh, Kjosavik and Bose on the Sundarbans (Chapter 5) and Adam *et al.* on Mumbai (Chapter 6) show how these binaries get fed into institutional responses that are too often short-sighted, reactive and anti-poor, as well as antithetical to inherent variability intrinsic to these environments. For example, in Mumbai, the building of structural defence mechanisms and concretisation efforts against flooding are a display of this partial approach to addressing complex environmental concerns and uncertainties, with the result that flooding proliferates and often worsens the situation (Chapter 6). A similar techno-centric approach is driving the embankment politics in the Sundarbans (Chapter 5).

However, uncertainties are not only about the absence of knowledge; they also have diverse material and embodied manifestations often articulated through cognitive, emotive and behavioural reactions (Scoones and Stirling 2020). In this sense, uncertainty is irreducible; something active, present and modulated through actors' "sense of confidence and control" (Penrod 2007: 664). Actors attach meanings to certain events, create plots (Hastrup 2013) and conviction narratives (Tuckett and Nikolic 2017) to make sense of uncertainty, and devise a future course of action.

Several studies have documented how communities who are highly exposed to climate variability adapt to uncertainty (Scoones 1994; Mehta 2005; Rudiak-Gould 2009; Hastrup 2013). In Kutch, for example, local communities have conventionally been equipped to deal with drought-related uncertainties and have adopted diverse strategies to cope and live with water scarcity (Mehta 2005). This is also linked to the practices of anticipation (Hastrup 2013), whereby people attempt to predict, forecast and prepare for both immediate and distant futures drawing on local cosmologies and indigenous traditions. However, the increasingly radical nature of uncertainties is creating manifold challenges for these IK systems.

Although policymakers and scientists tend to concede that more accurate information may help "tame" the radical nature of these uncertainties, the confounding factor of scale remains a challenge because the socio-political unknowns of climate change are massive and these often intersect with other "uncertain" drivers of change that compound or cascade into existing problems related to environmental conditions, such as water quality, health, and food and energy security (Chapter 2; also see Conway et al. 2019). This has also led many scholars to recognise that climate is much more than a mere "scientific" fact; it is a combination of social and natural processes (Hastrup 2013). Thus, the prevailing scientific knowledge needs to be understood as a convergence of broader processes, coalitions, motivations, meanings, social and ethical framings, rather than just a natural scientific framing (Shackley and Wynne 1996).

As demonstrated in Chapter 2, there is now a growing acknowledgement that climate science is better at dealing with uncertainties arising due to macro trends such as temperature extremes and sea-level rise than understanding effects at the local level due to downscaling challenges and intersections with other drivers of change (Bhave et al. 2016; see Chapter 2). These include impacts of land use change, water management trends and socio-political and economic processes, which can increase uncertainties for local people (see Swart et al., 2009). These can be described as the "envelope of uncertainty" (Wilby and Dessai 2010) that intersects with social, political, economic, cultural and scientific drivers that are multi-scalar in nature (Gajjar et al. 2018). These drivers also limit the adaptive capacity and pathways to address climate-induced uncertainties (Tschakert 2007; Solecki et al. 2017). It is for these reasons that the abstraction of climate as an objective and a distanced phenomenon has been criticised and the need for more nuanced approaches underlined. It is critical to unpack the understandings of what counts as climate change, how it is known and unevenly experienced, and how power and political economy mediate these interactions (Eriksen et al. 2015; Nightingale 2016; Watts et al. 2017).

The political economy of uncertainty

As much as uncertainty is natural to a system, it is also created and sustained as the human, ecological and socio-political systems interact in discreet ways. Uncertainties have differential impacts on local people because these are mediated and experienced differently by axes of difference arising due to gender, ethnicity and class, thus exacerbating the vulnerabilities of ordinary people (Adger 1999; Tschakert 2007; Lemos et al. 2016).

In many ways, and to paraphrase Wynne (1992), climate change may not be as apocalyptic as it is made out to be in the models, or, for some, the "apocalypse" (caused by other political, social or economic factors and exacerbated by climate change) has already happened or they have learned to cope or adapt to these changes. These may be a product of intersectional differences arising due to gender, sexuality, age, ableism, caste, class or race, historical or political arrangements such as citizenship, insecure land tenures as well as ownership and access to natural resources. Thus, climate change responses and impacts at the local level are often mediated through holistic experiences of wider ecologies concerning land, water and forests, markets and the economy and institutions and governance across scales (Puri 2015). For example, Damodaran *et al.* (Chapter 3) show how colonial interventions and imaginaries of the environmental "normal" were experienced and discussed differently by layers of society, communities, experts and government officials across the colonial and early post-colonial periods.

Various chapters across the volume explore the diverse range of institutions, processes and structures (climate-related and otherwise) which influence and are shaped by ecological uncertainties such as floods, droughts, cyclones, rainfall variability and extreme weather events. In all three sites, dominant pathways to deal with uncertainty and climate change range between capitalist and growth-driven trajectories (Mumbai and Kutch) to apathy and neglect of the vulnerabilities of poor people (the Sundarbans). To understand these intersections, we build on Douglass and Miller's (2018) conception of compounded disasters, looking at how spatial and/or temporal proximity of ecological, epistemic and political economy uncertainty can have compounding and cascading effects. For example, in the Sundarbans (Chapter 5), slow stressors such as salinity intrusion and coastline erosion gradually erode livelihood resources, culminating in varying forms of distress diversification and leading to compounded uncertainties. This, as we elaborate in various chapters, is a diversification towards less profitable, more precarious and more marginal livelihood activities.

Most of the research was concluded in 2018, but, wherever possible, we have tried to update our findings in light of the COVID-19 pandemic. In all three sites, existing climate uncertainties are compounded as they intersected with the COVID-19 pandemic. For example, cyclones Amphan and Yash which struck in May 2020 and 2021 destroyed agricultural lands and shelter, and severely increased the vulnerabilities of the islanders who were struggling simultaneously from the fallout of COVID-19-related measures. Between March and May 2020, in particular, the pandemic-induced lockdown phases contributed to reverse migration, reduced remittances, food insecurity and livelihood loss by limiting trade and reducing employment opportunities across sites.

Bridging perspectives: towards transformative politics and pathways

Various chapters of the book demonstrate how uncertainty has created a form of anxiety and alarm for various actors across scales, thus shaping social and political responses. Through different examples of colonial interventions (Chapter 3), or present policy discourses around pastoralism (Kutch), flood governance (Mumbai) or embankment politics (the Sundarbans), various chapters demonstrate that an excessive focus on techno-managerial solutions has provided only limited solutions in addressing uncertainties in these marginal environments. Usually, the perspectives from the "above" and their solutions prevail and governments have largely tended to ignore the more place-based experiences and assessments and the more critical voices from the "middle".

In Chapter 7, Movik *et al.* demonstrate how stakeholder dialogues and roundtables were organised as an attempt to break down disciplinary and other divides and bring diverse actors together (also see Bhatt *et al.* 2018). However, these bridging spaces are also not power neutral and the power imbalances between and across the "above", "middle" and "below" are critical. Methodologically, roundtables became an effective way of understanding the discursive, material and institutional configurations that shape the understanding and response to uncertainty. Thus, a sustained effort is required in bringing to the fore hidden and alternative perspectives, plural ways of valuation and epistemic diversity to foster transformative, socially just and inclusive development.

What does transformative change look like and what practices, politics and knowledges are required? While there are many diverging views of what constitutes transformation, a general consensus is that it goes beyond marginal or incremental change, is non-linear and challenges the status quo of existing development structures and paradigms (Pelling 2011; O'Brien 2012; Mehta *et al.* 2021). How are these changes enacted or facilitated? Scoones *et al.* (2020) refer to three approaches to understanding transformation: structural (fundamental ways in which production and consumption are organised and governed), systemic (intentional change to steer complex systems towards normative goals) and enabling approaches (fostering values of agency, justice and capabilities), and emphasise that embracing enabling approaches is key to transformative change.

Building on the notion of systemic change, in this volume, we attempt to seek out bottom-up pathways of transformation in marginal environments that are characterised by radical uncertainty. Although unequal structural conditions shape people's perception, experience and response to climatic uncertainty locking them into maladaptive pathways or distress diversification (Chapters 4–6), we also observe inspiring initiatives that are seeking to challenge incumbent knowledge systems and power relations. In this regard, we follow Few *et al.* (2017) in underlining transformation as initiatives and practices that go beyond incremental changes and challenge systemic inequalities and ultimately resulting in a fundamental reorientation of power relations, governance regimes, value systems and conceptions of well-being (Pelling *et al.* 2015).

In this vein, various chapters discuss the notion of hybrid knowledge (Chapters 7 and 8) and hybrid alliances from the "above", "middle" and "below" that are emerging to respond to various climate-related uncertainties, by offering alternative pathways that are attempting to bridge perspectives and experiences across the domains. Here, the role of the "middle" as interlocutors is key. For example, in the Sundarbans, collaborative efforts between NGOs and local communities are helping restore deltaic ecology and livelihoods. Similarly, in Kutch, civil society organisations and pastoralists are challenging dominant state paradigms regarding drylands and pastoralism and working towards ensuring livelihoods security while enhancing biodiversity (Mehta and Srivastava 2020; see Chapter 4).

Although such initiatives provide the scope to reframe nature–society relations, they also involve a delicate power relationship between different stakeholders, thus begging the question of who is imagining what and for whom? Which perspectives remain hidden and why, and what needs to be done to bring them to the fore? More importantly, how can bottom-up practices foster socially just pathways in the face of regressive politics, authoritarianism and shrinking civic spaces? How can opaque institutional practices of incumbent powers concerning the state, business and science be opened up and made accountable to the needs of the poor and marginalised sections? We argue that transformations are by their very nature multiple and contested and are closely associated and shaped by understandings of culture, place, identity and contingent conditions within the political economy (Brown and Westaway 2011; Scoones et al. 2015). For example, while local communities are affected by the here and now, transformation is usually associated with changing wider systems that are historically enmeshed in unequal power relations, landscape imaginaries and ecological changes (Mehta et al. 2021). Thus, what counts as transformation is not straightforward. It involves critical questions about scale, attribution, temporality, accountability, responsibility and ethics.

In this book, we highlight some of these tensions and dilemmas as the "above", "middle" and "below" shape and respond to different dimensions of climate-related uncertainties in diverse settings in India. We also offer emerging evidence on bridging these divides, while being alert to the structural drivers of power and inequity. Ultimately such bridging efforts will help facilitate more plural, inclusive and decentralised ways of understanding, embracing and living with uncertainty that can potentially open up pathways for socially just transformative engagement and politics around climate change.

★★

Note

1 Living on $1.9 consumption a day (Lee et al. 2021).

References

Achutarao, K. 2016. 'Uncertainty from Above: Can It Be Reduced?'. Paper presented at the STEPS Centre Workshop: Climate Change and Uncertainty from Above and Below, New Delhi, 27–28 January.

Adam, H.N. 2015. 'Mainstreaming Adaptation in India–the Mahatma Gandhi National Rural Employment Guarantee Act and Climate Change. *Climate and Development*, 7.4: 142–152.

Adam, H.N., D.J. Kjosavik, and N. Shanmugaratnam. 2018. 'Adaptation Trajectories and Challenges in the Western Ghats: A Case Study of Attappady, South India'. *Journal of Rural Studies*, 61: 1–11. doi.org/10.1016/j.jrurstud.2018.05.002

Adger, W.N. 1999. 'Social Vulnerability to Climate Change and Extremes in Coastal Vietnam'. *World Development*, 27(2): 249–269. doi.org/10.1016/S0305-750X(98)00136-3

Adger, W.N., P.M. Kelly, and N. Huu Ninh, eds. 2001. *Living with Environmental Change: Social Vulnerability, Adaptation and Resilience in Vietnam*. London: Routledge.
Beck, S. and M. Mahony. 2017. 'The IPCC and the Politics of Anticipation'. *Nature Climate Change*, 7: 311–313. doi.org/10.1038/nclimate3264.
Berkes, F. and M. Berkes. 2009. 'Ecological Complexity, Fuzzy Logic, and Holism in Indigenous Knowledge'. *Futures*, 41(1): 6–12. https://doi.org/10.1016/j.futures.2008.07.003.
Bhatt, M.R., L. Mehta, S. Bose, H.N. Adam, S. Srivastava, U. Ghosh, S. Movik, N.C. Narayanan, L.O. Naess, D. Parthasarathy, C. Wilson, and V. Pathak. 2018. *Bridging the Gaps in Understandings of Uncertainty and Climate Change*. Ahmedabad: AIDMI.
Bhave, A.G., D. Conway, S. Dessai, and D.A. Stainforth. 2016. 'Barriers and Opportunities for Robust Decision Making Approaches to Support Climate Change Adaptation in the Developing World'. *Climate Risk Management*, 14: 1–10. https://doi.org/10.1016/j.crm.2016.09.004
Bhave, A.G., D. Conway, S. Dessai and D.A. Stainforth. 2018. 'Water Resource Planning Under Future Climate and Socioeconomic Uncertainty in the Cauvery River Basin in Karnataka, India'. *Water Resources Research*, 54(2): 708–728. https://doi.org/10.1002/2017WR020970
Bidwai, P. 2012. *The Politics of Climate Change and the Global Crisis: Mortgaging Our Future*. New Delhi: Orient Black Swan.
Bourdieu, P. 1977. *Outline of a Theory of Practice*. Cambridge: Cambridge University Press.
Brown, K. and E. Westaway E. 2011. 'Agency, Capacity, and Resilience to Environmental Change: Lessons from Human Development, Well-being, and Disasters'. *Annual Review of Environment and Resources*, 36: 321–342. https://doi.org/10.1146/annurev-environ-052610-092905
Brugnach, M., A. Dewulf, C. Pahl-Wostl, and T. Taillieu. 2008. 'Toward a Relational Concept of Uncertainty: About Knowing Too Little, Knowing Too Differently, and Accepting Not to Know'. *Ecology and Society*, 13(2): 30.
Campbell, B.L. 1985. 'Uncertainty as Symbolic Action in Disputes Among Experts', *Social Studies of Science*, 15(3): 429–453.
Chattopadhyay, S. 2014. *Climate Change in India: Views on the Concerns of Adaptation and Survival in a Fast Changing World*. New Delhi: Iris Publications Ltd.
Conway, D. and K. Vincent. 2021. *Climate Risk in Africa: Adaptation and Resilience*. Cham: Palgrave Mcmillan.
Conway, D., R.J. Nicholls, S. Brown, M.G.L. Tebboth, W.N. Adger, B. Ahmad, H. Biemans, F. Crick, A.F. Lutz, R.S. De Campos, M. Said, C. Singh, M.A.H. Zaroug, E. Ludi, M. New, and P. Wester. 2019. 'The Need for Bottom-Up Assessments of Climate Risks and Adaptation in Climate-Sensitive Regions'. *Nature Climate Change*, 9: 503–511. https://doi.org/10.1038/s41558-019-0502-0
Coulthard, S. 2008. 'Adapting to Environmental Change in Artisanal Fisheries – Insights from a South Indian Lagoon'. *Global Environmental Change*, 18(3): 479–489. https://doi.org/10.1016/j.gloenvcha.2008.04.003
Crate, S.A. and M. Nuttall. 2009. 'Epilogue: Anthropology, Science, and Climate Change Policy'. In *Anthropology and Climate Change: From Encounters to Actions*, edited by S.A. Crate and M. Nuttall, 394–400. Walnut Creek, CA: Left Coast Press Inc.
Curry, J.A. and P.J. Webster. 2011. 'Climate Science and the Uncertainty Monster'. *Bulletin of the American Meteorological Society*, 92(12): 1667–1682. https://doi.org/10.1175/2011BAMS3139.1

Das, P.V. 2021. 'People's Climate Knowledge Versus Scientists' Climate Knowledge: A Study of Apple Farming Communities in Western Himalayas, India'. *GeoJournal*. https://doi.org/10.1007/s10708-021-10371-z

Dessai, S. and J. van der Sluijs. 2007. *Uncertainty and Climate Change Adaptation: A Scoping Study*. Utrecht: Copernicus Institute.

Dessai, S., K. O'Brien, and M. Hulme. 2007. 'Editorial: On Uncertainty and Climate Change'. *Global Environmental Change*, 17(1): 1–3. https://doi.org/10.1016/j.gloenvcha.2006.12.001

Douglass, M. and M.A. Miller. 2018. 'Disaster Justice in Asia's Urbanising Anthropocene', *Environment and Planning E: Nature and Space*, 1: 271–287. https://doi.org/10.1177/2514848618797333

Dubash, N.K. 2012. *Handbook of Climate Change and India: Development, Politics and Governance*. Oxford: Earthscan.

Dubash, N.K., Khosla, R., Kelkar, U. and Lele, S. 2018. India and climate change: Evolving ideas and increasing policy engagement. *Annual Review of Environment and Resources*, 43: 395-424.

Dubash, N.K. 2019. 'An Introduction to India's Evolving Climate Change Debate'. In *India in a Warming World: Integrating Climate Change and Development*, edited by N.K. Dubash, 1–28. New Delhi: Oxford University Press.

Dubash, N.K. and A. Jogesh. 2014. 'From Margins to Mainstream? State Climate Change Planning in India'. *Economic & Political Weekly*, 49(48): 86–95. https://doi.org/10.1093/oso/9780199498734.003.0020

Dubash, N.K., R. Khosla, U. Kelkar and S. Lele. 2018. 'India and Climate Change: Evolving Ideas and Increasing Policy Engagement'. *Annual Review of Environment and Resources*, 43: 395–424. https://doi.org/10.1146/annurev-environ-102017-025809

Eriksen, S., E.L.F. Schipper, M. Scoville-Simonds, K. Vincent, H.N. Adam, N. Brooks, B. Harding, D. Khatri, L. Lenaerts, D. Liverman, M. Mills-Novoa, M. Mosberg, S. Movik, B. Muok, A. Nightingale, H. Ojha, L. Sygna, M. Taylor, C. Vogel, and J.J. West. 2021. 'Adaptation Interventions and their Effect on Vulnerability in Developing Countries: Help, Hindrance or Irrelevance?'. *World Development*, 141: 105383. https://doi.org/10.1016/j.worlddev.2020.105383

Eriksen, S.H., A.J. Nightingale, and H. Eakin. 2015. 'Reframing Adaptation: The Political Nature of Climate Change Adaptation'. *Global Environmental Change*, 35: 523–533. https://doi.org/10.1016/j.gloenvcha.2015.09.014

Few, R., D. Morchain, D. Spear, A. Mensah, and R. Bendapudi. 2017. 'Transformation, Adaptation and Development: Relating Concepts to Practice'. *Palgrave Communications*, 3: 17092. https://doi.org/10.1057/palcomms.2017.92

Funtowicz, S.O. and J.R. Ravetz. 1993. 'Science for the Post Normal Age'. *Futures*, 25(7): 739–755. https://doi.org/10.1016/0016-3287(93)90022-L

Gajjar, S.P., C. Singh, and T. Deshpande. 2018. 'Tracing Back to Move Ahead: A Review of Development Pathways that Constrain Adaptation Futures'. *Climate and Development*, 11(29): 1–15. https://doi.org/10.1080/17565529.2018.1442793

García-del-Amo, D., P.G. Mortyn and V. Reyes-García. 2020. 'Including Indigenous and Local Knowledge in Climate Research: An Assessment of the Opinion of Spanish Climate Change Researchers'. *Climatic Change*, 160: 67–88. https://doi.org/10.1007/s10584-019-02628-x

Government of India. 2008. *National Action Plan on Climate Change (NAPCC)*. New Delhi: Prime Minister's Office.

Government of India. 2020. *Assessment of Climate Change Over the Indian Region: A Report of the Ministry of Earth Sciences (MoES), Government of India*. Germany: Springer Singapore.

Haraway, D. 1988. 'Situated Knowledges: The Science Question in Feminism and the Privilege of Partial Perspective'. *Feminist Studies*, 14: 575–599. https://doi.org/10.2307/3178066

Hastrup, K. 2013. 'Anticipating Nature: The Productive Uncertainty of Climate Models'. In *The Social Life of Climate Change Models: Anticipating Nature*, edited by K. Hastrup and M. Skrydstrup, 1–29. London: Routledge.

Hastrup, K. and M. Skrydstrup. 2013. *The Social Life of Climate Change Models: Anticipating Nature*. New York: Routledge.

Heisenberg, W., and F.S.C. Northrop. 1958. *Physics and Philosophy: The Revolution in Modern Science*. New York: Harper & Brothers.

Hulme, M. 2013. 'How Climate Models Gain and Exercise Authority'. In *The Social Life of Climate Change Models: Anticipating Nature*, edited by K. Hastrup and M. Skrydstrup, 30–44. London: Routledge.

Hulme, M. 2015. 'Climate and Its Changes: A Cultural Appraisal', *Geo: Geography and Environment*, 2(1): 1–11. https://dx.doi.org/10.1002/geo2.5

Hulme, M. 2017. *Weathered: Cultures of Climate*. London: Sage.

IPCC-SREX . 2012. 'Managing the risks of extreme events and disasters to advance climate change adaptation: A Special Report of Working Groups I and II of the Intergovernmental Panel on Climate Change', In edited by C.B. Field., V. Barros, T.F. Stocker, D. Qin, D.J. Dokken, K.L. Ebi, M.D. Mastrandrea, K.J. Mach, G.-K. Plattner, S.K. Allen, M. Tignor, and P.M. Midgley, 1–582. Cambridge, United Kingdom and New York: Cambridge University Press and IPCC.

IPCC. 2014. 'Climate Change 2014: Synthesis Report'. Switzerland: IPCC.

IPCC. 2018. 'Summary for Policymakers'. In *Global Warming of 1.5°C. An IPCC Special Report on the Impacts of Global Warming of 1.5°C Above Pre-Industrial Levels and Related Global Greenhouse Gas Emission Pathways, in the Context of Strengthening the Global Response to the Threat of Climate Change, Sustainable Development, and Efforts to Eradicate Poverty*. Switzerland: IPCC.

Jasanoff, S. 2010. 'A New Climate for Society'. *Theory, Culture & Society*, 27(2–3): 233–253. https://doi.org/10.1177/0263276409361497

Joseph, J., S. Ghosh, A. Pathak, and A.K. Sahai. 2018. 'Hydrologic Impacts of Climate Change: Comparisons between Hydrological Parameter Uncertainty and Climate Model Uncertainty'. *Journal of Hydrology*, 566: 1–22. https://doi.org/10.1016/j.jhydrol.2018.08.080

Kale, E. and M. D'Souza. 2018. *Using Transformative Scenario Planning to Think Critically About the Future of Water in Rural Jalna, India*. Ottawa: International Development Research Centre.

Kandlikar, M., J. Risbey, and S. Dessai. 2005. 'Representing and Communicating Deep Uncertainty in Climate-Change Assessments'. *Comptes Rendus Geoscience*, 337(4): 443–455. https://doi.org/10.1016/j.crte.2004.10.010

Klinke, A. and O. Renn. 2002. 'A New Approach to Risk Evaluation and Management: Risk-Based, Precaution-Based, and Discourse-Based Strategies'. *Risk Analysis*, 22(6): 1071–1094. https://doi.org/10.1111/1539-6924.00274

Knight, F.H. 1921. *Risk, Uncertainty and Profit*. Chicago, IL: Chicago University Press.

Kumar, P. and A. Naik. 2019. 'India's Domestic Climate Policy Is Fragmented and Lacks Clarity', *Economic & Political Weekly*, 54(7): 1–13.

Leach, M., I. Scoones and A. Stirling. 2010. *Dynamic Sustainabilities: Technology, Environment, Social Justice*. London: Earthscan.

Lee, J., O. Taherzadeh and K. Kanemoto. 2021. 'The Scale and Drivers of Carbon Footprints in Households, Cities and Regions across India'. *Global Environmental Change*, 66: 102205. https://doi.org/10.1016/j.gloenvcha.2020.102205

Lemos, M.C., Y.-J. Lo, D. Nelson, H. Eakin, and A.M. Barbieri Bedran Martins. 2016. 'Linking Development to Climate Adaptation: Leveraging Generic and Specific Capacities to Reduce Vulnerability to Drought in NE Brazil'. *Global Environmental Change*, 39: 170–179. https://doi.org/10.1016/j.gloenvcha.2016.05.001

Levin, K., B. Cashore, S. Bernstein, and G. Auld. 2012. 'Overcoming the Tragedy of Super Wicked Problems: Constraining Our Future Selves to Ameliorate Global Climate Change'. *Policy Sciences*, 45(2): 123–152.

Mahdi, S.S. 2018. *Climate Change and Agriculture in India: Impact and Adaptation*. New York: Springer International Publishing.

Mani, M., S. Bandyopadhyay, S. Chonabayashi, A. Markandya, and T. Mosier. 2018. *South Asia's Hotspots: Impacts of Temperature and Precipitation Changes on Living Standards*. Washington, DC: World Bank.

Marschke, M. and F. Berkes. 2006. 'Exploring Strategies that Build Livelihood Resilience: A Case from Cambodia'. *Ecology and Society*, 11(1): 42.

Mehta, L. 2005. *The Politics and Poetics of Water: Naturalising Scarcity in Western India*. New Delhi: Orient Longman.

Mehta, L., M. Leach, P. Newell, I. Scoones, K. Sivaramakrishnan, and S.A. Way. 1999. 'Exploring Understandings of Institutions and Uncertainty: New Directions in Natural Resource Management'. *IDS Discussion Paper 372*. Brighton: IDS.

Mehta, L. and S. Srivastava. 2020. 'Uncertainty in Modelling Climate Change: The Possibilities of Co-production Through Knowledge Pluralism'. In *The Politics of Uncertainty: Challenges of Transformation*, edited by I. Scoones and A. Stirling, 99–112. London: Routledge.

Mehta, L., S. Srivastava, H.N. Adam, S. Bose, U. Ghosh, and V.V. Kumar. 2019. 'Climate Change and Uncertainty from 'Above' and 'Below': Perspectives from India'. *Regional Environmental Change*, 19(6): 1533–1547. https://doi.org/10.1007/s10113-019-01479-7

Mehta, L., S. Srivastava, S. Movik, H.N. Adam, R. D'Souza, D. Parthasarathy, L.O. Naess and N. Ohte. 2021. Transformation as Praxis: Responding to Climate Change Uncertainties in Marginal Environments in South Asia. *Current Opinion in Environmental Sustainability*, 49, 110–117. https://doi.org/10.1016/j.cosust.2021.04.002

MoEFCC. 2015. *India's Intended Nationally Determined Contribution: Working towards Climate Justice*. New Delhi: Ministry of Environment, Forest and Climate Change.

Mohanty, A. 2020. *Preparing India for Extreme Climate Events: Mapping Hotspots and Response Mechanisms*. New Delhi: Council on Energy, Environment and Water.

Naess, L.O. 2013. 'The Role of Local Knowledge in Adaptation to Climate Change'. *Wiley Interdisciplinary Reviews: Climate Change*, 4(2): 99–106. https://doi.org/10.1002/wcc.204

Nightingale, A.J. 2016. 'Adaptive Scholarship and Situated Knowledges? Hybrid Methodologies and Plural Epistemologies in Climate Change Adaptation Research'. *Area*, 48(1): 41–47. https://doi.org/10.1111/area.12195

Nightingale, A.J., S. Eriksen, M. Taylor, T. Forsyth, M. Pelling, A. Newsham, E. Boyd, K. Brown, B. Harvey, L. Jones, R. Bezner Kerr, L. Mehta, L.O. Naess, D. Ockwell, I. Scoones, T. Tanner, and S. Whitfield. 2020. 'Beyond Technical Fixes: Climate

Solutions and the Great Derangement'. *Climate and Development*, 12(4): 343–352. https://doi.org/10.1080/17565529.2019.1624495

O'Brien, K. 2012. 'Global Environmental Change II: From Adaptation to Deliberate Transformation'. *Progress in Human Geography*, 36: 667–676. https://doi.org/10.1177/0309132511425767

Pahl-Wostl, C., M. Craps, A. Dewulf, E. Mostert, D. Tabara, and T. Taillieu. 2007. 'Social Learning and Water Resources Management'. *Ecology and Society*, 12(2): 5.

Panda, A. 2016. 'Exploring Climate Change Perceptions, Rainfall Trends and Perceived Barriers to Adaptation in a Drought Affected Region in India'. *Natural Hazards*, 84(2): 777–796. https://doi.org/10.1007/s11069-016-2456-0

Pelling, M. 2011. *Adaptation to Climate Change: From Resilience to Transformation*. London: Routledge.

Pelling, M., K. O'Brien, and D. Matyas. 2015. 'Adaptation and Transformation'. *Climatic Change*, 133: 113–127. https://doi.org/10.1007/s10584-014-1303-0

Penrod, J. 2007. 'Living with Uncertainty: Concept Advancement'. *Journal of Advanced Nursing*, 57: 658–667. https://doi.org/10.1111/j.1365-2648.2006.04008.x

Puri, R. 2015. 'The Uniqueness of the Everyday: Herders and Invasive Species in India'. In *Climate Cultures: Anthropological Perspectives on Climate Change*, edited by J. Barnes and M.R. Dove, 249–273. New Haven, CT: Yale University Press.

Rein, M. and D. Schön. 1993. 'Reframing Policy Discourses'. In *The Argumentative Turn in Policy Analysis and Planning*, edited by F. Fischer and J. Forester, 145–166. Durham, NC: Duke University Press.

Rudiak-Gould, P. 2009. *The Fallen Palm: Climate Change and Culture Change in the Marshall Islands*. Riga: VDM Verlag Dr. Müller.

Rudiak-Gould, P. 2013. '"We Have Seen It with Our Own Eyes": Why We Disagree about Climate Change Visibility'. *Weather, Climate, and Society*, 5(2): 120–132.

Saran, S. and A. Jones. 2016. *India's Climate Change Identity: Between Reality and Perception*. Cham: Palgrave Macmillan.

Scoones, I. 1994. *Living With Uncertainty: New Directions in Pastoral Development in Africa*. London: Intermediate Technology Publications.

Scoones, I. 2004. 'Climate Change and the Challenge of Non-Equilibrium Thinking', *IDS Bulletin*, 35: 114–119. https://doi.org/10.19088/1968-2020.116

Scoones, I. and A. Stirling. 2020. 'Uncertainty and the Politics of Transformation'. In *The Politics of Uncertainty: Challenges of Transformation*, edited by I. Scoones and A. Stirling, 1–30. London: Routledge.

Scoones, I., M. Leach and P. Newell. 2015. *The Politics of Green Transformations*. London: Routledge.

Scoones I., A. Stirling, D. Abrol, [...] L. Yang. 2020. Transformations to Sustainability: Combining Structural, Systemic and Enabling Approaches. *Current Opinion in Environmental Sustainability*, 42: 65–75. https://doi.org/10.1016/j.cosust.2019.12.004

Srivastava S. 2018. Action in the 'middle': Mid-level actors, climate change and intersectoral collaboration in urban India: Literature Review (unpublished)

Stirling A., M. Leach, L. Mehta [...] J. Thompson. 2007. Empowering designs: towards more progressive appraisal of sustainability. STEPS Working Paper 3, STEPS Centre, Brighton.

Shackley, S. and B. Wynne. 1996. 'Representing Uncertainty in Global Climate Change Science and Policy: Boundary-Ordering Devices and Authority'. *Science, Technology & Human Values*, 21: 275–302.

Sigel, K., B. Klauer, and C. Pahl-Wostl. 2010. 'Conceptualising Uncertainty in Environmental Decision-Making: The Example of the EU Water Framework Directive'. *Ecological Economics*, 69: 502–510. https://doi.org/10.1016/j.ecolecon.2009.11.012

Singh, R., & K. AchutaRao. 2019. Quantifying uncertainty in twenty-first century climate change over India. *Climate Dynamics*, 52(7): 3905–3928.

Singh, C., M. Madhavan, J. Arvind, and A. Bazaz. 2021. 'Climate Change Adaptation in Indian Cities: A Review of Existing Actions and Spaces for Triple Wins'. *Urban Climate*, 36: 100783. https://doi.org/10.1016/j.uclim.2021.100783

Singh, C., P. Dorward, and H. Osbahr. 2016. 'Developing a Holistic Approach to the Analysis of Farmer Decision-Making: Implications for Adaptation Policy and Practice in Developing Countries'. *Land Use Policy*, 59: 329–343. https://doi.org/10.1016/j.landusepol.2016.06.041

Singh, C., T. Deshpande, and R. Basu. 2017. 'How Do Ee Assess Vulnerability to Climate Change in India? A Systematic Review of Literature'. *Regional Environmental Change*, 17(2): 527–538. https://doi.org/10.1007/s10113-016-1043-y

Solecki, W., M. Pelling, and M. Garschagen. 2017. 'Transitions between Risk Management Regimes in Cities'. *Ecology and Society*, 22(2): 38. https://doi.org/10.5751/ES-09102-220238

Srivastava, S. and L. Mehta. 2017. *The Social Life of Mangroves: Resource Complexes and Contestations on the Industrial Coastline of Kutch, India*. Brighton: ESRC STEPS Centre.

Stainforth, D.A., M.R. Allen, E.R. Tredger, and L.A. Smith. 2007. 'Confidence, Uncertainty and Decision-Support Relevance in Climate Predictions'. *Philosophical Transactions of the Royal Society of London A: Mathematical, Physical and Engineering Sciences*, 365: 2145–2161. https://doi.org/10.1098/rsta.2007.2074

Star, S.L. and J.R. Griesemer. 1989. 'Institutional Ecology, 'Translations' and Boundary Objects: Amateurs and Professionals in Berkeley's Museum of Vertebrate Zoology, 1907–39'. *Social Studies of Science*, 19: 387–420. https://doi.org/10.1177%2F030631289019003001

Stein, C., C. Pahl-Wostl, and J. Barron. 2018. 'Towards a Relational Understanding of the Water-Energy-Food Nexus: An Analysis of Embeddedness and Governance in the Upper Blue Nile region of Ethiopia'. *Environmental Science and Policy*, 90: 173–182. https://doi.org/10.1016/j.envsci.2018.01.018

Stirling, A. 1999. 'On "Precautionary" and "Science-Based" Approaches to Risk Assessment and Environmental Appraisal'. In *On Science and Precaution in the Management of Technological Risk*, edited by A. Klinke, O. Renn, A. Rip, A. Salo and A. Stirling. Brussels: ECSC-EEC-EAEC.

Stirling, A., M. Leach, L. Mehta, I. Scoones, A. Smith, S. Stagl, and J. Thompson. 2007. 'Empowering Designs: Towards More Progressive Appraisal of Sustainability'. STEPS Working Paper 3, Institute of Development Studies, Brighton.

Swart R., L. Bernstein, M. Ha-Duong and J. Petersen. 2009. 'Agreeing to disagree: uncertainty management in assessing climate change, impacts and responses by the IPCC'. *Climatic Change*, 92: 1–9.

Taylor, M. 2014. *The Political Ecology of Climate Change Adaptation: Livelihoods, Agrarian Change and the Conflicts of Development*. London: Routledge.

Totin, E., J.R. Butler, A. Sidibé, S. Partey, P.K. Thornton, and R. Tabo. 2018. 'Can Scenario Planning Catalyse Transformational Change? Evaluating a Climate Change Policy Case Study in Mali'. *Futures*, 96: 44–56. https://doi.org/10.1016/j.futures.2017.11.005

Tschakert, P. 2007. 'Views from the Vulnerable: Understanding Climatic and Other Stressors in the Sahel'. *Global Environmental Change*, 17: 381–396. https://doi.org/10.1016/j.gloenvcha.2006.11.008

Tuckett, D. and M. Nikolic. 2017. 'The Role of Conviction and Narrative in Decision-Making under Radical Uncertainty'. *Theory & Psychology*, 27: 501–523. https://doi.org/10.1177/0959354317713158

Unmüßig, B., W. Sachs and T. Fatheuer. 2012. *Critique of the Green Economy: Towards Social and Environmental Equity*. Berlin: Heinrich Böll Foundation.

van der Sluijs, J. 2005. 'Uncertainty as a Monster in the Science-Policy Interface: Four Coping Strategies'. *Water Science & Technology*, 52: 87–92.

Vasavi, A.R. 1999. *Harbingers of Rain: Land and Life in South India*. Delhi: Oxford University Press.

Vedwan, N. and R.E. Rhoades. 2001. 'Climate Change in the Western Himalayas of India: A Study of Local Perception and Response'. *Climate Research*, 19: 109–117.

Venkatesh, S. 2018. 'Union Budget 2018: Climate Action Funds Lying Unused is a Concern'. *Down to Earth*, New Delhi, 17 January.

Walker, W.E., P. Harremoës, J. Rotmans, J.P. van der Sluijs, M.B.A. van Asselt, P. Janssen, and M.P. Krayer von Kraus. 2003. 'Defining Uncertainty: A Conceptual Basis for Uncertainty Management in Model-Based Decision Support'. *Integrated Assessment*, 4(1): 5–17. https://doi.org/10.1076/iaij.4.1.5.16466

Watts, N., W.N. Adger, S. Ayeb-Karlsson, Y. Bai, P. Byass, D. Campbell-Lendrum, T. Colbourn, P. Cox, M. Davies, M. Depledge, A. Depoux, P. Dominguez-Salas, P. Drummond, P. Ekins, A. Flahault, D. Grace, H. Graham, A. Haines, I. Hamilton, A. Johnson, I. Kelman, S. Kovats, L. Liang, M. Lott, R. Lowe, Y. Luo, G. Mace, M. Maslin, K. Morrissey, K. Murray, T. Neville, M. Nilsson, T. Oreszczyn, C. Parthemore, D. Pencheon, E. Robinson, S. Schütte, J. Shumake-Guillemot, P. Vineis, P. Wilkinson, N. Wheeler, B. Xu, J. Yang, Y. Yin, C. Yu, P. Gong, H. Montgomery, and A. Costello. 2017. 'The Lancet Countdown: Tracking Progress on Health and Climate Change', *The Lancet*, 389(10074): 1151–1164. https://doi.org/10.1016/S0140-6736(16)32124-9

Weick, K.E. 1995. *Sensemaking in Organizations*. Thousand Oaks, CA: Sage Publications.

Wilby, R.L. and S. Dessai. 2010. 'Robust Adaptation to Climate Change'. *Weather*, 65: 180–185. https://doi.org/10.1002/wea.543

Wynne, B. 1992. 'Uncertainty and Environmental Learning: Reconceiving Science and Policy in the Preventive Paradigm'. *Global Environmental Change*, 2: 111–127. https://doi.org/10.1016/0959-3780(92)90017-2

Wynne, B. 2010. 'Strange Weather, Again: Climate Science as Political Art'. *Theory, Culture & Society*, 27: 289–305. https://doi.org/10.1177/0263276410361499

Yenneti, K., R. Day and O. Golubchikov. 2016. 'Spatial Justice and the Land Politics of Renewables: Dispossessing Vulnerable Communities through Solar Energy Mega-Projects', *Geoforum*, 76: 90–99. https://doi.org/10.1016/j.geoforum.2016.09.004

Zeiderman, A., S.A. Kaker, J.D. Silver, and A. Wood. 2015. 'Uncertainty and Urban Life', *Public Culture*, 27: 281–304. http://dx.doi.org/10.1215/08992363-2841868

2
UNCERTAINTY FROM "ABOVE"
Diverse understandings, politics and implications

Lyla Mehta, Hans Nicolai Adam, Mihir R. Bhatt, Synne Movik, Lars Otto Naess and Shilpi Srivastava

FIGURE 2.1 Flooding in Mumbai during the monsoon (Photo credit: Wikimedia commons).

Introduction

Uncertainty is often considered to be a *super wicked problem* or a *monster* by scientists and policymakers (van der Sluijs 2005; Curry and Webster 2011). In climate change policymaking, approaches to handle uncertainty have been dominated

DOI: 10.4324/9781003257585-2

by efforts to minimise and control it, and "attempts to quantify it in one way or another" (Hallegatte et al. 2012: 10). This approach has been increasingly critiqued for neither providing a useful basis for meaningful policy responses nor reflecting the lived realities of people (Wilby and Dessai 2010). Alternative perspectives have emerged over recent years that have focused on embracing uncertainty through "robust" decision-making (Lemos et al. 2016; Kirchhoff et al. 2015) or engaging with and integrating local or indigenous understandings through citizen science (Panda 2016; D'Souza and Kale 2018) (Figure 2.1).

While there is now quite a rich literature focusing on indigenous experiences and knowledges of climate change and uncertainty (Crate and Nuttall 2009; Carey 2010; Rudiak-Gould 2013), there are still gaps in how uncertainties are understood across a range of actors involved in envisioning climate scenarios and models and translating them into policy. In this chapter, we examine how uncertainty is understood by climate scientists and policymakers at national and sub-national levels considered the "above" in this volume. This complements studies of how individuals, households and organisations at local levels (the "below") understand uncertainty and climate change, which is the focus of most of the chapters in this volume. We are particularly interested in how uncertainties are represented in policy debates and whether conceptualisations of climate-related uncertainties from the "below" are taken into account in scientific assessments. To do this, we draw on insights from existing literature, complemented by data from semi-structured interviews and roundtable discussions in Norway, India and the United Kingdom.

As discussed in the introduction to this volume, conceptualisations of uncertainty are varied and are embedded in different realms of knowledge and disciplinary traditions. Three types of uncertainties are relevant for our discussion (see Mehta and Srivastava 2020 and Chapter 1, this volume). Firstly, aleatoric uncertainties referring to natural fluctuations, high degree of variability and disequilibrium dynamics having unknown effects (cf. AchutaRao 2016); secondly, knowledge or epistemic uncertainties, which refers to indeterminate knowledge about changes and their impacts (Field et al. 2012; Scoones and Stirling 2020); and thirdly, uncertainties linked to larger political economy conditions, including unanticipated outcomes due to socio-political interventions and how they are experienced by diverse groups (Wynne 1992; Mehta et al. 1999). All these uncertainties are experienced, framed and interpreted differently by different actors and are linked to relations of power that justify different institutional practices and responses (Rein and Schön 1993).

Uncertainty is at the core of the climate change problem. The IPCC has slowly changed its stance on uncertainty. From a preoccupation with **reducing** and **mastering** uncertainty, it is now focusing more on how to **manage** and **cope** with uncertainty and defines uncertainty as "[a] state of incomplete knowledge that can result from a lack of information or from disagreement about what is known or even knowable" (IPCC 2014b: 128). Hawkins and Sutton (2009) distinguish three main sources of uncertainty in climate projections: firstly, the natural fluctuations or internal variability of the climate system; secondly, the fact that different models give different climate projections to the same radiative forcing[1]; and the third is scenario uncertainty, which are uncertainties around future demographic change and emissions pathways. These are sometimes referred to as aleatoric, epistemic and policy uncertainty, respectively (Hallegatte *et al.* 2012). For shorter timescales, the two former dominate, whereas for longer timescales of many decades, model and scenario uncertainty are dominant. From a climate science perspective, the potential to reduce uncertainties in climate projections is seen to be only in internal variability and model uncertainty; the former only over a decade or so through the integration of observational data (Hawkins and Sutton 2009) While aleatoric uncertainty over the longer term is, by its very nature, something that cannot be "dealt with" in any meaningful sense of the word, epistemic uncertainty can be identified, acknowledged and reflected on in policy processes.

Hallegatte *et al.* (2012: 4) describe climate change as a situation with "deep uncertainty", namely, where one of the following conditions is met: "(1) a range of possible futures without known relative probabilities; (2) multiple divergent but equally-valid world-views, including values used to define criteria of success and (3) decisions which adapt over time and cannot be considered independently". They argue that as these uncertainties cannot be eliminated, in either the short or most likely longer term, new approaches to deal with these uncertainties are needed. This has given rise to a growing "family of approaches" focused on providing robust outcomes in the face of a range of possible changes, ranging from large computer-based models to qualitative assessments (Interview with a climate scientist, UK, January 2017). Approaches include a focus on "no regrets", reversibility and flexibility in the face of uncertainty, building safety margins and reducing decision-making time horizons (Hallegatte *et al.* 2012). Common to these approaches is that they acknowledge and "embrace" uncertainty, rather than trying to avoid or minimise it and building in planning responses that are robust and resilient in the face of a range of possible future climates.

How climate change uncertainty is understood from the "above" matters because it is experts, policymakers and scientists who frame how we see climate change and related policy decisions and funded priority actions. Decisions are made today that will affect future vulnerabilities – and, in turn, impacts – from climate change and decisions will have to be made and, indeed, are made, based on incomplete information. This chapter, thus, explores how uncertainty is understood and represented by the "above", by whom and how decisions are made. We draw on over 30 interviews in India (Delhi, Mumbai, Kolkata and Gandhinagar) and 10 in Norway and the United Kingdom. Additionally, we also draw on insights generated from four roundtable events carried out with scientists, policymakers as well as representatives from academia and civil society, including their reflections on issues concerning inter- and transdisciplinary working and social science perspectives (see Chapter 7, this volume). While the roundtables had a good mix of men and women, apart from about four women scientists, all the other interviewees were men, highlighting the need for more women in climate science/climate decision-making. The findings are organised around the following broad questions: (1) how is uncertainty understood by climate scientists and experts? (2) how is uncertainty presented and represented in policy debates, including the integration of local knowledges and understandings? and (3) what are the possible options for generating a more social understanding of uncertainty?

We hope to demonstrate that while the "above" is deeply aware of the challenges of integrating uncertainty in scientific understandings, most groups in the "above" are largely wedded to conventional scientific assessments such as modelling and predictions and "mastering" uncertainty instead of embracing uncertainty. The "above" is of course very diverse and this chapter teases out this heterogeneity. We also focus on the challenges and frustrations that many scientists and experts have with the politics of uncertainty and the challenges of communicating uncertainty to decision-makers who do not care for such nuances and seek predictability. Finally, despite some attempts to bridge gaps between the "above" and "below", we found that in the Indian context, there is significant resistance to construct alternative approaches and systems that embrace plural knowledges and experiences from "below".

Understandings of uncertainty

The question of how uncertainty is understood by climate scientists, policymakers and boundary workers relates not only to whether it is considered as an epistemic or ontological issue but also if, and to what extent, local understandings of uncertainty are incorporated. We discuss these themes first by looking at issues concerning modelling and parameters and then by investigating the sources and nature of uncertainty at different spatial and temporal scales. This includes challenges concerning downscaling models to finer resolutions as well as dealing with uncertainties in long-term projections.

Uncertain models

Climate change has traditionally been conceived as a global phenomenon and conventionally one of the pervasive ways to understand it has been through computer models. The "globalising instinct" in knowledge making and the tendency to focus on the global scale can, in part, be attributed to the fact that the climate system is hugely complex and efforts to gain an understanding of the dynamics have largely been driven by the construction of General Circulation Models or GCMs (Edwards 2010). Because Greenhouse Gases (GHGs) influence systems of circulation, modellers argue that it is a tricky exercise to scale down models to lower levels such as the regional or the local. This is the premise on which the algorithms and parameters underpinning GCMs are based (Lahsen 2005).

All models, including GCMs, are simplified representations of complex systems and as such are never the "real" thing, a fact that is often ignored (Pollack *et al.*

2005). At the centre of the scientific practice is the creation of boundaries and distinct binaries (Douglas 1986) between the subjective and the objective, between the abstract climate and the particularities of weather (Hulme 2016; Heymann 2018). The abstract and supposedly "objective" is represented by the hard science of modelling which can ignore or externalise the subjective dimensions of uncertainties or neglect their political dimensions (Jasanoff 2009). Such scientific approaches are just one of the many ways people anticipate and prepare for the future and need to be viewed together with the day-to-day strategies of people who live with the uncertainties of climate (Hastrup 2013, see Chapters 3–6, this volume). However, a certain politics of knowledge results in particular domains with so-called hard science gaining authority over the others. Yet, all forms of knowledge (including so-called expert knowledge) are culturally and socially embedded and moulded by particular social, power and gender relations (as demonstrated in previous chapters). Models are also embedded in narratives and storylines about a future based on certain assumptions (Hajer 1995) but gain authority over other forms of knowledge through a range of political practices and boundary-ordering devices (Shackley and Wynne 1996; Heymann 2018).

These models, however, are ridden with uncertainty as it is a fraught exercise to represent the complexity of processes and climate in future. For example, GCMs aim to represent the relationship between two fluid and chaotic systems: the oceans and the atmosphere. Characterising such systems is virtually impossible using current theories of non-linear dynamic systems, particularly in situations involving transient changes of parameter values (Dyson 2015; Curry 2017). Sources of uncertainty include the structure of the model, the selection and function of particular parameters included in models as well as uncertainties related to the data used which are also derived from a variety of sources. In climate change, much uncertainty derives from imprecision, also through attempts to deal with disparate sources and sets of data. Furthermore, measuring devices and instruments can be unreliable or change over time and these are themselves models of a kind. Only 10% of the information gathered is raw data, and the rest has been processed through some sort of model, a phenomenon Edwards (2010) describes as "shimmering". Added to these sources of uncertainty is technical uncertainty regarding the computational implementation of these models.

The challenges of modelling such fluid and complex interlinked systems are exemplified by what Dyson (2015) terms "fudge factors" such as clouds and, to some extent, aerosols. The stochastic nature of clouds makes it extremely hard to incorporate cloud behaviour into models. This was reflected in several interviews with Indian scientists working on climate change models, who stated that even "one cloud in a model is difficult to model" (Interview with scientist, New Delhi, May 2017, NCMRF). By contrast, a scientist in the Ministry for Earth Sciences was optimistic about gaining knowledge about how "how clouds react, develop and interact. While these processes need to be understood from a range of disciplines including physics and mathematics, I am optimistic about it" (Interview May 2017). Another such "fudge factor" and notorious source of uncertainty is aerosols. These are "tiny particles in solid/liquid phase ubiquitously dispersed in the atmosphere" (Moorthy et al. 2016, 53) and have climate forcing potential due to their optical, microphysical and chemical properties (ibid.). Aerosols impact climate directly by interacting with incoming solar and outgoing terrestrial radiations. They also have indirect effects as they alter cloud properties (Srivastava 2017). Their dispersion and effects on climate are extremely challenging to model, not least due to lack of data on emissions that are a significant source of aerosols. According to a scientist in Kutch (Gujarat), models have a weak emission inventory in India because emission inventories have mainly developed in Europe. In Kutch, for example, industrial expansion has led to an increase in aerosols, which, in turn, can increase cloud cover but not necessarily more rain. It could influence the incidence of extreme weather events such as tropical cyclones (Srivastava 2017). A scientist from Kutch argued:

> Aerosols are challenging in the Indian context. They are difficult to understand and need more time and computational models. How are these particles parametrized with rainfall? If this is not done, predictions are not possible. The dangers of ignoring this is that prediction reliability is less than 40% […]. Clouds for example may exist according to meteorological parameters but if aerosols are not taken into consideration, predictions could fail.
>
> *(Scientist October 2016, Kutch)*

As stated earlier, the challenge according to the IPCC is to learn to manage uncertainty. In the *Fifth Assessment Report*, the IPCC (2014a) acknowledges that there are uncertainties that we will never know and that the best response is to understand and cope with them. For the IPCC,

> uncertainties arise at the level of observations (measurements for natural phenomena and some socio-economic statistics, possibly survey data for other socio-economic, political and cultural issues) and from how the data from observations are turned into indicators used in the assessment (e.g. by combinations of variables, statistical methods) (Swart et al. 2009: 4).

Scientific assessments and results are weighed across this spectrum of confidence, but here too, there is room for bias and value judgements (Curry and Webster 2011). Computer simulations are used to represent "aspects of the climate that are extremely difficult to observe […] and explore the system that would otherwise be impenetrable" (Curry and Webster 2011: 1668).

The challenges of modelling uncertainty

Nobody we interviewed denied the problem of climate change. All interviewees acknowledged climate change as a major global challenge and recounted their own observations of climate change examples. A meteorologist in Norway observed that:

> The main characteristic of the weather in Norway is variability and temperature differences can be rather large. From our measurements and data over a span of 50 years we see that the temperature is rising, and that precipitation generally has increased. Flash flooding and intense precipitation over limited areas for 1–3 hours causing a lot of damage has also increased. These need to be taken into account for future planning, e.g. in cities, drainage etc. The trends we are observing were not there earlier, and they are in tune with what is coming out of the IPCC reports.
> *(Expert from the Norwegian Meteorological Institute August 2016, Oslo)*

A central question is what can – and cannot – models cover? A crucial choice that modellers have to make is to choose what parameters to include and how. Given that modellers cannot capture the whole range of issues and uncertainties in their models, how do you accommodate the effects of land use changes, for instance? There are diverse sources of epistemic uncertainty which may cascade into other types of uncertainty related to models, parameters and assumptions. A climate researcher in a government institution in Gujarat highlighted this as follows:

> In research, all predictions are based on projections. My research is on Greenhouse Gases (GHGs) and how uncertainty is accounted in emissions. The IPCC's emission scenarios are based on the natural course of emissions in the atmosphere and energy (direct fossil fuel burning) accounts for 70 percent of GHG emissions. But there is a lot of uncertainty in these emission scenarios due to the limitations of models and the baselines. So, if there is so much uncertainty in the data, methodology and also emission factor (e.g. the ash contents are different for different resources and depend on how they are burnt, namely, aerobically, anaerobically or incomplete burning), how does it influence and guide our projections?
> *(Interview September 2016, Gujarat)*

Another modeller based at a research institute in Norway told us that the uncertainties associated with physiographic parameters, affected by socio-economic factors such as urban development plans and patterns of land use change, will affect modelling; however, tackling them remains challenging:

> We have no idea how different development scenarios take place – for example, if a hotel will be built on the coast in Greece and how will it affect land use changes? All the uncertainty I can deal with is reduced to the distribution of non-probability [...] We don't capture change when it comes to land/water change or changes due to infrastructure and

population dynamics. We make large-scale global assumptions; we don't capture these kinds of (socio-economic) changes.

(Modeller August 2016, Oslo)

In India, climate models are a relatively recent development. India's nodal department for weather- and climate-related information and analysis, the Indian Meteorological Department's (IMD) models have only evolved relatively recently which limits their applicability in terms of establishing baselines and useful, long-term trends. According to two scientists from a forecasting institute in New Delhi:

> We want to predict everything, but our models are old and hence our predictions are based on old models. We are using information from old satellites from the 1980s and 1990s. Only recently do we have better data and improved models. Before the 1990s, the IMD only used observational data and charts, hence the experience of IMD with models has been very limited. Currently there is a cult like faith in modelling and hence there is a major demand for our models. However, there will always be uncertainty. For example, if data is collected within 1 and half hour and it is 150 km away from Delhi there will be uncertainty. Even with the best model, surprises can happen even with the best input/data. I am sure even in 200 years there will be uncertainty. Modelling is not a perfected science.
>
> *(Interviews May 2017, New Delhi)*

For a climate scientist in Norway, uncertainty stems from models (and parameterisation), natural variability and social systems. "Some uncertainties can be narrowed down but there are limitations in the modelling exercise. Even though models have improved a lot over the past 20 years and are now finer in scale, there is still a lot of complexity" (Interview August 2016, Oslo). Despite acknowledging these complexities, most climate scientists we interviewed hoped that with better knowledge, better modelling and better parameters uncertainties could be reduced or addressed since they are keen to provide certainty and data to make decisions. Our interviews suggest that many modellers in practice remain committed to reducing and mastering uncertainty rather than aiming to have models that speak to coping and learning to live with uncertainty.

The challenge of downscaling

Climate change models are associated with a cascade of uncertainties that increase with downscaling (Wilby and Dessai 2010). These relate to uncertainties of future emissions of GHGs and sulphate aerosols as discussed above; uncertainties of the response of the climate system to these changes at global and national scales and the spatial and temporal distribution of these impacts (Dessai and Sluijs 2007). In a scalar view of uncertainty, the cascade of uncertainty proceeds from different demographic and socio-economic pathways and then translates into GHG emissions, gets picked up by models by way of outcomes, which then translate into various human and natural impacts that further trickle into the adaptation responses (Wilby and Dessai 2010). However, socio-economic pathways are particularly hard to capture. Thus, the socio-political unknowns of climate change are massive, and these often intersect with other "uncertain" drivers of change and may exacerbate or snowball into existing problems related to environmental conditions such as water quality, health and food and energy security (Hastrup 2013). The chapters that follow demonstrate this cascading view of uncertainty in Mumbai, Kutch and the Sundarbans. As noted earlier in this chapter, there has been a distinct "globalising instinct" in climate change science, as scientists working on constructing GCMs have mainly been preoccupied with the global dynamics of CO_2 emissions, circulation and effects (Curry 2017). There is another dimension to scaling down as well, what Schneider and Walsh refer to as the "politics of zoom" (2019). This emphasises how downscaled visualisations of the impact of climate change tend to replicate the "hegemonic dynamics of their global sources" and tend to "cancel out conflicting local data" (Schneider and Walsh 2019: 5). Scaling down to lower spatial scales is, therefore, considered challenging.

The temporal scales in climate change models are another challenge. The climate models are made to look at the effects of emissions or scenarios, and these differences only come into play after about 30 years so every uncertainty before that is not really dealt with. The models often also do not capture all the changes and uncertainties at the local level. There is a fundamental misconception that climate models can do anything in the here and now, locally.

Interviews reflect that uncertainties are particularly problematic at regional and local scales. For the most part, uncertainties are described in epistemic terms, for example, that models and science are "not up to it yet" or that science still needs to improve. Uncertainty in models, therefore, can potentially reduce the veracity of claims around climate change and limit the potential to meaningfully inform policy (see "below"). Most of the scientists we interviewed acknowledge the uncertainties associated with downscaling. This is especially true in dense urban settings. A hydro-climatologist from Mumbai stated:

> Downscaling from global circulation models to finer resolutions is a failure because the science is not properly understood. At a finer resolution they are failing at a miserable scale. For example, take Mumbai. There is much talk about links between urban island heat effect and extreme rainfall. But there are so many multiple factors: the buildings and city structure have much to do with this. That Mumbai is getting more extreme rainfall due to the urban heat island is actually a wrong hypothesis and scientists have started to realise this. When the monsoon starts there is nothing, all temperature goes down, so urban heat island doesn't really level up.

> What is exactly happening is that there is huge flux of moisture [coming in from the Arabian sea and that creates lots of problems because of the urban structure (i.e. very tall buildings that change the patterns of wind and rainfall). Even two buildings between roads can have an effect on urban precipitation. The resolution will be in the range of 2–5 km. But in climate models the resolution is more than 100 km. Even if we are going for regional models and the range is 4 km there will still be huge uncertainty. These phenomena are not really captured in models and even if we have the scientific understanding it is very difficult to represent that understanding into models. Different models try and parametrize these cases in a coarse scale and when we use different parameter scales, this also leads to sources of uncertainty whilst looking at the urban scale.
>
> *(Interview with scientist April 2016, Mumbai)*

Singh and AchutaRao (2018) highlight the aleatoric and epistemic uncertainties inherent in modelling rainfall, especially monsoon (see below) behaviour and emphasise the challenges of downscaling especially since GCMs are coarse in resolution since they cover up to 200 kilometres in grids. Regional Climate Models (RCMs) are supposed to address some of these challenges; however, they also add further to the uncertainty existing in GCMs due to the "high computational costs resulting in a limited number of simulations being available. Also, downscaling further adds to the uncertainty that already exists in the global coupled model simulations" (Singh and AchutaRao 2018: 2). For example, a scientist from Gandhinagar told us that in India, Gujarat is one state that has produced an inventory of regional-level emissions. But she concurs that planning regarding adaptation and mitigation can be difficult based on regional-level data, as these are not communicated to global bodies. The international organisations rely on national-level data and this can be misleading. For instance, the state of Gujarat has a different emissions scenario from the rest of the country. The per capita consumption of electricity is almost double that of the national average due to the high number of industries and the very industrialised and developed coastline (Scientist September 2016, Gandhinagar).

These challenges of uncertainty come clearly to the fore in drylands such as Kutch, which are characterised by high variability in precipitation and where rainfall patterns vary every few kilometres. Global projections on climate change are not particularly helpful when it comes to state-level planning, argues an IMD scientist in Gandhinagar:

> Though it is projected that there would be an average rise of 1–1.5 degrees in the global temperature, that is not helpful for decision-making when you have to plan for this kind of warming at local stations. You need to make a proper strategy, probably to make people aware of the grilling heat that is likely to affect people in coming future.
>
> *(Interview January 2018, Gandhinagar)*

Automatic Weather Stations (AWS) can help provide more locally attuned forecasts, but there are only three in a large district such as Kutch that function well (Interview, October 2016, Kutch), while there are about 60 in Mumbai (Interviews with Bombay Municipal Corporation official, January 2016, Bombay). Due to the massive weather variability and massive changes happening every 10 kilometres, a dense network is required every 10–15 km to record variability. However, in remote places in areas like Kutch, poor internet connectivity and limited funding impede the efficiency of AWS. This discussion highlights that global and RCMs have limits when it comes to predicting impacts at the local level and managing with local-level uncertainties and variations, especially in highly variable locations such a drylands. India, at least, is still far off in having robust systems at the local level to improve weather and climate forecasts in order to provide predictions and support to agencies working on the impacts of climate change in areas such as water security, food security and vector-borne diseases (Interview, October 2016, Kutch).

Forecasts and projections: uncertainty in the short, medium and long term

While climate modellers are concerned with the long-term projections of what is likely to happen in the future, the science of weather forecasting is dealing with the short-term, day-to-day predictions of precipitation patterns, temperature changes, wind speeds and other weather features. For meteorologists, weather and climate are often considered to be a seamless continuum. An expert from the Norwegian meteorological office told us: "When scientists talk about climate change, they talk about the past and they talk about the future. Weather forecasting is a few days in between". By contrast, lay people rarely distinguish between "weather" and "climate" (see quote below). The same meteorologist discusses the temporal aspect of climate change and the distinction between weather and climate change:

> I talked with a taxi driver some weeks ago. He did not know that I was a meteorologist, so he told me that they had had three different climates that day. It is difficult for lay people to distinguish between weather and climate, and I don't think it is necessary to expend much effort to make people see the difference. I think we should rather look at it as a continuum, a sort of seamless change between the past climate, the current weather, and future climate projections. Of course, we are providing the weather forecasts, as professionals, we are distinguishing very much. But in fact, it is a seamless change. For me, the analysis of climate change, the weather and climate projections for the future are part of the seamless production of information and services.
>
> *(Interview August 2016, Oslo)*

While short-term weather forecasting is a less uncertain endeavour than speculating about long-term effects of GHG emissions, uncertainty looms large. In particular, the problem of resolution is a key issue for many weather forecasters. As discussed above, rainfall is intrinsically tricky to predict, due to the stochastic nature of cloud cover. Several interviewees also mentioned particular challenges in forecasting rainfall, both due to extremes and also the uncertainties around the monsoon in the Indian context. The following quote from a Mumbai-based scientist captures this nicely:

> There are two challenges when we talk about India: The monsoon is one and the second one is extremes in rainfall patterns. Temperature is not so difficult and we get good projections on forecast, but precipitation is tricky. When we heat corns we know when the temperature is high, we know what will happen, but we don't know what will pop up. up[...] Rainfall is like popcorn [...] Over and above the challenges of resolution and parametrization, we just don't know which corn will pop up or not. With temperature there is less uncertainty but with moisture we never know when it precipitates and how. It could precipitate here or there, now or after 12 hours and these patterns can disturb the entire balance. So from a climate/weather perspective these are the uncertainties we are talking about.
>
> *(Scientist October 2016, Mumbai)*

This often makes forecasting difficult for the IMD, given the challenges in predicting the Indian monsoon. The same scientist stated that climate

> models are failing to simulate the monsoon trends and climate projections thus often do not work. It perhaps makes sense to focus on a shorter scale for models so that they can be more of user and also lead to decision making.
>
> *(Scientist October 2016, Mumbai)*

This implies, thus, the need to cope and manage uncertainties around the monsoon and also communicate them appropriately rather than assuming that there is confidence in predicting the longer scale.

Uncertainty in policy and public debates

The science–policy interface, that is, how scientific practice/projections are translated into decision outcomes also has implications for how uncertainty is addressed. While scientists work with uncertainty in terms of probability, decision-makers often like to be certain about the outcomes (Bradshaw and Borchers 2000) and governments are typically very unresponsive to uncertainty, see Chapter 4 for the case of senior bureaucrats in Gujarat. As discussed earlier, decision-making is less about mastering uncertainty prerogative of natural science and more about managing uncertainty (Schneider and Kuntz-Duriseti 2002). In real terms, there could be two kinds of paradoxes that policymakers encounter: excess of information and the lack of time to determine policy options, or the time scale lag between resolution of uncertainty and policy decisions (Schneider and Kuntz-Duriseti 2002).

No one disputes that effective communication between science and policy is necessary to make informed choices regarding decisions on climate change (Dessai and Sluijs 2007). One of the foremost challenges of climate change decision-making is to "translate" and make sense of the models and integrate this into policy- and decision-making and justify such decisions. As Dosi and Egidi (1991: 152) argue that – "with uncertainty, information is imperfect and possibly asymmetric, agents hold different beliefs and 'priors', and their knowledge of the future is limited. They can interpret correctly the signals that they receive (and try to do so), but they do not [and cannot] receive all the signals necessary to make those optimal choices that would have been taken under perfect information". This point relates to the epistemic uncertainty whereby imperfect knowledge leads to uncertainty. However, these decisions are often located and embedded in structures and contexts that function, harness and use information in particular ways. These may be (1) the epistemic networks, (2) financial networks, (3) political networks, (4) discursive networks and (5) performative networks (Hulme 2013). The focus on quantitative and statistical uncertainty most often hides or ignores the "policy relevant uncertainty information about the deeper dimensions of uncertainty that cannot be quantified" (ibid.: 5). The uncertainties in forecasting and modelling lead to difficulties in translating these issues into policy and public debates. Several patterns emerged from the interviews that we outline below. These include:

- The conflation of variability and climate change in popular discourse
- Critique of relevance of models to policymaking
- Decision-makers may not accept the forecasts from scientists, especially if they are uncertain
- The media may not present the nuances inherent in the forecasts
- Approaches like 'robust decision-making' or similar tend to be more at the academic level and do not seem to be gaining much traction in India

We now examine these issues in depth with the help of the interview material. An important distinction, which is often conflated in popular discourse as well as decision-making, is between climate variability and climate change (Hulme 2016). Local people and decision-makers tend to focus on "the here and now" and on the variability that they experience, rather than long-term climate change. This can be frustrating for scientists as expressed by a climate scientist in Kutch:

> Climate change and variability are often conflated. We need at least 30 years of data to talk about climate change and one cannot talk about climate change with a few years of data.
>
> *(Interview October 2016, Kutch)*

Many of the scientists interviewed spoke of the problems in translating scientific knowledge to decision-making.

> Ministers and others always push scientists for estimates and figures regarding climate change impacts. Climate change science gives you a range but they want a figure for planning crops, breeding programmes etc. This is a problem for us working in climate change. How to deal with the complexity in models?
>
> *(Scientist January 2015, Kolkata)*

Largely, policymakers tend to focus on what's happening in microclimates in order to be able to act accordingly. For example, they look at predictions for agriculture so that they can provide inputs to farmers regarding decisions to plant crops (Social scientist 2014, UK). However, they seem to want a lot of certainty which is often not possible due to the reasons mentioned above.

This often leads to difficult relationships between scientists and officials. Officials complain when forecasts are wrong and fail to understand that uncertainty is always embedded in forecasts and that we need to live with it and work around it. In part, the problem is also that scientists have failed to communicate issues concerning uncertainty to the public, the media and the government and the probabilistic nature of forecasts.

In the roundtable held in Oslo, observations in a similar vein were made:

> We often represent research on climate change as a flower, with the climate system and changes in the climate system, in the middle. Then the next circle is about impacts on nature and society, and then there are the petals of the flower, where we get into more sectoral research – adaptation and mitigation in transport, adaptation and mitigation in agriculture, things like that. There is a danger that this view leads to climate research being a bit like a drunken man who has lost his keys – he will look under the light of a lamppost, because that is where he can see something, but it is not necessarily where the keys are. In the same way, climate science can say something about probabilities of extreme rainfall, average temperatures, and so on, but that may not necessarily be what matters to people.
>
> *(Roundtable discussion August 2017, Oslo)*

A geologist working on climate change in the Sundarbans feels very frustrated by policymakers who only focus on short-term gains, whilst ignoring climate change and also completely lack long-term thinking and planning:

> In 2002, I started talking about sea level rise in the Bay of Bengal and vanishing islands but nobody listened to me. The government said: "it's

under control so the sea cannot rise". Now with all the plans and data in place, they are saying: "let it rise". Despite sea level rise, islands are still forming but this is due to geological factors. Everything is unknown and we cannot quantify uncertainty. The monsoon forecasts for the Sundarbans have failed miserably since 2008. Farmers are now committing suicide all over India due to floods and droughts combined. We cannot fight with the sea and nature. Even in Japan the tsunami wall failed. Why are cities being built in such vulnerable coastal areas, e.g. Bombay? There is no proper long-term planning. The government only thinks 10 km around Delhi. They focus on scenarios and on lowering costs and less on benefits. Which dams or embankments in the country have given the desired results? Has anybody been punished for wasting public money?

(Interview January 2014, Sundarbans)

He also argued that mainstream science in India, including engineering, has tended to ignore uncertainty. This is because Indian science tends to focus on modifying and controlling nature rather than accepting that "we don't know enough [...]". Observing and experiencing nature are both very important. This training is absent in Indian science. To understand a place like the Sundarbans, one needs a different orientation or mindset" (Interview January 2014, Sundarbans).

Most scientists also complained that there is a marked lack of political and bureaucratic will to engage with climate science and research. The scientist working in Gujarat comments:

Our research will always have recommendation for the government but they keep it and forget it! Even in Gujarat which has all the policies in place around climate change, integration is not happening – I think the Climate Change Department operates only as fund managers, but the policy has not yet come (See also Chapter 4 on Kutch, this volume).

We also interviewed social scientists who work on climate change who feel that the problem is that policymakers are always looking for easy solutions and that natural scientists and social scientists also often cannot agree about uncertainty. In a group discussion with natural and social scientists, a social scientist contended that

Natural and social sciences ask completely different questions. Natural scientists want to provide information to economists, whereas economists ask what decisions to take under uncertainty [...] It is very difficult to translate a natural scientists uncertainty formulation into decision making.

(Interview August 2016, Oslo)

They all acknowledged that communicating uncertainty is difficult, especially when you begin to quantify uncertainties:

> There are cascading uncertainties and we can't quantify all of them. In climate change temperature forecast ranges from 2.5 C – 5 C. We need to ignore some uncertainties in order to say anything and don't want to live completely in an uncertainty scenario. Of course, a lot depends on communicating what we put in our models and quantification is only one aspect here. We need better communication.
>
> *(Modeller August 2016, Oslo)*

> We try to work within standard errors but there exists a dilemma of how much uncertainty one should communicate. Natural scientists bring facts-based observations. Economists interpret information and we tell policymakers what to do. Too much of focus on whether it is 3, 4 or 5 degrees (i.e., uncertainty) can distract attention from key issues.
>
> *(Economist working on climate change, August 2016, Oslo)*

Natural scientists told us that social scientists tend to focus too much on complexity which does not allow decisions to be taken and does not help problems to be solved ultimately. By contrast, social scientists said that natural scientists have a too narrow view of what uncertainty is and that there is a need to work around "uncertainty" as a problem of communication. In the Oslo roundtable, a participant, with experience from the IPCC, argued that there are a lot of scientists who think we should just ban the word uncertainty altogether and instead talk about "how certain are you"?

Attribution and the uptake of forecasts and projection

An issue that came up in most interviews concerned problems in attribution, over and above the complexity and uncertainty in forecasts and projections. We have already discussed the problems of forecasts around the monsoon; however, there are little long-term data and trends that provide sufficient evidence that the monsoon has changed in response to climate change in terms of average precipitation as evident in this statement from a meteorologist at the IMD.

> We do not see long term trends linking climate change with the monsoon. Of course, in different Indian states, there are differences in rainfall patterns, e.g. Rajasthan has seen changes in rain frequency. There is an increase in monsoonal heavy rain and an increasing number of days with heavy rain with lighter and moderate rain decreasing. But still on average the totals are still roughly the same.
>
> *(IMD expert, May 2016, Delhi)*

India has organised events related to attribution which are attended by delegates from other countries in the global South. However, attribution can also be harnessed for political uses. The attribution of heatwaves and other climatic events is increasingly becoming a contested area as it deals with questions of responsibility, equity and justice as well as adaptation (see below). In an interview with two officials at the Ministry of Earth Sciences (MoESs), we were told:

> We need more research on how to do attribution, at present it is experimental. We recently had an African Development Bank meeting in Ahmedabad looking at attribution of heatwaves and floods. Attribution involves use of all available models and assesses historical data over a period of time plus different variables related to specific climate events. For example, the recent heat waves are attributed to climate change. India is leading research on the question of attribution. The use of outputs from attribution science can be deployed also in the global arena. India wants to use attribution science in climate negotiations.
>
> *(Officials Ministry of Earth Science May 2016)*

Attribution issues, however, seem to matter less at the national, state and district level. Policymakers and politicians in India are not necessarily concerned about whether a certain weather event is attributable to climate change or not in the first place. What matters is the type and nature of response and displaying that the prevailing government/state is in control. Largely, the cause of the event does not matter to the local electorate (IIT climate scientist January 2018). This again underscores the disconnect between the "above" that still has a tendency to reduce and master uncertainty v/s the "below" that is finding ways to live with and manage climate and other related uncertainties.

Also, in dynamic environments like Kutch and the Sundarbans, attribution is more difficult because climate change is one of the many issues that people have to grapple with in their daily struggle for survival (see Chapters 4 and 5). According to a social scientist working on climate change:

> Usually it's best not to rush to conclusions regarding climate change though of course much depends on how ecosystems change and adapt and a lot of other relationships. Locals tend to have a far more nuanced perspective [...] But NGOs tend to attribute and relabel lots of things as climate change in order to access money. All development work is now climate change. By contrast, people at the forefront of climate change are less likely to label it as such.
>
> *(Social scientist UK, July 2014)*

Scientists also struggle with dealing with simplistic views from NGOs.

> Local NGOs are foolish to blame local people for all the problems in the Sundarbans, e.g. 'overfishing' and forest loss. Locals cannot be blamed for salinity and flooding [...] Sea level rise is the main reason why the islands are disappearing. Even tigers are getting homeless in islands where there are no people. We need to convince NGOs that local people cannot be blamed for a lot of these changes.
>
> *(Scientists January 2014, Kolkata)*

From a development point of view, such simplistic perceptions are also unhelpful because local people are vilified and often not allowed to pursue their traditional livelihoods in the name of climate change, often increasing their vulnerabilities and insecurities.

On a positive note, with respect to disaster management, some government scientists are happy about the scope for forecasting and are optimistic regarding the potential for further improvements. This is especially the case with respect to the usefulness of narrowed down uncertainty (scenario bands), in particular predicting cyclones:

> We have done well in disaster prediction and threats are detected even though there can be some difference between actual intensity compared to prediction. With cyclone Aila in 2009, the trend was different from prediction though with cyclone Phailin in 2013 we did very well. The science has improved a lot and is now part of a co-ordinated system and network with disaster management authorities. Disaster management cells co-ordinate functioning and there are now far lower casualties than 20 years ago. Of course, we can still improve the models and forecasting but overall, I am optimistic about our progress.
>
> *(Scientist at MoES May 2016)*

Hybrid knowledges and social understandings of uncertainty

As discussed in this volume, approaches are growing that focus on embracing rather than seeking to avoid uncertainty. They are based on the realisation that uncertainty should not, and need not, lead to paralysis in action. Thus, while the traditional view of uncertainty that we have described so far persists both globally and in the Indian context, there is now an emerging alternative framing that is gaining ground. According to one of the leading researchers working in this field:

> We are looking at frameworks and what options we have that are immune to uncertainty. [It] is supported by institutions such as the World Bank, Rand corporation and so on (...) there are obstacles still in costs, data availability etc., but it is developing.
>
> *(UK Researcher January 2017)*

The "Decision-making under uncertainty society"[2] consists of political scientists, modellers and others actors who are trying to move away from the "predict and act" framework. Robust decision-making is a group of tools, anything from "back of the envelope" tools to RAND corporation's big dataset approaches (UK Researcher January 2017; see also Bhave et al. 2016). From a methodological perspective, the alternative framing has come a long way in changing the focus of adaptation planning away from scenario-led approaches and towards decision-led approaches that emphasises the need for flexibility in future planning (echoing responses that we have described from the "below" in many chapters of this volume). But it is less clear whether and how much traction these approaches have beyond academia. Some argue that approaches like "robust decision-making" have very little traction among governments who tend to revert to familiar and dominant frameworks based on risk assessment. Another UK researcher put it this way: "Climate change is not special […] policy makers are not interested if you say you do not have an answer, [you] have to pick a model or a scenario and go with that" (Interview, February 2017, UK).

Heymann (2018) contends that the discursive trend to concentrate on global models and averages runs counter to the history of climatology as a discipline anchored in local experience of climate and weather. The importance of downscaling and validating local knowledge is to "humanise" climatology, making it accessible and link it to everyday live, knowledge and practice. We now turn to focus on the scope to include forms of knowledge that are often overlooked or undervalued by the "above". These include embodied, emotional and tacit ways of knowing and representing the world which requires a pluralist sensitivity and appreciation for a persistent diversity of understandings (Stirling et al. 2018). Social scientists studying the "social life of models" tell us that climate modelling takes place according to diverse reasoning and across different scales (Hastrup 2013). While this so-called hard science has largely gained authority over other forms of knowledge, all forms of knowledge (including so-called expert knowledge) are culturally and socially embedded and moulded by particular social, power and gender relations. Indeed, the preceding sections have focused on the different scientific and socio-political rationalities that have moulded the "above's" understandings of climate-related uncertainties. Historically, local communities have developed practices and strategies to plan for and live with ecological uncertainty and variability (Hastrup 2013). Hastrup (2013) argues that dealing with climate change involves practices of anticipation, that is, how people anticipate the future and prepare for it. For her, scientific approaches are just one of the many modalities of this anticipation alongside the day-to-day strategies of people who live with uncertainty or make decisions regarding changes in climate. These could be seasonal mobility, crop diversification or risk-averse behaviours to cope with resource fluctuation.

According to Berkes and Berkes (2009), many indigenous systems have developed highly appropriate ways to deal with complexity and uncertainty. Indigenous knowledge (IK) evolves through adaptive learning based on developing a complex knowledge base of the environment and lessons from past mistakes and is thus a kind of post-normal science (Funtowicz and Ravetz 1993). According to Berkes and Berkes (2009), both kinds of knowledge are desirable because they have different relative strengths and a potential for complementarity. IK can also complement more macro perspectives by filling in the local scale. However, as argued in Chapter 4 on Kutch, climate change and new radical uncertainties profoundly alter previous indigenous anticipations and often test tested indigenous system might not help in tackling the new range of unpredictability and unknowns.

Indeed, climate scientists we interviewed working in an interdisciplinary institution in Norway acknowledged the limitations of engineering and technologically oriented solutions which cannot solve everything.

> Unfortunately, 'techno-management' and pipe thinking are very problematic and there is too much faith in technological solutions to 'rescue us'. Instead, we need to have more learning and mutual, exchanges across different groups and levels of expertise. For example, scientists could learn from farmers at what temperature it is when crops die and then improve threshold scenarios. Policy makers could also make use of this information and give guidance to farmers to change their cropping patterns. But it is difficult for humans to grasp all of this complexity and learning processes embracing uncertainty are key.
>
> *(Discussion with scientists August 2016, Oslo)*

Plural knowledge systems can act as the "bridge". Historical work by Carey (2010) demonstrates how scientific knowledge about glacial changes in the Andes is moulded by power dynamics, economic outcomes, local worldviews and social relations. Thus, even the so-called modern forms of knowledge based on western science are thoroughly dynamic and imbued with local culture and practice (Feyerabend, 1996; Wynne 1996). Thus, neither scientists nor local people are homogeneous. The dynamic view of the nature of uncertainty from "below" and "above" that we have pursued in this volume opens up the possibility of identifying convergences between certain actors and perspectives in local and scientific worlds. Hybrid knowledges can, thus, be a suitable way to tackle uncertainty challenges, and a growing number of scientists are seeking to work in transdisciplinary and interdisciplinary ways (see also Movik *et al.*, Chapter 7). As argued by a professor from Kolkata:

> I have moved out from the conventional academic domain. When we started only 2% of fishers used GPS, now 60% use it. Scientists are now working with farmers in Kutch and the Sundarbans to revive local crops that are resistant to droughts, salinity etc and can survive better in the face of cyclones, droughts etc In Mumbai, IIT researchers are developing

a flood forecasting system. Different experts from tidal, atmospheric and hydrological sciences will work together and develop a model which will have a probabilistic forecast on floods. It will be opened up to community (urban people) to get their feedback on what way they can improve it further.

(Interview, January 2014, Kolkata)

The Met office in Norway works in close co-operation with different authorities – for example, roads, water, energy, agriculture, fisheries, transport and coast – who all depend on the weather for their work. They also consult the public about how best to provide weather forecasts and information (e.g. mobile apps). The 90-minute weather forecast is based on user feedback. We did not find this same level of user engagement in the IMD in Delhi even though there was acknowledgement of the strengths of local weather information and traditional knowledges:

Yes, they [local weather forecasts based on perceptions] are useful in many respects, we can find out whether local people understand our 'language'. We can also learn how to prepare better, how our information is used and what the local confidence in our warnings is. Traditional knowledge can be useful for some situations, e.g. a local person based on understanding of cloud formation can predict whether there will be thunderstorms etc. Farmers through this knowledge can utilise historical evidence, memory and observation. This knowledge can work but not always. Animal behaviour is similarly to have shown ability to react/predict weather but similarly cannot be used much or relied on. But traditional knowledge can be use especially for wider communication.

(Scientists at IMD, Delhi, Interview May 2016)

Clearly, despite appreciating local traditions and knowledge, this official did not see an integration of this knowledge/and perceptions into models as feasible. By and large, the scientists we interviewed seemed to imply that scientific knowledge was perhaps better or of a higher level.

[...] ordinary people may be also decision-makers but it is our duty as scientists to explain about the possibilities for the future. The possibilities are based on historical records that you really have to take into account that the future will not be like the past. I think that is a sort of mission we have as scientific people, to try to explain that. I do not think we will manage to convince everybody Religion is something you believe, that is good for many people, but science is not a religion, it is about good hypotheses for the future, which are based on scientific work.

(Interview with scientist in Oslo Met office, August 2016, Oslo)

A scientist working in Gujarat says he has learnt a lot from farmers regarding the agriculture–climate interface. His organisation has organised "listening sessions" with farmers and training programmes with farmers, however, with the aim to educate the farmers about climate change and also to improve forecasting "so we can help farmers". Even though he acknowledges limits to modelling exercises, he thinks local knowledge is in itself difficult if not impossible to quantify and feed into models. In that way, rather than hybrid knowledges, most of the scientists we interviewed see an unbridgeable epistemic and ontological divide between expert and lay knowledge. Scientists in the MoESs plainly stated that local knowledge is "not useful in modelling. I don't think local people can give feedback on weather/climate related information […] and don't think it is possible to use local knowledge to further develop models" (Interview with MoES Scientists, Delhi May 2016). This was echoed by scientists from the National Centre for Medium Range Forecast (NCMRF) on the issue of local knowledge and its integration into modelling exercises: "No, they cannot be integrated. Model development is very different from local perceptions. There is so much subjectivity when it comes to observed weather. We are scientists want some objectivity and can't rely on sentiments or emotions" (Interview with NCMRF Scientists May 2016).

Similarly, scientists from a national research institute in Delhi said that it was difficult to integrate sociological dimensions in climate models since it was not possible to bring narratives together with quantification of data, with the exception perhaps of Representative Concentration Pathways (RCPs) which can incorporate development aspects and integrate different data sources, for example, scientific data with socio-economic aspects (Scientists interviewed May 2016, Delhi). Most of our interviewees expressed similar reservations although one US-based scientist said that bringing in local-level field information is very challenging but might be viable. By contrast, scientists did appreciate that interdisciplinary research (especially in the natural sciences) is vital to "connect the dots' and improve scientific findings and models across fields, though here too it depends on "what skills can tolerate other skills" and the ability of models to be re-examined with respect to incorporating feedback" (US-based scientists interviewed January 2018, Mumbai IIT).

In the political realm, a top-down structuring of governance seems to be an impediment towards local perceptions making their way into decision-making processes, as a former Minister of Environment and Forests in India highlights:

> No, it is not possible at the moment to include local perceptions though NGOs as mediators are important. When I was minister, we listened to the people and civil society organisations but currently 95% of the information flow is top down especially at the centre.
>
> *(Interview with former Minister of Environments and Forests May 2017, Delhi)*

This highlights the importance of instituting structural processes at the political level if local climate information were to be of greater relevance in macro- as well as micro-level decision-making.

In sum, while the experts we interviewed seemed to acknowledge limits to their models and approaches, most of them seem to imply that science or scientists have a "mission" regarding climate change. Barring a few exceptions, we did not see much evidence of scientists actively trying to incorporate local-level knowledge and history into their models and methods. In fact, while doing the research, we did not find much evidence in the Indian context of climate scientists working closely with local communities and their indigenous knowledge systems to understand climate change-related uncertainties. This is unlike emerging alliances in the Arctic and beyond, where scientists are working closely with local communities and indigenous peoples to co-produce knowledge and understandings of climate change in a bottom-up and democratic manner.[3] There are growing attempts to create plural climate studies frameworks to embrace place-based experiences of local people and insights from the critical social sciences (see Chakraborty *et al.* 2021) and also attempts to decolonise climate sciences by using indigenous peoples' experiences and knowledges as the starting point (Johnson *et al.* 2021). We hope these will gradually make their way into mainstream climate science and climate policymaking.

Conclusions

This chapter has explored how uncertainty is understood by scientists, decision-makers and boundary workers and how it is presented and represented in models and scientific understandings. We also discussed the science/policy interface and the challenges in communicating uncertainty before discussing the possibility of integrating local knowledges and understanding in order to generate a socially grounded understanding of uncertainty. We found that despite an acknowledgement of the problems of modelling in capturing and understanding uncertainty, particularly at regional and local scales, there is a major drive to improve modelling and predictions to embrace uncertainty and complexity. Scientists also struggle due to the conflation of uncertainty in weather and climate in popular discourse and the media and the fact that the media do not portray the nuances of forecasting well, which also impedes future work. Many scientists were also constrained because their work on forecasts and models was often not taken seriously or because the probabilistic nature of the models is not deemed relevant to policymaking.

The chapter also discussed the growing community of natural and social scientists, boundary actors and policy actors, working to develop approaches to better reflect the "deep uncertainty" in relation to climate change and some efforts on the part of a growing community of natural scientists, social scientists and policy actors trying to bridge the gap between the "above" and "below".

However, our interviews show that while there has been significant progress in developing concepts, large gaps exist in the understanding across the different groups, due, in part, to different starting points, languages and priorities (UK researcher, March 2017).

We also discussed how the scientific models and scientific data largely focus on biophysical factors. However, as the case studies in this book demonstrate, biophysical changes interact with socio-economic and other trajectories of change causing new vulnerabilities for people and their ecologies. Thus, models may lack the local perspectives, socio-historical components and human dimensions that confront communities at the forefront of climate change as they adapt and respond to climate change. It is, thus, important to validate models with micro-level detail, local perceptions and histories in a way that is non-instrumental in order to fill crucial gaps in knowledges and understandings of uncertainty. As we have discussed in this chapter, scientists are clearly aware of the political nature of climate change and the limits to their knowledge and also the problems with translating their knowledge into policy and practice. However, they still appear to be resistant to construct alternative models and approaches that are more plural and draw on other skill sets and repertoires. Most of the scientists interviewed were men. In general, there are fewer women in senior roles in climate science and policymaking, but the few women we interviewed in all three countries, acknowledged some of the limitations of perspectives from "above" and the need to take on board local perspectives and realities in their work. This highlights the importance to have more plural and gendered perspectives in, otherwise, very male-dominated research and policy environments.

In conclusion, while the scientists we interviewed acknowledge uncertainty and there are signs of increasing appreciation of "deep uncertainty", traditional approaches to uncertainty still dominate in the understandings and policy debates among the "above". There remains a tension between the "above" still trying to master and reduce uncertainty through modelling and scenario building and the "below" that is seeking to cope with and live with uncertainty. While most of the scientists we interviewed acknowledge local understandings of uncertainty and the need for local expertise to inform climate models, and hybrid engagements emerging, there is as yet not much evidence of mainstream climate science or policymakers in India embracing alternative knowledges.

Acknowledgements

The authors would like to thank all the policymakers and scientists in India, Norway and the United Kingdom who were generous with their time and insights during our interviews with them. We also thank all those who participated in the roundtables carried out in Norway and India for their participation and insights.

Notes

1 Radiative forcing is defined as "the net change in the energy balance of the Earth system due to some imposed perturbation (...) and quantifies the energy imbalance that occurs when the imposed change takes place" (Myhre et al., 2013).
2 http://www.deepuncertainty.org/, accessed July 2021.
3 See http://www.unesco.org/new/en/media-services/world-heritage-37th-session/whc37-details/news/global_change_in_the_arctic_and_co_production_of_knowledge/, accessed March 2020.

References

AchutaRao, K. 2016. 'Uncertainty from Above: Can It Be Reduced?'. Paper presented at the STEPS Centre Workshop: Climate Change and Uncertainty from Above and Below, New Delhi, 27–28 January.
Berkes, F. and M. Berkes. 2009. 'Ecological Complexity, Fuzzy Logic, and Holism in Indigenous Knowledge'. *Futures*, 41(1): 6–12. https://doi.org/10.1016/j.futures.2008.07.003.
Bhave, A.G., D. Conway, S. Dessai, and D.A. Stainforth. 2016. 'Barriers and Opportunities for Robust Decision Making Approaches to Support Climate Change Adaptation in the Developing World'. *Climate Risk Management*, 14: 1–10. https://doi.org/10.1016/j.crm.2016.09.004
Bradshaw, G.A., and J.G. Borchers. 2000. 'Uncertainty as Information: Narrowing the Science-Policy Gap'. *Conservation Ecology*, 4(1): 7.
Carey, M. 2010. *In the Shadow of Melting Glaciers: Climate Change and Andean Society*. Oxford: Oxford University Press.
Chakraborty, R., M. Gergan, P. Sherpa, and C. Rampini. 2021. 'A Plural Climate Studies Framework for the Himalayas'. *Current Opinion in Environmental Sustainability*, 51: 42–54. https://doi.org/10.1016/j.cosust.2021.02.005
Crate, S.A. and M. Nuttall, eds. 2009. *Anthropology and Climate Change: From Encounters to Actions*. London: Routledge.
Curry, J. 2017. *Climate Models for the Layman*. London: The Global Warming Policy Foundation.
Curry, J. and P.J. Webster. 2011. 'Climate Science and the Uncertainty Monster'. *Bulletin of the American Meteorological Society*, 92(12): 1667–1682. https://doi.org/10.1175/2011BAMS3139.1
D'Souza, M. and E. Kale. 2018. 'Using Transformative Scenario Planning to Think Critically About the Future of Water in Rural Jalna, India'. Second TSP Report, CARIAA Programme, University of Cape Town, South Africa.
Dessai, S. and J.V.D. Sluijs. 2007. *Uncertainty and Climate Change Adaptation*. Utrecht: Copernicus Institute.
Dosi, G. and M. Egidi. 1991. 'Substantive and Procedural Uncertainty'. *Journal of Evolutionary Economics*, 1(2): 145–168. https://doi.org/10.1007/BF01224917
Douglas, M. 1986. *How Institutions Think*. New York: Syracuse University Press.
Dyson, F. 2015. *Dreams of Earth and Sky*. New York: New York Review of Book.
Edwards, P.N. 2010. *A Vast Machine: Computer Models, Climate Data, and the Politics of Global Warming*. Cambridge, MA: MIT Press.
Feyerabend, P. 1996. *Against Method (Third Edition)*. London and New York: Verso.
Field, C.B., V. Barros, T.F. Stocker, D. Qin, D.J. Dokken, K.L. Ebi, M.D. Mastrandrea, K.J. Mach, G.-K. Plattner, S.K. Allen, M. Tignor, and P.M. Midgley, eds. 2012.

Managing the Risks of Extreme Events and Disasters to Advance Climate Change Adaptation, a Special Report of Working Groups I and II of the Intergovernmental Panel on Climate Change (IPCC). New York: Cambridge University Press.

Funtowicz, S.O. and J.R. Ravetz. 1993. 'The Emergence of Post-Normal Science'. In *Science, Politics and Morality*, edited by R. Von Schomberg, 85–123. New York: Springer.

Hajer, M. A. 1995. *The Politics of Environmental Discourse: Ecological Modernization and Policy Process*. Oxford: Clarendon Press.

Hallegatte, S., A. Shah, R. Lempert, C. Brown, and S. Gill. 2012. *Investment Decision Making Under Deep Uncertainty: Application to Climate Change*. World Bank Policy Research Working Paper, 6193., Washington, DC: The World Bank.

Hastrup, K. 2013. 'Anticipating Nature: The Productive Uncertaibty of Climate Models'. In *The Social Life of Climate Change Models: Anticipating Nature*, edited by K. Hastrup and M. Skrydstrup. London: Routledge.

Hawkins, E. and R. Sutton. 2009. 'The Potential to Narrow Uncertainty in Regional Climate Predictions'. *Bulletin of the American Meteorological Society*, 90(8): 1095–1108. http://doi.org/10.1175/2009BAMS2607.1

Heymann, M. 2018. 'The Climate Change Dilemma: Big Science, the Globalizing of Climate and the Loss of the Human Scale'. *Regional Environmental Change*, 19(6): 1549–1560. https://doi.org/10.1007/s10113-018-1373-z

Hulme, M. 2013. 'How Climate Models Gain and Exercise Authority'. In *The Social Life of Climate Change Models: Anticipating Nature*, edited by K. Hastrup and M. Skrydstrup, 30–44. London: Routledge.

Hulme, M. 2016. *Weathered: Cultures of Climate*. London: Sage.

Intergovernmental Panel on Climate Change (IPCC). 2014a. *Climate Change 2014: A Synthesis Report, Contribution of Working Groups I, II and III to the Fifth Assessment Report of the Intergovernmental Panel on Climate Change*. Geneva: IPCC.

Intergovernmental Panel on Climate Change (IPCC). 2014b. 'Annex II: Glossary'. In *Climate Change 2014: Synthesis Report. Contribution of Working Groups I, II and III to the Fifth Assessment Report of the Intergovernmental Panel on Climate Change*, edited by Mach, K.J., S. Planton and C. von Stechow, 117–130. Geneva: IPCC.

Jasanoff, S. 2009. *The Fifth Branch: Science Advisers as Policymakers*: Cambridge, MA: Harvard University Press.

Johnson, D., M. Parsons, and K. Fisher. 2021. 'Indigenous Climate Change Adaptation: New Directions for Emerging Scholarship'. *Environment and Planning E: Nature and Space*. https://doi.org/10.1177/25148486211022450

Kirchhoff, C.J., M.C. Lemos, and S. Kalafatis. 2015. 'Narrowing the Gap between Climate Science and Adaptation Action: The Role of Boundary Chains'. *Climate Risk Management*, 9: 1–5. https://doi.org/10.1016/j.crm.2015.06.002

Lahsen, M. 2005. 'Seductive Simulations? Uncertainty Distribution around Climate Models'. *Social Studies of Science*, 35(6): 895–922. http://doi.org/10.1177/0306312705053049

Lemos, M.C., Y.J. Lo, D.R. Nelson, H. Eakin, and A.M. Bedran-Martins. 2016. 'Linking Development to Climate Adaptation: Leveraging Generic and Specific Capacities to Reduce Vulnerability to Drought in NE Brazil'. *Global Environmental Change*, 39: 170–179. https://doi.org/10.1016/j.gloenvcha.2016.05.001

Mehta, L., M. Leach, P. Newell, I. Scoones, K. Sivaramakrishnan, and S.A. Way. 1999. 'Exploring Understandings of Institutions and Uncertainty: New Directions in Natural Resource Management'. IDS Discussion Paper 372, Institute of Development Studies, Brighton, UK.

Mehta, L. and S. Srivastava. 2020. 'Uncertainty in Modelling Climate Change: The Possibilities of Co-Production Through Knowledge Pluralism. In *The Politics of Uncertainty: Challenges of Transformation*, edited by I. Scoones and A. Stirling, 99–112. London: Routledge.

Moorthy, K., S.K. Satheesh, and V.R. Kotamarthi. 2016. 'Evolution of Aerosol Research in India and the RAWEX–GVAX: An Overview'. *Current Science*, 11(1): 53–75.

Myhre, G., D. Shindell, F.M. Bréon, W. Collins, J. Fuglestvedt, J. Huang, D. Koch, J.F. Lamarque, D. Lee, B. Mendoza, T. Nakajima, A. Robock, G. Stephens, T. Takemura and H. Zhang. 2013. 'Anthropogenic and Natural Radiative Forcing'. In *Climate Change 2013: The Physical Science Basis. Contribution of Working Group I to the Fifth Assessment Report of the Intergovernmental Panel on Climate Change*, edited by Stocker, T.F., D. Qin, G.K. Plattner, M. Tignor, S.K. Allen, J. Boschung, A. Nauels, Y. Xia, V. Bex and P.M. Midgley, 659–740. Cambridge: Cambridge University Press.

Panda, A. 2016. 'Exploring Climate Change Perceptions, Rainfall Trends and Perceived Barriers to Adaptation in a Drought Affected Region in India'. *Natural Hazards*, 84(2): 777–796. https://doi.org/10.1007/s11069-016-2456-0

Pollack, H.N., J.E. Smerdon, and P.E. Van Keken. 2005. 'Variable Seasonal Coupling between Air and Ground Temperatures: A Simple Representation in Terms of Subsurface Thermal Diffusivity'. *Geophysical Research Letters*, 32(15). https://doi.org/10.1029/2005GL023869

Rein, M. and D. Schön. 1993. 'Reframing Policy Discourses'. In *The Argumentative Turn in Policy Analysis and Planning*, edited by F. Fischer and J. Forester, 145–166. Durham, NC: Duke University Press.

Rudiak-Gould, P. 2013. '"We Have Seen It with Our Own Eyes": Why We Disagree about Climate Change Visibility'. *Weather, Climate, and Society*, 5(2): 120–132.

Schneider, S.H. and K. Kuntz-Duriseti. 2002. 'Uncertainty and Climate Change Policy'. In *Climate Change Policy: A Survey*, edited by S.H. Schneider, A. Rosencranz and J.O. Niles, 53–87. Washington, DC: Island Press.

Schneider, B., and L. Walsh. 2019. 'The Politics of Zoom: Problems with Downscaling Climate Visualizations'. *Geo: Geography and Environment*, 6(1): e00070. https://doi.org/10.1002/geo2.70

Scoones, I. and A. Stirling. 2020. 'Uncertainty and the Politics of Transformation'. In *The Politics of Uncertainty: Challenges of Transformation*, edited by I. Scoones and A. Stirling. London: Routledge.

Shackley, S. and B. Wynne. 1996. 'Representing Uncertainty in Global Climate Change Science and Policy: Boundary-Ordering Devices and Authority'. *Science, Technology, & Human Values*, 21(3): 275–302. https://doi.org/10.1177/016224399602100302

Singh, R., and K. AchutaRao. 2018. 'Quantifying Uncertainty in Twenty-First Century Climate Change over India'. *Climate Dynamics*, 52: 3905–3928. https://doi.org/10.1007/s00382-018-4361-6

Srivastava, R. 2017. 'Trends in Aerosol Optical Properties over South Asia'. *International Journal of Climatology*, 37(1): 371–380. https://doi.org/10.1002/joc.4710

Stirling, A., F. Marshall, and A. Ely. 2018. 'How Is Transformative Knowledge 'Co-Produced?'. Available at: https://i2insights.org/2018/04/03/co-producing-transformative-knowledge/ (accessed on 08 February 2021)

Swart, R., L. Bernstein, M. Ha-Duong, and A. Petersen. 2009. 'Agreeing to Disagree: Uncertainty Management in Assessing Climate Change, Impacts and Responses by the IPCC'. *Climatic Change*, 92(1–2): 1–29. https://doi.org/10.1007/s10584-008-9444-7

van der Sluijs, J. 2005. 'Uncertainty as a Monster in the Science-Policy Interface: Four Coping Strategies'. *Water Science & Technology*, 52(6): 87–92.

Wilby, R. L., and S. Dessai. 2010. 'Robust Adaptation to Climate Change'. *Weather*, 65(7): 180–185. https://doi.org/10.1002/wea.543

Wynne, B. 1992. 'Uncertainty and Environmental Learning: Reconceiving Science and Policy in the Preventive Paradigm'. *Global Environmental Change*, 2(2): 111–127. https://doi.org/10.1016/0959-3780(92)90017-2

3
UNCERTAINTY AND ENVIRONMENTAL CHANGE

Kutch and the Sundarbans as environmental histories of climate change

Vinita Damodaran, Rohan D'Souza and Subir Dey

Introduction

This chapter explores understandings of uncertainty in South Asian environmental history scholarship. Environmental histories of South Asia have mostly evolved their plot lines around the theme of environmental change (Kumar, Damodaran and D'Souza 2011: 1–13). The overall mood in such narratives has often been described as being "declensionist" – that is, emphasising environmental decline and irretrievable ecological loss. While providing compelling insights and careful documentation of the environmental impacts brought on by European modernisation and western colonialism, these declensionist frameworks have been inadequate in their scrutiny of the pre-colonial period in South Asia (Grove, Damodaran and Sangwan 1998). In part, this striking limitation has been driven by the belief that pre-colonial societies aimed for ecological harmony, and this led them to strive for achieving relatively stable environments as they pursued resource prudence rather than profligacy (cf. D'Souza 2019).

Although a number of revisionist accounts have subsequently demolished the environmental stability thesis, recent anxieties about global warming have, understandably, pressed for another rethink over how South Asia's environmental pasts may be understood (Damodaran and D'Souza 2020). In particular, this includes the need to debate how understanding weather events and long-term climate trends can help us grasp how states and societies have responded to radical environmental uncertainties. Thus, we suggest a rethinking of the plausible environmental history plot lines and narratives for South Asia in the context of climate change and global warming and the possibility for de-centring the previous emphasis on environmental change and replacing it with the notion of "uncertainty".

Uncertainty, as pointed out in the introduction to this volume, can be discussed in terms of its *epistemic* (knowledge-making) and *ontological/aleatory* (how Nature exists) dimensions (Chapter 1). And integral to uncertainty is what Sheila Jasanoff felicitously describes as the tensions between "global fact" and "local value" (Jasanoff 2010). While the global fact would refer to the high science of model building and the universal abstract protocols for collecting meteorological data (see Chapter 2), the local value, in Jasanoff's estimate, draws out how local communities experience and make sense of weather events and phenomena and the need to recover the local in our global regimes (Jasnoff and Martello, 2004). This is nicely illustrated through the empirical chapters in this volume (see Chapters 4–6). In effect, there is a friction between the qualitative that is borne by the everyday experience and the quantitative, which speaks for the abstract and distant assessment mainly by experts.

To illustrate and deepen our understanding of the notion of uncertainty as a framing device for writing environmental histories of South Asia, we focus in this essay on two dynamic environments in British India – the princely state of *Kutch* (in present-day Gujarat) and the *Sundarbans* (Bengal). For the colonial authorities, Kutch and the Sundarbans were overwhelmingly marked as being "marginal environments" and treated as being distinctly different from places and regions that were, in contrast, considered as the "environmental normal".

While marginal environments, especially for colonial officialdom, meant environments that were subject to frequent extreme weather and natural events such as droughts, floods, earthquakes and violent river behaviour, the "environmental normal" referred to the relatively productive, stable, predictable and revenue-yielding zones (Heredia and Ratnagar 2003; Prasad 2003; Bhattacharya 2018; Saikia 2019). These contrasts between the "marginal" and the "normal" not only shaped different types of colonial administrative interventions and institutional capacities but, critically, there emerged as well a set of sociological and economic distinctions that were elaborated by the colonial authorities that helped further define these zones. Notably, the marginal was about subsistence communities that were characterised by mobility, vulnerability and regular environmental distress, while the normal comprised settled agrarian communities, revenue-paying cultivators and referred to spaces which saw markets and commerce flourish.

A second set of contrasts was over the notion of the environmental shock as opposed to that of gradualist environmental change. The regions of Kutch and the Sundarbans, we point out, were described and discussed within the administrative lexicon in terms of sudden and dramatic natural shocks such as earthquakes, cyclones or extreme floods, which not only resulted in the radical landscape change but could potentially cause the drastic erosion of livelihood possibilities and even the total abandonment of lands. In normal environments, on the other hand, environmental changes could be more gradualist and could be brought on by long-term activities such as steady forest clearances or even a persistent drought but without irreversible landscape change.

The "marginal environments" (Kutch and the Sundarbans) having experienced limited interventions by the colonial state were substantially documented and studied between the 18th and 19th centuries. The town of Bhuj in the Kutch princely state had suffered from drought and scarcities of water while the Sundarbans remained vulnerable to recurrent extreme flooding, drastic landform erosion and ferocious cyclones. Both colonial and post-independent state initiatives in these two sites were instituted to turn them into "normal" and "secure" geographies (also see Chapters 4 and 5). Tracing the trajectory of such stabilising initiatives can help deepen our understandings of how uncertainty was experienced and discussed differently by layers of society, communities, experts and government officials across time periods, and how these translate into present-day response. In particular, we are keen to explore how the responses from communities, experts and the state or "below", "middle" and "above" differed in their approaches to viewing environmental change and the differing perspectives they provided for understanding how environments were represented and understood. The pastoralists in Kutch, for example, saw seasonal migration and mobility as critical adaptation strategies for their livelihoods, while in the normal zones, migration was mostly seen as a distress strategy or as desperate efforts to cope with an irregular or a one-off event (Mehta 2005). Similarly, communities in the Sundarbans remained agile to the moods of the rivers, as they hopped across islands and *diaras* or *chars* as part of their portfolio of livelihood strategies.

This essay, in effect, will seek to underline not only how the notion of the margin was, in several respects, framed as being a deviation to the normal and, therefore, caused British administrators to often misread local livelihoods, coping mechanisms and strategies aimed at harnessing uncertain environmental conditions. While the lack of environmental predictability meant a loss of control over territory and the populace for the colonial state, local knowledges, syncretic histories and pastoralist narratives can draw our attention to how certain kinds of social worlds could be more adept at handling environmental shocks. Below, we review the colonial archival record (from 1800 onwards) on what got described as calamitous events, natural catastrophes and environmental shocks in Kutch and the Sundarbans. The effort, in essence, is to read against the grain in order to explore and capture the varied conceptual tensions that ran through colonial efforts to frame marginal environments in terms of the normal through the lens of uncertainty.

Discovering Kutch

Kutch acquired political coherence from the late 12th century when the *Jadeja* Rajputs came to rule the tract. In 1819, the ruling house, accepted the suzerainty of the British East India Company (hereafter, EIC) with Captain James Macmurdo becoming the first political resident. Amongst the topographical peculiarities that Macmurdo quickly noted was the striking physical feature of a salty marshland of close to 10,000 square miles that comprised the *Rann* of Kutch, which alternated between being a seasonally dry sandy desert and a marshy inland lake with only small stretches of freshwater.[1] He also recalled from memory in 1820, the impact of the earthquake of 1819 that had ravaged the entire province.[2] In 1824, James Burnes, a doctor, posted in Bhuj and his brother, Alexander Burnes, also wrote about Kutch. Their initial writings were focused mainly on the regional history of Kutch and were essentially a subtle justification for British rule. In 1829, James Burnes began to pen his observations of the land and people of Kutch.

> The general appearance of Cutch is barren and uninteresting. Most of the villages are ruinous and dilapidated, bearing marks alike of the shocks of nature and the destructive powers of man. A few fields in their neighbourhood are cultivated, while the remainder of the country presents nothing to the view but a rocky and sandy waste, which in many places is scarcely relieved by a show of vegetation. Water is scarce, and often brackish; and although the population does not exceed three hundred and fifty thousand souls, the produce of the land under cultivation is insufficient for their support; so that Cutch, even in the best seasons, is dependent on Sinde for supplies of grain.
>
> (James Burnes 1830a)

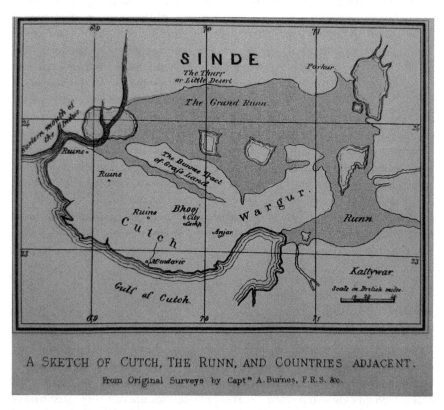

FIGURE 3.1 A sketch of the history of Cutch (Burnes 1830).

In addition to the fairly grim assessment of the resources and people, the brothers also advanced an understanding of the various castes, tribes, their customs, habits and social hierarchies[3] and noted the unique Banni grasslands.[4] In 1839, drawing upon the accounts of the Burnes, the writer Marianne Postans described Kutch as a "barbaric and primitive polity" that was marred by unfair and exploitative customs, which, she went on to conclude, could only be saved by the East India Company, who possessed "industrious sciences and the Christian faith".[5]

It is only in the memoir of S.N. Raikes of 1854, that we finally note that Kutch is unhesitatingly described as a colonial administrative territory.[6] Now geographically demarcated from the neighbouring province of Sindh, Kutch was shown to comprise an area of 6,500 square miles. As for the Rann and the Banni grasslands, it was believed that seismic changes had created these salty marshes by converting a large water body into a seasonally dry seabed – a fact borne out by the periodic discovery of sea fossils.[7] There was also the building of the great embankment by Gholam Shah in 1770 on the Eastern branch of the *Indus* in *Sinde* (Sindh) and the building of canals for channelling the waters to the Kutch.[8] The Grand Runn (Great Rann of Kutch) on its northern boundary was 9,000 square miles. Mostly a rocky and hilly terrain comprising three irregular hill ranges:

a   Most northern range an irregular chain bordering the Runn, of rocks containing marine remains.
b   Charwar range passing through the centre of the province connected to the former at a northwest point.
c   Southern range connected to the centre of the Charwar range.

Apart from these ranges, Denodar was the highest peak among a cluster of irregular hills that contained volcanic material. Geologists had begun to take a keen interest in Kutch since an early period for this reason. Raikes reported that, in some seasons, generally when rain falls in July, the surface, particularly of the eastern portion of the Runn, would be stunningly covered with salt (see Figure 3.1). On one or two occasions, "I have observed the whole distance between Kutch and Parkur covered with salt as white as snow, which it exactly resembled. It had a most striking appearance".[9] The southern coast was fertile and all channels of water that flowed through the province were periodic and would swell during the rains, after which these would remain as detached pools of water. They were most prominent on the northern side of the city of Bhuj.[10]

The climate of Kutch was described as mild and agreeable compared to other parts of Bombay, the hot months being April and May. Along the coast these months were also found to be pleasant while the month of June could become cloudy before the preceding rains. Rains happened to be irregular and sometimes heavy and damaging to poorly designed housing. In 1850, it was reported that heavy rains fell claiming 50 inhabitants and led to the death of close to 20,000 cattle. After the heavy monsoon, fever and rheumatism were found to be common ailments in the province. It was observed that these ailments were particularly close to the Runn where the drying up of vegetation would release what was called "noxious vapours". The temperature would remain high until November and then winter would commence from December and last until March. The occurrence of cholera after the rains was, in fact, noted to be fairly regular. The average annual rainfall between 1848 and 1853 was 12 inches (59 centimetres), though even this amount could be very variable.[11] As the political agent Reeves, in an 1878 despatch, observed:

> Cutch is peculiarly situated as to rainfall being on the very edge of the South West Monsoon and getting a small and precarious rain, it is evident therefore that the sinking of numerous wells, whereby a permanent water supply is ensured, is of the first importance.[12]

The colonial narrative then was that, the Kutch was in dire need of improvements, especially through infrastructural interventions so as to be rendered into a productive and predictable landscape.

Despite the uncertain rainfall pattern, a variety of crops were grown that included coarse cereals such as *bajra*, *muth*, *gowar*, *jowary*, *moong* and even some amounts of wheat. Cash crops were also cultivated, such as castor oil and cotton. Cotton was exported to Bombay from the region, and in 1852, Kutch produced 75,000 *maunds*. Silk from Kutch found a substantial dedicated European clientele.[13] Most Kutch dwellers were reported as being subsistence cultivators and did not own their lands. Proprietary titles to land and its jurisdiction known as *Girasias* were recognised by the British. This was, however, essentially confined to a much smaller constituency of members mostly from the *Jharejah* clan, who formed the *Bhayyad* or the brotherhood. These landholders reserved the right to levy taxes and fines on cultivation and goods in transit through their towns and villages. A small constituency of religious and charitable institutions held a certain portion of these villages and lands, for which they received grants from the Kutch durbar. These were known as *Inamee* and *Khyratee*. The British East India Company recorded and recognised these landholdings as part of their policy of non-intervention in the domain of religion.

In these colonial surveys, agrarian conditions were also described as being adverse, owing not only to the uncertain rainfall pattern but also to the high levies by local authorities. Additionally, duties across towns and villages that were collected by the landholders led to a concentration of surplus at one end of the social spectrum. During the mid-19th century, a trend became noticeable, wherein the *durbar* of the court kept acquiring more lands from the nobility. Lands in Kutch, consequently, increasingly began to be held directly by the court.[14]

All ports of Kutch were under the *durbar* and foreign goods were only allowed to be imported through them. Sea customs were levied on all goods and the durbar and landholders of the nobility levied transit duties on merchandise in whichever direction they moved. By virtue of the treaty with the Kutch durbar, it is important to note that Company goods were exempted from the sea customs.[15]

Known for their maritime success, the Kutchis were intrepid seafarers and many fortunes were made from oceanic trade. Port towns like *Lakhpat, Jakhau, Mandvi* and *Mundra* retain even today, albeit to differing degrees, reminders of an earlier prosperity. While there have been studies focused on the seafaring traditions of Kutch that supported trade and migration, the overland migration that occurred across the Rann into Sindh and thence to Central Asia and beyond historically has been less studied (Simpson 2003).

Pastoralism and weather uncertainties

The Rann turned marshy during periods of rainfall and breaks into a collection of raised islands, where habitation becomes possible. These islands or *gauchar bets,* which were also regarded as common lands, moreover, were overrun by a vast carpet of lush nutritious grasses. The Banni grasslands often find mention as being one of the largest *bets* in the Rann and colonial accounts describe it as attracting a number of pastoral groups with their cattle, who were even able to enjoy a better lifestyle than the agriculturalists (Williams 1981: 222).

The colonial records, it should be noted do not refer to the pastoralists of Kutch in occupational terms, rather they were listed as nomadic tribes. While they did not have proprietary rights to the Banni, which was held by the Durbar, they had unlimited grazing rights. What they were taxed for was not grazing rights but their trade in butter. There were, moreover, strict grazing regulations for sheep and goats who were prevented from grazing in the earlier period which helped preserve the grassland resources for camels and cows (Ibrahim 2004). While recording land titles and ownership, Arthur Malet in 1842 remarked that in the district of Banni an estimated 100,000 cattle were tended to in this tract and five *kutchi kories* (local currency)[16] were levied on every *maund* of clarified butter that was produced. In that very year, the revenue that the durbar received from Banni was 70,000 *kutchi kories*. It is unclear if this revenue was accrued through levies on butter or some other means as well.[17] The Banni, moreover, was vulnerable to pillage from seafaring pirates and also suffered cattle theft. The British East India Company thus had to secure the property from such raids even as vulnerabilities from extreme weather events and famine regularly occurred.[18] In the 1880s, one colonial report on the Banni tellingly described it as follows:

> '[…] is all apt to be covered with water in times of high flood. The whole is scantily covered with coarse grass and *babul* trees, and supports large herds of buffaloes and other cattle, for whose use some wells and ponds have been dug. The herdsmen live in clusters of beehive shaped grass huts, and under the orders of their holy men use no sleeping cots and light no lamps after dark.' On the pastoralists they noted that the 'Rabaris 13,371 strong, also called *Bhopas* because many of them serve in *Mata* temples, a wandering tribe of shepherds are generally found in the *Banni* and other rich pasture lands of north Cutch'.[19]

One also gets the idea of the recalcitrant frontier in the colonial archive. "The Muhammadan herdsmen in the Banni (a tract of grasslands extending along the edge of the northern Rann) are reckoned fierce and unsettled" noted Macmurdo in 1820. When caravans laden with goods – rice, dates, silks and cloths – would cross the Rann during the trading season between mid-September and mid-June, their safety was not easily guaranteed.[20] Tribes along the way had to be mollified with payments to prevent the looting of goods.

The colonial state, perhaps not unsurprisingly, as part of their efforts to pacify and settle what increasingly appeared to them as a marginal, uncertain and volatile zone sought to transform the pastoralists into a sedentary community that could be more legible to their taxation regimes. Amongst the first initiatives was to enclose the commons and village forests. Local ecologies had various local terms identifying their importance to the common people: common lands which were termed as *gauchars bets*; islands in desert tracts termed as *Pung*, *Aaliya* and *Nada*; Grasslands like *Banni*, *Kaddr*, *Lakhpat* and *Vadhiya*; and Forests like *Gir*, *Bardas*, *Aalech*, *Vidis* and *Rakhal*. Pastoralism was adapted to the environment with mobility being key, with groups moving between Sindh and Kutch taking their herds where they would find fodder. The livestock included three native breeds of Oxon: *Bagadia* and *Bharbads* reared by *Rabaris* and the *Banniai* referring to Muslim herdsmen in the *Banni*. During the several famine episodes that were noted in the region, migration was the main response of local pastoralists. In 1823, it was recorded that there was a migration of people and death of cattle due to famine. In 1860, severe scarcity of provisions led to heavy migration to Sindh, Kathiawar and Bombay, and the cattle were even driven to Gujarat.

Colonial sources have recorded close to 102 episodes of what they would consider calamitous events in Kutch through the course of the 19th century. Aside from the earthquake of 1819, the remaining 101 instances counted relate to extreme weather events. The list mentions 48 years as being marred by poor or untimely rainfall leading to crop failure with some years tipping into becoming famines. In the remaining 52 years, though there were a range of weather uncertainties such as unintended showers, unexpected timings for rain and even shock floods that brought about scarcities in fodder and grass and especially increased the prices of food grains. Each event produced consequences for livelihood and economy, which lingered on for years. A closer look in Table 3.1 details these events.

In the first decade, barring the two years of 1803 and 1804, the decade witnessed predictable weather events. However, the next decade was a trend in reverse, barring 1814 and 1818, one or more calamitous events occurred. This decade began with "pestilence resulting in crop failure" and famine followed by an epidemic of plague in 1812. In 1813, the epidemic continued and was accompanied by famine. While the situation began to marginally improve in 1814, in May 1815, the cropped fields witnessed heavy rain and rats robbed the cultivators clean. The epidemic of plague reappeared in 1816 and continued in 1817. While 1818 provided some succour, June 1819 witnessed an earthquake, followed by a heavy monsoon that destroyed crops. Untimely, rain and poor

TABLE 3.1 Table showing climate-related events in 19th century Kutch

Decades of the 19th Century	Famines	Crop Failure	Pestilence	Epidemic	Rainfall Failure
1800–1810	1	1	1	2	2
1811–1820	3	4	2	5	5
1821–1830	1	1	1	0	2
1831–1840	0	1	1	0	1
1841–1850	0	2	0	0	3
1851–1860	0	1	0	0	1
1861–1870	0	4	2	1	5
1871–1880	0	3	1	3	5
1881–1890	0	0	0	0	0
1891–1900	2	0	0	5	4

Source: Authors' own using information from the Gazetteer of Bombay Presidency, Volume V 1880.

harvests closed the decade in 1820 and the period 1821–1830 had seven years that did not witness any widespread calamitous event.

The decade of 1831–1840 was comparatively free in terms of calamities, with only three years of adverse rainfall leading to poor harvest and crop failure. The following decade of 1841–1850 appears to be balanced with five years of primarily poor rainfall leading to crop failure but with two earthquakes in 1844 and 1845 noted as severe but without any additional details. The following decade had only two years known to have adverse rainfall and crop failure. This was followed by the decade of 1861–1870 in which frequencies of calamitous events were similar to the decade of 1811–1820. This state of affairs was only marginally reduced in the following decade of 1871–1880. In this decade, seven years saw active calamities which also included plague in cattle and animals in 1872 and 1878 that had serious consequences on livelihoods. The count of these events in the last decade of the 19th century stands at nine active years of climate events and one clear year. The earthquake episodes from 1892 to 1895 did not seem to have any drastic impact enough to have entered the colonial records. The plague epidemic outbreak between 1896 and 1900, however, caused huge casualties and was accompanied by untimely rains and poor harvests (see Table 3.1).[21]

State and people: the twain never meets

A close study of the pattern of responses, from "above" and "below" that these frequently occurring extreme weather events evoked, shows that people and the state responded in different and often contrasting ways. The colonial state after some initial hesitation began to reconcile itself to the idea of having to settle for a mixed bag of good and bad years. In particular, the administration had to ensure that their revenue collections had to be correctly indexed to the actual abilities of the local populace to pay after an extreme event. In 1842, when Arthur Malet, the political agent at Kutch surveyed and documented the towns and villages and their ownership, the aggregate of revenue including all items and of all revenue receiving entities was estimated at 62,95,745 *Kutchi Koris*. Malet remarked that in a good year at least 64 lakhs Kutchi Koris of revenue was realised and then proceeded to estimate the most probable trend of revenue realisation under three additional categories, namely, the following:

a   Sookal which meant a very good year.
b   Dookal which meant a year of famine.
c   Kurwara which meant a year of when one fall of rainfall has failed.

Against each kind of year, there was a proportionate adjustment in the scale of revenue realisation.[22] Nonetheless, prices for necessities often escalated in difficult years. A report in 1872 on the previous year's harvest, notes:

> [...] the monsoon has been unfavourable even for Kutch, where a precarious rainfall is the rule. The total number of inches was 3 inches and 47 centimetres, of which no less than 3 inches and 4 centimetres were registered during the first week in May, a most untimely fall. The consequences has been diminished harvests throughout the country, and high prices for grain, grass and the necessaries of life, with much distress.'[23]

Locusts sometimes could ruin a good harvest. In 1872, the year which recorded a good harvest owing to

> seasonable and copious rain during last monsoon throughout the province, after the previous year's unfavourable and scanty fall, has relieved much of the distress that prevailed [...] in consequence of the appearance of locusts when the crops were standing, and a good deal of damage was done in most of the districts thereby.[24]

One of the main responses of the populace to rain deficiency and such kinds of distress was to resort to strategic migration as noted in 1876:

> There was a deficiency of rain all over the Province, the average being only 7 inch 21 centimetres, or about half the usual supply. The three *pergannas* bordering on Sind were the greatest sufferers. The crops in them entirely failed, and a large portion of the population emigrated. The food supplies of the country were thus relieved. But severe scarcity has prevailed everywhere, and the water and forage supplies are dangerously low.[25]

The transitory nature of such migration was noted, in 1891, for example, it was reported that in Bhuj owing to poor rainfall "the grass preserves of the *Darbar* as well as the common pasture lands of the villages" failed to meet the demands of the domestic animals and immediately spurred the pastoralists to seek pastures elsewhere.[26] Almost a year later, however, the pastoralists who had migrated "drew back to Cutch several herds of cattle which had left the province for want thereof in the previous year".[27]

While temporary distress migration seemed part of the rhythm for coping with the vagaries and uncertainties of the inhabitants of Kutch, the colonial administration increasingly saw well irrigation as the solution to preventing mobility:

> Scarcity and rain and danger of famine in Cutch are not unfrequent, and special precautions are necessary, against the distress arising there from. Well irrigation has been long considered to afford a sure, certain and suitable remedy, especially in this Province. The Council of Regency who conducted the affairs of the principality during the minority of His Highness the Rao recognised the necessity of increasing well irrigation as much as possible; since his accession to full powers of State, his Highness the Rao has also spared no pains in increasing wells and encouraging improved cultivation of land.'[28]

Interestingly, since in most official reports the cause of famine in Kutch was seen to be a result of multiple years of bad weather, the administration linked migration not to pastoral rhythms and coping strategies but exclusively to rainfall deficit and weather uncertainty. Well irrigation, consequently, became the widely accepted official response which as a "[…] measure will not only keep compact and steady the subjects of the State in those parts, but will also bring to their doors a certain supply of water on which they can depend".[29] That is, the lack of cultivation in Kutch was seen as a natural calamity. The pursuit of a robust policy for sedentarisation, thus, also followed from the need to prevent migration and mobility.

The improvement of agricultural resources of the country was highlighted as being necessary and involved the administration in trying to ensure that there was an "abundance of manure, good cultivation and plentiful supply of water".[30] The State attempted to partially assist the cultivating classes by advancing money and granting remissions and also giving *Takavi* (loans) and grants-in-aid.[31] In effect, by the end of the 19th century, a set of interventions for the sedentarisation of the populace improving well irrigation, revoking transit duties, relief work in the form of construction and taking over wastelands was considered to be the main response of the colonial state, which stood in striking contrast to that of the local populace that sought to develop and orient their coping strategies around temporary and seasonal migration as they historically had always done. As the exactions of the colonial state intensified forcing sedentarisation on pastoralists, further changes in land use and boundary changes following the partition of India limited the range of responses to local climate events among these communities leaving them more vulnerable to uncertainty and climate change (Mehta and Srivastava 2019; also see Chapter 4 for postcolonial interventions in Kutch). We now turn to a similar examination of uncertainty in historical perspective in the Sundarbans.

Sundarbans' migratory rivers and mobile people

The Sundarbans comprises the most volatile deltaic portions that is borne out of the confluence of the massive Ganga, Brahmaputra and Meghna river systems. The region which overlaps both Bangladesh and India, has a unique ecology that is hedged in by mangroves, littered with mudflats and cut into innumerable islands by streams and channels. Given the fact that the Sundarbans is a highly unstable landscape that is recurrently moulded by tidal actions, floods and regular marine erosion, the early East India Company (EIC) officials, unsurprisingly, were overawed upon gaining possession of the territory in the final decades of the 18th century (see Figure 3.2).

Upon seizing the right to assess and collect revenue in the Sundarbans in 1764, the EIC officials first set their sights instead on containing the threats from the *Magh*, who were variously described as pirates and accused of plundering ships and carrying away populations for the slave trade in the *Arakans*. Apart from securing the routes of commerce that carried out through the many channels between the river Meghna and Hooghly, the Company also aimed to expand

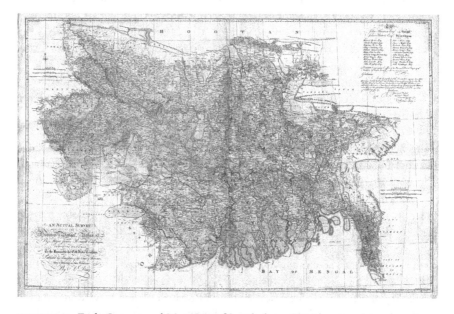

FIGURE 3.2 Early Survey and Mapping of Sundarbans 1794.

Source: Map of Bengal, Bahar & C. prepared by Major James Rennell, Engineer and Surveyor of East India Company, published on 12th May, 1794.

cultivation in the lower portion of the delta to prevent raiders from taking cover in the Sundarbans forests (Chatterjee and Sarkar 2010).

Colonial administrators amidst difficult efforts to settle the volatile deltaic tracts, however, were led to systematically document the forest and vegetation cover for close to 150 years. The importance of fisheries was also recognised earlier on when the Sundarbans were acknowledged as possessing the "most valuable of the estuarine fisheries in Bengal", with the numerous waterways being full of fish. But the "deterioration" of several channels in later years, it was noted, had caused the water to turn brackish in several places such that "carp have already deserted them".[32]

Three aspects of the Sundarbans, however, came to define the colonial documentary record in the region. First were the complications brought on by efforts to build and maintain embankments to secure the region from the regular devastations of the annual floods, an intractable issue that persists to date (see Chapter 5). Second were the tensions between ensuring forest conservation for timber, while, at the same time, encouraging the agrarian expansion and settlement in the deltaic tracts. The third involved the colonial anxieties bought on by cyclonic storms and their potential devastations.

Embankment construction

For the EIC, the project of building embankments and maintaining them proved to be a conflicted intervention that preoccupied colonial officials, landlords and cultivators throughout. From 1783 onwards, officials began to farm out schemes for reclaiming lands from forests and marshy terrain. The first attempt in this direction was by Mr. Tilman Henckell.[33] Apart from reclaiming forest lands for cultivation, Henckell intended to extend the agrarian frontier so as to deal with a potential situation of famine. The famine of the 1770s was still fresh in public memory as it had allegedly killed ten million people.

Initially, embankments in order to protect the reclaimed lots were undertaken by landlords and the cost of repairs was reimbursed by the Company. In 1785, the government resumed the *pulbandi* (embankment) charges and undertook maintenance on their own. However, in 1791, it decided to place the burden of the cost of repairs on landlords again and, not unexpectedly, faced considerable resistance from these groups. The landlords stated that if monetary assistance was not given by the Company, all losses in revenue incurred due to floods should be pardoned by the Company. As a result of this argument, this measure was withdrawn. The British government then farmed out the maintenance of embankments to Salt Agents who did so until 1803 when an Embankment Committee was formed. This Embankment Committee, however, failed to function properly, and in 1814, the government was obliged to rebuild embankments at their own expense. In 1816, a Sundarbans Commission was formed that operated till 1821. In 1819, the government asked the landlords to estimate and undertake repairs of the embankments under an embankments superintendent. In 1834, the government withdrew monetary support for this purpose but owing to protests and losses, resumed maintaining the embankments through its Public Works Department. The maintenance of embankments and their impacts on the environment, however, continued to draw debate and dissension throughout the colonial period.[34]

Forestry against Reclamation

Reclaiming the forest was part of the push by the Revenue Department for bringing tracts under cultivation. However, the period from 1870 to 1879, when new rules for the reclamation of wastelands in the Sundarbans were issued, a number of disputes erupted over the sale and lease of forest land. In part, this was because the forest department considered forests more useful than rice cultivation.[35]

The policy of Sir Richard Temple, the then Lieutenant Governor, was a case in point for he argued against any need for reclamation as the resources grown in the Sundarbans already were more valuable than creating more paddy fields. His policy resulted in the creation of the Reserved and Protected Forest in Jessore (Khulna) and the 24 Parganas. Temple chose to record his views about the importance of forest resources:

> Western Bengal is supplied partly from the Sunderbuns and partly from the high lands to its west. The southern districts of Central Bengal draw ample supplies of cheap wood from the Sunderbuns. In the city of Calcutta firewood is probably cheaper than in any large town of India; a short system of rivers and canals brings the products of the Sunderbuns to several parts of Calcutta and its environs. To the northern districts of Central Bengal, bamboos and timber are brought by river from the sub-Himalayan forests. Eastern Bengal is supplied by water from the Sunderbuns, from the frontier jungles, and from occasional private forests scattered over the country.[36]

But the impetus for cultivation continued and 3,305 acres were transferred to the civil authorities to be leased for cultivation.[37] The region soon became quite profitable and it was noted that

> It will be seen that there is a large and increasing surplus, so that the general result is satisfactory. The profit is very great in the Sunderbuns Division, from which Calcutta is supplied with fuel, and also the important sugar and other works scattered through Khoolna and Jessore.

It was further reported that

> After sal (*Shorea robusta*) we have to notice sundri (*Heritiera littoralis*), the important produce of the Sundarbans forests, which serves to construct most of the native river craft met with on the Hooghly and adjacent

channels. In the water-divided country of the 24-Parganas, Khulna, Backergunge, Noakhali, and neighbouring districts, the rivers and creeks to a great extent take the place of roads, and boats the, place of carts, so that the value of the Government forests of the Sundarbans to the country at large is immense. Again, all the firewood used in Calcutta is brought from these same forests. The financial results were reported by the Sundarbans Division as especially satisfactory. Besides expending only 28 per cent, of its receipts it furnishes no less than 45 per cent, of the revenue of the whole circle. The regularising of the work and the introduction of the monopoly sale system have so improved matters that the period of its administrative uncertainty may be considered to be a thing of the past. The revenue during the year increased by Rs. 51,000.[38]

It was further reported that the reclaimed tract to the north was entirely devoted to rice cultivation and winter rice of a fine quality was grown there; sugarcane and areca-palms were also cultivated in the tracts lying in Khulna and Backergunge districts. The methods of cultivation included the following:

> when land is cleared, a *bandh* or dike is erected round it to keep out the salt water and after two years the land becomes fit for cultivation; in normal years excellent crops are obtained, the out-turn being usually about 20 *maunds* of rice per acre.[39]

The debate on forests, however, remained very intense and often bitter. It was reported that by 1877 the limits of the forest reserve had been fixed, even as a considerable area of wasteland, the revenue administration believed had been excluded and was still available for reclamation,[40] causing them to aggressively declaim in a note that as late as 1853 the

> Government had declared that the paramount object of its policy in the Sundarbans was the speedy reclamation of the forest in order to improve the health of the neighbourhood of Calcutta and to deprive wild animals, smugglers and pirates of the shelter afforded by the jungle: the improvement of the revenue was of secondary and altogether subordinate importance.[41]

The history of forest demarcation, the debates on reclamation and cultivation and the responses of the Forest Department were to prove vital in partially protecting the region against cyclones. Although the Sundarbans forest was declared government property in 1817, it was not declared a protected forest area until 1878. At this time, 4,856 square kilometres in the south-eastern part of the Sundarbans was officially preserved by British authorities. This was an important victory not only for the Indian forest department but also for the deltaic stretch as well as these reserved and protected forests proved important in giving protection for cyclones and floods.

From the brief account "above", one can gauge the slow pace at which the Sundarbans was brought within the domain of the colonial administration and the competing claims of the forest and revenue departments. During the middle of the 19th century, there were many proposals made that sought to undertake reclamation and settlement at a mega scale through mobilising big capital and labour. In January 1865, Ferdinand Schiller presented one such proposal of reclaiming all the remaining "wastelands" of the Sundarbans that, as per his estimation, was about close to one million acres, which included tracts that were yet to be surveyed. He proposed to introduce settlers from China, Madras and other parts of the coast of India and also encourage the immigration of free labour from Zanzibar on as large a scale as possible. He proposed to grow cotton on these tracts. Ferdinand summed up his rationale thus and is indicative of how gigantic the scale of his enterprise was being envisioned:

> The object of my application is to provide for the speedy cultivation of the large tract of fertile country stretching to the Eastward between Canning and the River Megna. This would not only give a great additional impetus to the trade of Bengal, but materially improve the sanitary condition of both Canning and Calcutta. To accomplish this two things are required: *money and population.* The latter I could not hope to obtain by the mere withdrawal of excess population from other parts of India, as it is well known that India in many parts is suffering from great want of labor; and although it may seem strange that with such facts before us emigration to other distant Colonies is actually facilitated, yet I look upon this as a mere consequence of free trade and I do not complain of it as a grievance, claiming on the other hand the right and privilege to introduce the necessary labor for the accomplishment of my scheme from such parts of the world as may appear desirable. The first country I should direct my attention to is China, where the peaceful agricultural classes have long been suffering from the consequences of Civil wars, and where, I know a good class of laborers with their families could be obtained under the altered conditions of that country. In settling Chinese we should introduce a superior race, a race which would soon rise into a trading population and keep up by its own spontaneous action a constant and regular stream of immigration. With these men, we should have to deal to suit their peculiarities, and each family would probably have to be started as small farmers at once, being under bond to the Company for the refund of their passage money and paying such rents for the land they occupy as may be considered fair and equitable. San Francisco, the Straits, and many Islands in the Indian Archipelago have thus been successfully populated. Another class of labor I should propose to draw from various parts of the African Coast. With these men a different system would probably have to be adopted. In addition, we will, of course, obtain cultivators from other parts of India. Special Acts of Legislation will have to be passed for the introduction of what may be

termed foreign labour. In entering on this cultivation we should have to leave certain belts of jungle, say 10 miles inland facing the sea, untouched, partly with the view of protecting the inner cultivation against the storms in the Bay of Bengal, partly in order to preserve the supply of fuel for the surrounding population; but many of the outer grants would have to be protected by good bunds, similar to those which prevent the sea from washing over some of the richest portions of Holland.[42]

What Schiller was proposing was not within the rules of settlements and perhaps owing to a miscommunication the proposal remained shelved and led many investors to withdraw from the venture. However, something much more dramatic happened that put an end to any real prospects of such a proposal; this was the total destruction of Port Canning in a cyclone in 1867 to which we will now turn in the context of the cyclone history of the region.

Cyclones, uncertainty and devastation

The Sundarbans, for the early officials of the EIC, appeared almost deserted and it took them a while to connect the relative lack of habitation and settlement to the devastating impacts of the 1737 cyclone, which were still lingering:

> There remain yet to be considered the effects of a cyclone and its storm waves. This occurred in Calcutta in 1737, cyclone, "when a wave 40 feet higher than usual, came up. Such would have been sufficient to produce an almost total loss of life in the Sundarbans and its consequent abandonment."

It was debated in colonial sources whether it is the constant invasions by Portuguese and Mugs (sea pirates) that have created this condition of abandonment or whether it was the harsh environment of the Sundarbans and the argument was settled in favour of the latter. The extent of revenue collection in the past was also debated. It is believed that at one time the Sundarbans was far more extensively inhabited and cultivated than at the present; and possibly this may have been due to the fact that the shifting of the main stream of the Ganges from the Bhagirathi to the Padma, by diminishing the supply of fresh water from the north, rendered the tract less fit for human habitation.[43]

There is a strong indication that in the times of the Mughals (1526–1857), the Sundarbans was, indeed, inhabited. A cyclone of 1585, nonetheless, finds mention in the writings of Abul Fazl, where he notes that

> The Sarkar, or district, of Bagla, extends along the seacoast. The fort of the Sarkar is surrounded by a forest. From new moon to full moon, the waves of the sea rise higher and higher; from the fifteenth to the last day of the moon, they gradually decrease. In the 29th year of the present era

(A. D. 1585), one afternoon, an immense wave set the whole district under water. The chief of the place was at a feast; he managed to get hold of a boat, whilst his son Paramanand, with a few others climbed up a Hindu temple. Some merchants got on a *Tâlâr*★ For nearly five hours the waves remained agitated; the lightning and the wind were terrible; houses and ships were destroyed; only the Hindu temple and the *Tâlâr* escaped. About two hundred thousand souls perished in this hurricane.[44]

The cyclone of 1585 did not result in the depopulation of the Sundarbans because Abul Fazl, 11 years later, in 1596, mentions four towns as belonging to the Sarkar of Bagla, viz., Isma'ilpur, commonly called Baglachinj, Srirampur, Shahzadahpur and Adilpur. These four places must have been of some importance because the district then paid a revenue of nearly 70 lakhs of dams, that is, nearly 180,000 lis., and was besides liable to furnish 320 elephants and 15,000 *zamindari* troops.[45] Earlier debilitating cyclones, therefore, had not deterred people from settling in the area as one report noted the frequency of storms and the consequent suffering:

The colonies of settlers in Sundarbans are specially exposed to the fury of such storms. Their houses and their fields are only a foot or two above high-water mark and when the cyclone wave pours up the great streams of the Poseur and Haringhata, and from them spreads over the country, the inundation works cruel havoc among the low-lying isolated villages. The grain in their fields is spoiled their houses are torn away and all their stores are lost their cattle are carried away and drowned; and they themselves are reduced to extreme shifts to save their own lives.[46]

The frequency of cyclones was also apparent from the literature. In October 1895, which swept over both the Bagherhat and Satkhira subdivisions

On 16 May 1869, a cyclone destroyed 250 lives in Morrellganj alone and caused an immense loss of property.[47] It was reported in 1870 that the average annual rainfall varied from about 82 inches in the west to over 200 inches in the east. Cyclones and storm waves occurred from time to time. The worst of the calamities of this nature was in 1870 when a great part of the Backergunge and the adjoining districts was submerged, the depth of water in some places being over ten feet.

In the night of 31 October and 1 November 1876, another report noted that the most terrible cyclone and storm wave had been experienced since 1822. The greatest havoc was confined to Chittagong and the estuary of the Meghna and accordingly the Bakarganj portion of the Sundarbans suffered severely; in Galachipa thana, no less than 10th of the population was estimated to have been drowned. The calamity was described in detail by Sir Richard Temple, Lieutenant Governor of Bengal, who visited the affected area immediately after the occurrence and a vivid account is contained in the Gazetteer of the Bakarganj

District published in 1918. Crops and cattle were destroyed far and wide, and the immediate effect of the storm, so far as it effects this history, was the relapse of a vast area of the Sundarbans in Bakarganj to jungle.[48] The secondary effect of the cyclone was an enquiry into the possibility of erecting refuges to protect from loss of life in case of similar calamities. This cyclone heavily impacted land leases as several lands were submerged by the storm. Importantly, it was also reported that

> Khulna was affected only to a small extent by the terrible cyclone and storm wave of 1876 but its immunity was largely due to the protection afforded by the large area of forest and to the fact that no reclamation had been undertaken in the danger zone with the exception of lots 1 to 6 (Khaulia-Barisal) on the Haringhata estuary.[49]

In contrast to Bakarganj being severely impacted by the 1876 cyclone, it appears that the creation of more reserved forests in Khulna protected the district from the impact of the cyclone. Clearly, here the transformative potential of forests to protect against natural disasters was widely commented on.[50] The rich state of the forests was commented on frequently:

> It appeared to be clear, both from the look of the forests and from the statements of the wood-cutters, that the Sunderbuns forests reproduced themselves in ten to twenty years. One-twentieth of the forest area would yield about 700,000 tons of firewood and petty timber per annum, or more than would supply all the requirements of Calcutta and the Delta districts, and therefore the Sunderbuns forest might be trusted 'to supply the wants of the country without any interference'.[51]

Forests not only provided protection from cyclone but the colonial reports also give details about people livelihoods and how they were linked to the forest. Woodcutting and fishing were recorded as being part of people's livelihoods though the dangers of tiger attacks continued to be high. In 1908 it reported the practice of the woodcutters:

> These brutes, who will swim broad streams in search of prey, are justly dreaded by those whose business takes them into the forests. No woodcutter will go there to cut wood unless accompanied by a *fakir* who is supposed to have power over tigers and other wild animals. Before commencing work, the *fakir* assembles all the woodcutters of his party, clears a space at the edge of the forest and erects a number of tent-like huts, in which he places images of various deities, to which offerings are made. When this has been done, the allotment is considered free of tigers; and each woodcutter, before commencing work makes an offering to the jungle deities, by which act he is supposed to have gained a right to their protection. In the event

of any of the party being carried off by a tiger, the *fakir* decamps and the woodcutters place flags at the most prominent comers of the allotment to warn off others.[52]

Yet the number of tiger deaths continued and they themselves came under attack. In 1906, the number of persons reported to have been killed by tigers in the Sundarbans was 60 against 79 in the previous year with the number of tigers killed during the year being 35. In 1914, the number of persons reported to have been killed by tigers in the Sundarbans was 79 against 81 in the previous year and the number of tigers killed during the year was 39. In 1916, the number of persons reported to have been killed by tigers in the Sundarbans was 19 against 60 in the previous year and 86, the average of past five years. it was noted that "There was an appreciable increase in the number of deaths by tigers, the total figure being 81 in 1917 against 55 in 1916".[53] The number of tigers killed increased from 110 in 1916 to 123 in 1917. In 1919, the number of deaths caused by tigers showed a decrease, the number being 28 against 60 in the preceding year and the number of tigers killed decreased from 104 in 1918 to 86 in 1919. Tigers were clearly a force to be reckoned with in this period and were actively killed by the settlers.[54]

Two devastating cyclones hit the centre of the Sundarbans and Calcutta in the latter half of the 19th century. This was a period when colonial weather data and collecting cyclones had made a big step forward. It was realised by colonial scientists that climate and weather are complex phenomenon and vary through time and geographically. The colonial scientific network allowed for the possibility to collect useful data through lots of data points and an information flow network that spanned Australia, India and oceanic islands such as Mauritius and St. Helena. The "Monsoon" coined from Arabic *mawsin* (a season) was key to understanding world climate and, therefore, the Indian peninsula became key to understanding world climate. Between 1700 and 1924, main features of world climate discovered by Indian civil servants and officials, who were mostly Scots, Germans& Bengali.[55] They included the remarkable Henry Piddington who wrote the Law of storms and coined the word cyclone in 1848. By 1852, there were 123 weather stations in India with the Centre of Calculation being in Calcutta. The journal, *Asiatic Researches* published the data which included a detailed study of cyclones.[56]

The 1864 storm had a width of 100 miles and was proceeding at a speed of 10–17 miles per hour. The greatest damage on land was from a 15-foot storm surge. It was reported that at the end of the cyclone, 48,000 people were declared dead in Calcutta and environs about 1/3 of the population including those who died in the aftermath due to death by cholera. The official report of the 1864 cyclone by Henry Blanford is a biography of the cyclone.[57] The storm chart of the Bay of Bengal drawn up by Henry Piddington showed that the majority of the cyclones, the tracks of which are there laid down, proceeded from a line running from south to north by the Nicobars, Andamans and the islands of the

Arracan coast, following the westward side of the mountain axis, which, in part, submerged and a prolongation of the Sunda Islands.

Of these storms, several appear to have originated in the neighbourhood of the Andamans. The force of the cyclone was intensified by the formation of a tidal bore in the Hoogly breaching dykes in many places and leaving the interior flooded.[58]

Local ships like the *Alexander*, Clarance and the Comet gave details of the storm. On the impact of the 1864 cyclone itself, contemporary reports noted several details. Babu Chatterjee noted that in Tamluk Bazaar in Midnapur, the storm waves rose and the water stood 12 feet "above" the roadway and of the 1,400 houses and huts only 27 were left standing.[59] In Calcutta, heavy winds and the fall of barometric pressure to 29.7 accompanied the storm on the 6th of October felling several trees in Chowrangee.

> Wherever there were trees, they were either uprooted and fell, carrying with them in many cases walls, railings and buildings, or their branches were snapped off like reeds and hurried away with the wind. Carriages and *pulkees* were upset and strewed the roads, mingled with the debris of roofs, verandahs, gates and fallen trees; corrugated iron roofings were torn, doubled upand blown away like sheets of paper.[60]

The cyclone showed the differential impact on the rich and poor. In Calcutta alone, 102 pucca houses were destroyed, with 563 severely damaged. On top of that, 40,698 native huts were completely levelled. Reports from the ship Clarence also provided some of the details.[61] A scheme was being mooted to develop another port as an auxiliary to Calcutta, a place about 45 kilometres to the south-east of Calcutta, deeper in the Ganga–Brahmaputra delta, on the estuarine river, the Matlah. Piddington wrote to the Governor-General of India in 1853, warning the site would be extremely vulnerable to storm surges. Port Canning was commissioned in 1864, and in 1867, a storm of quite moderate intensity brought in six feet (1.8 metres) of water over the settlement. The damaged port was abandoned four years later. Port Canning was an ambitious venture that the government had taken up in Bengal, and this proposal had the approval from the apex office of the colonial administration. Since 1853, the government had undertaken the survey of the lands around river Matlah with the intention of building a subsidiary port to Kolkata and settling a municipality town as well. Work of survey, settlement and formation of a company occurred in rapid succession. That very year, Henry Piddington who had moved his residence in Kolkata to pursue his varied intellectual interests wrote to the Governor-General of India stating that the river Matlah as per his calculations was directly in the way of cyclones a term that he had coined for the sea storms and gales that he had been studying for a while now. His letter was received, and his proposition was reviewed in *The Calcutta Review* in which his reputation was commended, but his proposal was refuted on the premise that there were no facts to support his projection. His critics chose to ignore his warning and stated that given an upsurge in the river one could always resort to the good old system of embankments. The example of prosperous coastal ports and port towns in Europe was thrown in comparison for good measure.

In 1867, Piddington's claim turned out to be true. Port Canning after its grand inauguration in 1864 came in the way of a cyclone and was completely destroyed, never to be rebuilt again. This was one of factors that eventually shelved the proposal drawn up by Ferdinand Schiller. The state had ignored the warnings of experts like Piddington at its own expense. The Sundarbans, however, continued being reclaimed and populated and by the beginning of the 20th century had begun to be reclaimed in its lower reaches within the lease undertaken by Daniel Hamilton who introduced a cooperative system to communally maintain the embankments while he provided its financial cost.

During the long 19th century in the Sundarbans, the colonial state had to contend with floods and cyclones while trying to turn the Sundarbans into a productive geography. At the official level, in the responses from "above" embankments appear to be the answer to all calamities from water. The cyclones of 1864 and 1867 did not seem to have acted as any deterrent or any reference point for reflection as we can see the haste with which Port Canning was constructed despite advice from Henry Piddington. The pertinent question that appears to have engaged them was who would bear the incidence of maintaining and repairing the embankments?

Making the margin from the normal: concluding remarks

Environmental histories on Kutch and the Sundarbans, especially in terms of the colonial record, suggest that these environments were considered to be dynamic, unpredictable and subject to debilitating impacts from extreme natural events. For the colonial officials and the state consequently, both Kutch and the Sundarbans were considered and treated as marginal environments and, therefore, subjected to different regimes for monitoring and exploitation. Local communities, however, despite many of their vulnerabilities as subsistence cultivators and pastoralists turned mobility and a portfolio of livelihood generating capacities into adaptation strategies rather than simply as coping responses. For the Sundarbans, this disjuncture of responses from "above" and "below" give us insights into the ways in which these continue to be part and parcel of the nature of governance and local-level responses in the postcolonial period. Following the most recent cyclones in the region in the 21st century, Aaila, Titli and Amphan while communities have responded by migration, their options now are much more limited (see Chapter 5). In Kutch, similarly, the responses of the state to frequent droughts and the 2001 earthquake has not brought solace to communities whose water resources are being ever more reduced by dams upriver, water grabbing by the industries and increasing rainfall variability (see Chapter 4). Today in the Banni, the degradation of the grassland has been also partly due to the introduction of an alien species by the state, *Prosopis juliflora*. Nearly, 55% of the area is today invaded by *Prosopis*, a leguminous shrub, locally called *gandobaval*, imported from South America in the 1960s, in an attempt to keep desertification and salinisation at bay. The fragile eco-system of the Kutch is teetering on the edge of an environmental crisis.

Notions about uncertainty, as pointed out earlier, are critically informed by ideas about environmental change (Bennett 2010; Marris 2011;. Environmental histories, on the other hand, can help explore the layered social, economic and political responses to environmental shocks. Consequently, as out study shows, the colonial record on Kutch and the Sundarbans becomes particularly compelling in terms of how subsistence cultures by local communities can offer insights for assembling adaptation strategies in conditions of extreme environmental stress.

Notes

1 James Macmurdo quoted in Chhaya Goswami, 2011, *The Call of the Seas, Kachchhi Traders in Muscat and Zanzibar, 1800–1880*, 16: New Delhi Orient Black Swan.
2 James Macmurdo to William Erskine, Esq. & C. Bombay Feb 1824, *Papers Relating to the Earthquake Which Occurred in India in 1819*, in *The Transactions of the Literary Society of Bombay*, 63 (310) Feb, 1824, 105–119.
3 Burnes, *A Sketch of the History of Cutch*, Bombay, 1830.
4 Alexander Burnes, Memoir on the Eastern Branch of the River Indus, giving and Account of the Alterations produced on it by an Earthquake, also a Theory of the formation of the Runn, and some Conjectures on the Route of Alexander the Great; drawn up in the years 1827–1828 in *Transactions of the Royal Asiatic Society of Great Britain and Ireland*, 3 (3) (1834), p. 569.
5 Marianna Postans. *Cutch or Random Sketches of Western India interspersed with Legends and Traditions*, London, 1839.
6 Lieutenant S. N. Raikes, *Memoir on the Kutch State*, submitted to the Government of Bombay in November, 1854, in *Selections from the Records of Bombay Government* No. XXVII – New Series, National Archives of India (hereafter NAI), New Delhi.
7 S. N. Raikes, *Memoir on the Kutch State*, Submitted to Government, November, 1854, NAI, pp. 4–5.
8 James Burnes in *A Sketch of the History of Cutch*, Bombay, 1830, p. 30.
9 S. N. Raikes, *Memoir on the Kutch State*, Submitted to Government, November, 1854, NAI, p. 5.
10 Ibid., p. 84.
11 Ibid., pp. 78–80.
12 Letter from Major H.N. Reeves, Political Agent, Cutch, to C. Gonne, Esquire, Secretary to Government, Political Department, Bombay, No. 123, dated Bhuj, 30th July 1878, p. 3.
13 S. N. Raikes, *Memoir on the Kutch State*, Submitted to Government, November, 1854, NAI, p. 84.
14 Ibid., pp. 70–72.
15 Ibid., pp. 69–70.
16 The Kori was the currency of Kutch State until 1948. It was subdivided into 24 *Dokda* (singular *Dokdo*), each of 2 *Trambiyo*. Only coins were issued. Other copper coins in use were called *Dhabbu* and *Dhinglo*. The Kori was replaced by the Indian rupee. 1 Kori = 2 Adhio = 4 Payalo = 8 Dhabu = 16 Dhingla = 24 Dokda = 48 Trambiya = 96 Babukiya.

17 Arthur Malet, *Statement Containing Information Relative to the Names of the Towns and Villages in the Province of Kutch; Their Estimated Annual Revenue, and the Names of Their Respective Owners*, Submitted to Government on the 1st November, 1842, NAI, pp. 12–13.
18 In December 1819, 250 Kosias came to Banni carrying of 300–400 cattle. At that time, population combined and soldiers at the outpost combined to reclaim cattle and fight the plunderers as documented in S N Raikes, *Memoir on the Kutch State*, Submitted to Government, November, 1854, NAI, pp. 47–48.
19 Gazetteer of Bombay Presidency, Vol. 5, Kutch, Palanpur & Mahikanta, 1880, p. 80, NAI, New Delhi.
20 Gazetteer of Bombay Presidency, Vol. 5, Kutch, Palanpur&Mahikanta, 1880, p. 120, NAI, New Delhi.
21 Gazetteer of Bombay Presidency, Vol. V, 1880, NAI, pp. 17, 18, 107, 108, 155, 173–176, 207–208.
22 Arthur Malet, *Statement Containing Information Relative to the Names of the Towns and Villages in the Province of Kutch; Their Estimated Annual Revenue, and the Names of Their Respective Owners*, Submitted to Government on the 1st November, 1842, NAI, pp. 58–59.
23 Letter from Lieutenant Colonel S.C. LAW, Acting Political Agent, Kutch. To C. Gonne, Esq, Secretary to Government, Bombay. No. 40 of 1872, Camp Mandavi, 4th April 1872, p. 1. – Note: Cost of low rainfall measured in agricultural and revenue losses.
24 Letter from Captain G. R. Goodfellow, Acting Political Agent, Kutch. To C. Gonne, Esq, Secretary to Government, Bombay. No. 75 of 187, Bhuj, 15th June 1873, p. 1.
25 Letter from Colonel W.C. Parr, Political Agent, Cutch, to C. Gonne, Esquire, Secretary to Government, Political Department, Bombay, No. 93 of 1876, dated Bhuj, 20th June 1876, p. 6.
26 Report on the Administration of the Cutch State for 1891–1892, p. 21 Bhuj, 'Cutch Darbari' Press. 1892. Note: Clear suggestion of nomadic patterns.
27 Report on the Administration of the Cutch State for 1891–1892. Bhuj, 'Cutch Darbari' Press. 1893, p. 25.
28 Report on the Administration of the Cutch State for 1885–1886. Bombay: Printed at the Bombay Gazette Steam Press, Rampart Row. 1886, p. 18.
29 Letter from Major H.N. Reeves, Political Agent, Cutch, to C. Gonne, Esquire, Secretary to Government, Bombay, No. 73 of 1880, Political Department Bhuj, 12th July 1880, p. 6.
30 Report on the Administration of the Cutch State for 1885–1886. Bombay: Printed at the Bombay Gazette Steam Press, Rampart Row. 1886, p. 18.
31 Report on the Administration of the Cutch State for 1885–1886. Bombay: Printed at the Bombay Gazette Steam Press, Rampart Row. 1886, p. 19. – Note: Policy intervention to increase cultivation.
32 Bengal District Gazetteers: Khulna. L.S.S. O'Malley, Indian Civil Service. Calcutta: The Bengal Secretariat Book Depot. 1908, p. 23. Note: First mention of fishing as possibly being a lucrative activity.
33 Frederick E. Pargiter, *A Revenue History of the Sundarbans, 1765–1870*, 1885, Bengal Government Press, 1934–1935, Chapter 1, pp. 1–9. Available at http://www.southasiaarchive.com/Content/sarf.140487/201193/001 (accessed on 2 January 2020).
34 F. E. Pargiter, *A Revenue History of Sundarbans, 1765–1870*, Chapter 24, pp. 109–110.
35 F.D. Ascoli, *A Revenue History of the Sundarbans from 1870 to 1920*, Secretary to the Board of Revenue. Calcutta: Bengal Secretariat Book Department, 1921, p. 15.
36 *Report of the Administration of Bengal (1871–1872)*. Calcutta, Bengal Secretariat Press. 1873, p. 145. Notes: Describes Sunderbans as supplying key resources to Bengal.

37 *Report of the Administration of Bengal (1887–1888)*. Calcutta, Bengal Secretariat Press. 1889, p. 20.
38 *Report of the Administration of Bengal (1905–1906)*. Calcutta, Bengal Secretariat Book Depot. 1907, p. 20.
39 The Imperial Gazetteer of India. Volume 23. Meyer, William Stevenson, Sir, 1860–1922. Burn, Richard, Sir, 1871–1947. Cotton, James Sutherland, 1847–1918. New edition, published under the authority of His Majesty's secretary of state for India in council. Oxford, Clarendon Press, 1908–1931 [v. 1, 1909] Sir Herbert Hope, 1851–1911. p. 143.
40 F.D. Ascoli, *A Revenue History of the Sundarbans from 1870 to 1920*, Secretary to the Board of Revenue, Calcutta, Bengal Secretariat Book Department. 1921, p. 15. Notes: Disputed nature of distinguishing between valuable forest lands to be preserved versus wastelands to be brought under cultivation.
41 Ibid.
42 *Letter from S C Bayley, Esquire, Junior Secretary to the Government of Bengal, to the Secretary to the Board of Revenue, Lower Provinces*, 30 January, 1865, No. 396, NAI, New Delhi.
43 *Proceedings of the Asiatic Society of Bengal* Edited by the General Secretary, January to December 1868, Calcutta: Printed by C.B. Lewis, Baptist Mission Press, p. 265.
44 *Proceedings of the Asiatic Society of Bengal* Edited by the General Secretary, January to December 1868, Calcutta: Printed by C.B. Lewis, Baptist Mission Press, pp. 266–267. Please note, Talar means an erected platform near temples and palaces for musicians.
45 L.S.S. O'Malley, *Bengal District Gazetteers: Khulna*, Calcutta: The Bengal Secretariat Book Depot. 1908, p. 107.
46 Ibid., 107
47 F.D. Ascoli, *A Revenue History of the Sundarbans from 1870 to 1920*, Secretary to the Board of Revenue, Calcutta, Bengal Secretariat Book Department, 1921, p. 66. Note: Cyclone of 1878 documented. Gazetteer of Bakarganj District 1918.
48 Ibid., p. 66.
49 Ibid.
50 Ibid., p. 71.
51 L.S.S. O'Malley, *Bengal District Gazetteers*, Khulna, Calcutta: The Bengal Secretariat Book Depot. 1908, p. 20. Notes: Practices around cutting wood and tigers are discussed extensively.
52 *Report of the Administration of Bengal (1914–1915)*. Calcutta: The Bengal Secretariat Book Depot. 1916, p. 67. Notes: The trajectory of how the large number of people being killed by tigers in the Sundarbans declines as the number of tiger killings increases.
53 *Report of the Administration of Bengal (1915–1916)*. Calcutta: The Bengal Secretariat, Book Depot. 1917, p. 66.
54 The world's biggest weather phenomena are: The Pacific Ocean, the monsoon, the atmosphere, the seasons.
55 Henry Piddington, Law of Storms in India, (An Eighteenth Memoir on the) being the Cyclone of the 12th to 14th Oct. 1848, in the Bay of Bengal, *Journal of the Asiatic Society of Bengal*, Vol. XVIII, Part II,–July to December 1849, pp. 826–869.
56 Lieut. Col. J. E. Gastrell and Henry F. Blanford, A.R.S.M, 'Report on the Calcutta Cyclone of the 5th October 1864, *with Maps and Diagrams Illustrating the Origin and Progress of the Storm and the Track of the Storm Wave*. Calcutta, O.T. Cutter, Military Orphan Press, 1866.
57 Blanford, 1864 Calcutta Cyclone, pp. 110–112.
58 Blanford, 1864 Calcutta Cyclone, p. 56.
59 *India: The Cyclone at Calcutta*, account printed in *The Calcutta Englishman,* October, 10 reprinted in General News column in New York Times, November 24, 1864, https://www.nytimes.com/1864/11/24/archives/general-news-india-the-cyclone-at-calcutta.html last accessed on 20 December, 2019.

60 Ship log of Clarence kept by James Watson, 1858–1873, MSS Coll 832, University of Pennsylvania.
61 Henry Piddington, 'On the Cyclone Waves in the Soonderbuns – A Letter to the Most Noble the Governor-General of India' 1853. Calcutta Review, Vol. XXIV, January to June, 1855, pp. 330–342.

References

Ascoli, F.D. 1921. *A Revenue History of the Sundarbans from 1870 to 1920*. London: Routledge.
Asiatic Society of Bengal. 1849. *Journal of the Asiatic Society of Bengal Vol. XVIII, Part II, – July to December 1849*. Kolkata: The Asiatic Society of Bengal.
Bengal Government. 1865. *Board of Revenue Proceedings Records Room*. New Delhi: Records Room of the National Archives of India.
Bennett, J. 2010. *Vibrant Matter: A Political Ecology of Things*. Durham, NC: Duke University Press.
Bhattacharya, N. 2018. *The Great Agrarian Conquest: The Colonial Reshaping of a Rural World*. Ranikhet: Permanent Black.
Burnes, J. 1830a. *A Narrative of a Visit to the Court of Sinde; A Sketch of the History of Cutch, from Its First Connexion with the British Government in India till the Conclusion of the Treaty of 1819; and Some Remarks on the Medical Topography of Bhooj*. Edinburgh: John Stark 1831 at Asia Pacific & Africa Collection, British Library, UK.
Burnes, J. 1830b. *A Sketch of the History of Cutch*. New Delhi: Asian Educational Services. Accessed via PragMahal Archives, Bhuj, Gujarat.
D'Souza, R. 2019. 'Scarcity, Environmentalism and the Politics of Pre-Emption: Reconsidering the Environmental Histories of South Asia in the Epoch of the Anthropocene'.*Geoforum*, 101: 242–249. https://doi.org/10.1016/j.geoforum.2018.09.033
Damodaran, V. and R. D'Souza, eds. 2020. *Commonwealth Forestry and Environmental History: Empire Forests and Colonial Environments in Africa, the Caribbean, South Asia and New Zealand*. New Delhi: Primus Books.
Gastrell, Lieut. Col., J. E. and H.F. Blanford. 1866. *Report on the Calcutta Cyclone of the 5th October 1864, with Maps and Diagrams Illustrating the Origin and Progress of the Storm and the Track of the Storm Wave*. Calcutta: O.T Cutter, Military Orphan Press.
Gazetteer of the Bombay Presidency. 1880. *Volume V, Cutch, Palanpur, and Mahikanta*. Bombay: Government Central Press. Accessed via the National Archives of India, Library, New Delhi.
Grove, R., V. Damodaran, and S. Sangwan. 1998. *Nature and the Orient: The Environmental History of South and Southeast Asia*. New Delhi: Oxford University Press.
Heredia, R.C. and S.F. Ratnagar, eds. 2003. *Mobile and Marginalized Peoples: Perspectives from the Past*. New Delhi: Manohar.
Ibrahim F. 2004. 'No place like home, History, politics and mobility among a pastoral nomadic community in Western India'. *Nomadic Peoples*, New Series, Special Issue: Whither South Asian Pastoralism? 8(2): 168–190.
Jasanoff, S. 2010. 'A New Climate for Society'. *Theory, Culture & Society*, 27(2–3): 233–253. https://doi.org/10.1177/0263276409361497
Jasanoff, S. and M.L. Martello, eds. 2004. *Earthly Politics: Local and Global in Environmental Governance*. Cambridge, MA: MIT Press.
Journal of the Asiatic Society of Bengal, Vol. XVIII, Part II,-July to December. 1849. Accessed via The Asiatic Society Library, Kolkata.

Kumar, D., V. Damodaran, and R. D'Souza, eds. 2011. *The British Empire and the Natural World: Environmental Encounters in South Asia*. New Delhi: Oxford University Press.

Lieutenant, A. 1834. 'Memoir on the Eastern Branch of the River Indus, Giving an Account of the Alterations Produced on It by an Earthquake, Also a Theory of the Formation of the Runn, and Some Conjectures on the Route of Alexander the Great; Drawn up in the Years 1827–1828'. *Transactions of the Royal Asiatic Society of Great Britain and Ireland*, 3(3): 550–588. Available here: https://www.jstor.org/stable/25581779?seq=1#metadata_info_tab_contents (Accessed 15 August 2018).

Malet, A. 1842. *Statement Containing Information Relative to the Names of the Towns and Villages in the Province of Kutch; Their Estimated Annual Revenue, and the Names of their Respective Owners*. Accessed via the National Archives of India, New Delhi.

Malley, L.S.S.O. 1908. *Bengal District Gazetteers, Khulna*. Calcutta: The Bengal Secretariat. Accessed via the Diectorate of State Archives, Kolkata, West Bengal.

Marriss, E. 2011. *The Rambunctious Garden: Saving Nature in a Post-Wild World*. Bloomsbury.

Mehta, L. 2005. *The Politics and Poetics of Water: The Naturalization of Scarcity in Western India*. Hyderabad: Orient Blackswan.

New York Times. 1864. 'General News Column'. *The New York Times*, New York, November 24.

Pargiter, E.F. 1885. *A Revenue History of the Sundarbans, 1765–1870*. Kolkata: Bengal Government Press. Available at: http://www.southasiaarchive.com/Content/sarf.140487/201193/001 (Accessed 20 December 2019).

Postans, M. 1839. *Cutch or Random Sketches of Western India Interspersed with Legends and Traditions*. Kachchh: Smith, Elder and Company. Accessed via London, Library and The Asiatic Society, Mumbai.

Prasad, A. 2003. *Against Ecological Romanticism: Verrier Elwin and the Making of an Anti-Modern Tribal Identity*. New Delhi: Three Essays Collective.

Proceedings of the Asiatic Society of Bengal, January to December 1868. 1868. Calcutta: C.B. Lewis, Baptist Mission Press. Accessed via the Asiatic Society Library, Kolkata.

Raikes, S.N. 1854. *Memoir of the Kutch State*. Submitted to Government, New Delhi. Accessed via the National Archives of India, New Delhi.

Rennell, J. 1794. 'A Map of the North Part of Hindostan or a Geographical Survey of the Provinces of Bengal, Bahar, Awd, Ellahabad, Agra and Delhi'. Available at: https://apps.lib.umich.edu/online-exhibits/exhibits/show/india-maps/item/5156 (Accessed on 28 July 2021).

Report of the Administration of Bengal 1871–1872. 1872. Calcutta: Bengal Secretariat Press. Accessed via the Directorate of State Archives, Kolkata, West Bengal.

Report of the Administration of Bengal 1887–1888. 1888. Calcutta: Bengal Secretariat Press. Accessed via the Directorate of State Archives, Kolkata, West Bengal.

Report of the Administration of Bengal 1905–1906. 1907. Calcutta: The Bengal Secretariat Book Deposit. Accessed via the Directorate of State Archives, Kolkata, West Bengal.

Report of the Administration of Bengal 1914–1915. 1916. Calcutta: Bengal Secretariat Book Deposit. Accessed via the Directorate of State Archives, Kolkata, West Bengal.

Report of the Administration of Bengal 1915–1916. 1917. Calcutta: Bengal Secretariat Book Deposit. Accessed via the Directorate of State Archives, Kolkata, West Bengal.

Report of the Administration of Cutch State for 1871–1872; 1875–1876; 1877–1878; 1879–1880; 1885–1886; 1891–1892. Accessed via the British Library, India Office Records, Asia, Pacific & Africa Collection, UK.

Saikia, A. 2019. *The Unquiet River: A Biography of the Brahmaputra*. Oxford: Oxford University Press.

Simpson, E. 2003. 'Migration and Islamic Reform in a Port Town in Western India'. *Contributions to Indian Sociology*, 37(1–2): 83–108. https://doi.org/10.1177/006996670303700105

STSC 077. 2015. 'Sailing the British Empire: The Voyages of The Clarence, 1858–73'. Seminar by STSC 077, University of Pennsylvania, USA.

The Calcutta Englishman. 1864. 'India: The Cyclone at Calcutta'. *The Calcutta Englishman.* Calcutta, 10 October.

The Calcutta Review, Vol. XXIV, January to June, 1855. 1855. Calcutta: Sanders, Cones and Co. Accessed via the University Library, University of Calcutta.

The Imperial Gazetteer of India, Vol. XXIII Singhbhum to Trashi-Chod-Zong. 1909. Oxford: Clarendon Press. Available at: https://dsal.uchicago.edu/reference/gazetteer/ (Accessed on 10 January 2019).

Transactions of the Literary Society of Bombay. 1824. Mumbai: Asiatic Society of Bombay.

4
BETWEEN THE MARKET AND CLIMATE CHANGE

Uncertainty and transformation in Kutch

Shilpi Srivastava, Lyla Mehta, Lars Otto Naess, Mihir R. Bhatt and V. Vijay Kumar

FIGURE 4.1 Coastal infrastructure projects undermine pastoralism in Kutch (Photo credit: Shilpi Srivastava).

Introduction

"Kudrat ek karishma hai, uske apne tareekein hain, Malik dekh lega!" (Nature is miraculous, it has its ways. God will keep us) – said Omar *bhai*, former fisher

DOI: 10.4324/9781003257585-4

now Sufi mystic, when we met him in a small fisher hamlet in Kutch in August 2016. He was referring to the changes in seasonal cycles and attributed these to the miracles and also at times to the wrath of nature. But beneath his sense of poise and calm was an anxiety about the future, about his family, village and their livelihoods. "We have to get by", he said and smiled. This anxiety about the "unknown" is often laced with a staunch belief in divination, be it God or *karma*, as life and livelihoods become increasingly precarious for these marginal communities in Kutch. This district in Gujarat, western India, has witnessed massive ecological, economic, demographic and social changes in the 21st century. These include aggressive industrialisation and a boom in business activities which have not only led to economic growth for some but also dispossessed many local people from their traditional lands and livelihoods (see below; also see Figure 4.1).

For most rural communities in Kutch, living with uncertainty has been an intrinsic part of their daily lives. For example, droughts have been a part of the ecological rhythm in Kutch and something people living there have been used to dealing with (see Mehta 2005). However, many now say they are struggling to cope due to a combination of, on the one hand, changing rainfall patterns and intensities of droughts and, on the other hand, the compromised ability to tackle these extremes due to wider social and economic changes which have increased precarity and vulnerability.

Once considered to be the backyard of the developed and prosperous state of Gujarat and a "punishment post for bureaucrats" (Mehta 2005: 314), Kutch, especially after the 2001 earthquake, has been slowly and strategically turned into a corporate enclave (Srivastava and Mehta 2017). This new landscape has also made way for a new set of actors. These include big corporate houses that are increasingly laying claims to coastal and marine resources and a vibrant network of civil society organisations (CSOs) working in diverse areas of reconstruction, rights and development (Kohli and Menon 2016).

Thus, this landscape, hitherto considered "remote" and "backward" with respect to mainstream development in India, is now servicing the engines of the capitalist economy through various interventions such as the Special Economic Zones (SEZs)[1] and renewable energy parks that are making these marginal areas legible to the state and corporate actors (see Damodaran *et al.*, Chapter 3; Scott 1998). In parallel, climate change is also posing a threat to the traditional livelihoods in the district (Mehta *et al.* 2019). Due to rapid groundwater depletion and poor rainfall, saltwater intrusion has emerged as a major challenge (GUIDE 2014). Furthermore, industrial development in some eco-sensitive zones has affected local livelihoods such as dryland agriculture, fishing and pastoralism (Kohli and Menon 2016).

In this chapter, we investigate how uncertainty is characterised by these diverse actors in Kutch. As discussed in Chapter 1, we use the Kutch case to argue that the increase of extreme events, together with the many ecological, economic and political changes taking place in this remote district, has given rise to a more radical form of uncertainty. By radical uncertainty, we mean a situation where the past is no longer a good guide to what the future might hold (Kay and King 2020). This, we argue, creates situations that are not only pushing people to the limits of coping but also reducing their adaptive capacity to live with current as well as future climatic uncertainties. Thus, new ways of anticipating and reimagining these landscapes may be required for socially just transformation in the context of climate change.

After laying out the conceptual framework and methodology, we discuss the varying perceptions of uncertainty from the "above" and "below". This is followed by a short discussion on the role of intermediaries (the "middle") who are instrumental in entrenching or reframing the development narratives, thus becoming the potential facilitators of transformative change in Kutch. We discuss one such example at the end of the chapter.

Radical uncertainty and transformation

Changing rainfall patterns caused by climate change can increase the severity and frequency of both droughts and floods (Lehmann *et al.* 2018). This is a cause for concern when these historically new patterns occur in drought-prone areas. While local people may be attuned to coping with climate variability in Kutch, the rapid rise of extreme weather events and high climatic variability has constrained their traditional responses, especially when wider forces in the political economy also limit their adaptive capacity and pathways to address climate-induced uncertainties (Tschakert 2007; Solecki *et al.* 2017). This intersection of epistemic uncertainty with wider drivers of change leads to what we have called radical uncertainty in this chapter.

In this chapter, we draw on Walker *et al.*'s (2003) distinction between ontological (uncertainty due to inherent variability of the system) and epistemological uncertainty (uncertainty due to imperfect knowledge) and argue that perceptions of and responses to uncertainty are shaped by diverse factors. These range from dynamic and variable ecological systems (rainfall, temperature, salinity intrusion) to the incumbent knowledge systems and systemic drivers of change (such as industrialisation, water and land grabs) which lead to situated perspectives on uncertainty and also shape particular responses (Haraway 1988; Mehta *et al.* 2019).

This intersection between these different drivers has material effects and is at the heart of radical uncertainty, which either pushes local people to the limits of coping or compels them to adopt maladaptive pathways that compromise their or others' well-being in different ways (Gajjar *et al.* 2018; Mehta *et al.* 2019). It creates what Ribot (2014: 673) has referred to as the "pre-existing precarity that climate change finds in place", which then (re)produces vulnerabilities and may limit future adaptation pathways and choices. For example, we show how the denigration of pastoralism has led several herders to take up precarious and insecure employment and also compromised on their identity and sense of well-being (Mehta and Srivastava 2019).

Uncertainty and transformation

As argued in the introduction, uncertainties can often create feelings of anxiety and precarity, these should not always be viewed negatively. They may present opportunities, policy windows and spaces that trigger change, disrupt incumbent systems that lock in social inequalities and provide an opportunity to address root causes and in effect "to reconfigure the meaning and trajectory of development" (Pelling 2011: 231). These are broadly characterised as transformations in this chapter.

For example, in the context of climate adaptation, Pelling (2011: 88) notes that "the most profound act of transformation facing humanity as it comes to live with climate change requires a cultural shift from seeing adaptation as managing the environment "out there" to learning how to reorganise social and socio-ecological relationships, procedures and underlying values "in here"". In this chapter, we look at transformation as a contested process that may be triggered by various uncertainties but is directed towards social justice, ensuring recognition of livelihood rights of the marginal communities and is attuned to production processes and ecological realities that attempt to re-orient value systems towards social and economic justice. Transformations require moving away from top-down and techno-centric approaches to more plural, place-based and diversified ways of embracing and living with uncertainty which are sensitive to human–environment relationships and target the root causes of vulnerability (Eriksen *et al.* 2015). We argue that such deliberately created spaces can offer possibilities to reimagine radical socio-economic change, which also incorporates ecological considerations (health and quality of the ecosystem) as discussed through the pastoral initiative in this chapter.

Methodology

This chapter draws on a multi-sited qualitative study, which brings in a long durée perspective going back many decades by two of the authors. Following a literature review on climate change, environmental politics and development in Kutch, fieldwork has been taking place since 2015. To capture the diverse ecosystem and livelihoods profile of Kutch, the ethnographic fieldwork focused on two geographical sites: Merka in Rapar *taluka* (sub-district) and the coastal village of Jalva and adjoining hamlets in Abdasa *taluka*. This was complemented by extended field observations in these sites and by an additional short research study undertaken in Tasu and Phuleri *vands* (hamlets) in Mundra. These sites represent the diverse ecosystems of Kutch (coastal-marine, wetland and dryland) and the predominant livelihoods of the region which are fishing, agriculture and pastoralism. Our field visits aimed to capture uncertainty in different seasons (winters, summers and post-monsoon). Over 70 semi-structured interviews were conducted with herders, farmers and fishers. This local-level fieldwork was complemented by stakeholder interviews, which were conducted in Naliya

(Abdasa), Bhuj, Gandhinagar and Ahmedabad. Geographically, the "above" and "middle" are spread across the *taluka* headquarters (Rapar and Naliya), the district headquarter (Bhuj) and the twin cities of Gandhinagar and Ahmedabad. In total, 100 interviews were conducted across the various field sites in Gujarat.[2]

Site description

Kutch, derived from the Gujarati word Kachua (tortoise), was formed out of the former native State of Kutch and ten enclave villages of the former native State of Morvi (Mehta 2005). Kutch is the largest district in the country covering an area of 45,674 sq km, of which 51% is covered by the Rann (salt desert) and 15.67% by forests (Government of Gujarat 2020). It has nine ecological zones that range from the Ranns to the lush green irrigated fields and the Banni. The main occupations are pastoralism, agriculture and fishing, but these are in transition due to changes in the local economy after the 2001 earthquake (discussed "below").

Off the Bhuj–Ahmedabad Highway and bordering the Little Rann of Kutch is the compact village of Merka in Rapar *taluka*. Merka is a medium-sized village with over 1,000 households that are multi-religious and multi-caste. Caste, wealth, gender, ownership of land and water resources form the important axes of social differentiation (Mehta 2005). Prominent social groups include the erstwhile feudal lords (the Darbars or the Jadeja Rajputs), the Rjputs (also from the so-called warrior castes, but traditionally considered "lower Jadejas" because they gave up certain restrictive feudal and gender practices (cf. Mehta 2005)), the herders (Rabaris and Bharwads) and Dalits (referred to as Harijans in the village), Kolis and Muslims. The Darbars and the Rjputs occupy the village centre and the Harijan, Koli and Muslim *vas* (settlements) are on the margins. Kolis live in the *vand* on the periphery of the village. They are one of the least developed communities in Merka with little access to health, water, sanitation and other basic amenities.

The village has a semi-arid climate, and the average annual rainfall is about 365 mm (Samerth Trust 2013). The prominent livelihood activities are agriculture (which is largely rain-fed), livestock rearing and charcoal making. Like other villages in the district, water is the backbone of the rural economy in Merka. Previously, the villagers depended on open wells and community ponds (*gaon talabs*) for drinking and livelihood activities, but most of these water sources are either depleted or have fallen into disuse in the last 15 years. With the expansion of settled agriculture, and depletion of other water sources such as ponds, wells and dug wells, groundwater resources are severely strained. Although the village falls within the catchment of the Sardar Sarovar project, which is considered a "lifeline" for Gujarat (see Mehta 2005), water has not yet reached this village and "people are still waiting" (Interviews, January 2016, Merka). For drinking water, people usually rely on the piped water supply but fall back on the wells, especially during the summer months, when the supply is irregular since water is only available once in three days.

Towards the north-west frontier of the district is Jalva, a large coastal village located in Abdasa *taluka*, with a population of 5,369 people (Government of India 2011). Since medieval times, the Jalva port has assumed central importance owing to trade links with west Asian and African countries (Ibrahim 2009). Being the last port on the western frontier of India, Jalva has significant strategic importance and the activities are continuously monitored by the Border Security Force (BSF). The village is predominantly Muslim, with the majority of the population belonging to the Vagher community. Other social groups include the Jains or the Vania, Bhanushalis, Lohana, Darbars and Kolis. Given its proximity to the coast, fishing is one of the major livelihoods in Jalva largely practised by the Vaghers and the Kolis. Livestock rearing is also an important livelihood in the village. The *maldharis* (one who owns and rears livestock) usually live in the *simara* (the boundary of the village) or small hamlets adjacent to the main Jalva village. One such hamlet is Jimlivand, which is the site for our focused study on Jalva.

Jimlivand, a hamlet of approximately 35 families, is a compact community of Fakirani Jats (different from the Jats of Northern India), a sect influenced by the Sufi tradition, who have settled in various hamlets across the Gujarat coast (Soneji 2017). They claim their ancestral links to the Halaf region in Iran (Bharwada and Mahajan 2007). Although fishing is one of the predominant livelihoods in the community, Jimlivand's identity is closely linked to camel and cattle-rearing, that is, being *maldharis*. However, the residents have given up on camel breeding and rearing and now keep buffaloes instead. The village now has about 600–700 buffaloes (Srivastava and Mehta 2017).

The average rainfall of the *taluka* is 371.67 mm and there has been a slight increase in the rainfall (by 17%) from 1932 to 2010 (Gujarat Ecology Commission 2011). Declining water quality is a serious issue in Jalva. Most wells in Jalva have now turned saline and are unfit for drinking or irrigation purposes. Piped water supply is irregular and unreliable. With very few freshwater wells, women and young girls have to make several trips to the wells and wait for hours to collect water.

About 150 km away from Jimlivand is Mundra, a coastal town, which survived the destruction from the 1998 cyclone due to its "thick" mangrove shield (Srivastava and Mehta 2017). A sprawling SEZ has now replaced the mangrove shield. Due to the construction of the SEZ (including the private port), it is estimated that about 3,000 hectares of mangroves were cleared by the Adani Group, and in some cases, as in Mundra and Hazira, they virtually disappeared overnight (Singh quoted in Asher 2008). On the margins of the SEZ are the small-scale fishers (*pagadias* and boat fishers) and the Rabari camel herders whose livelihoods are at risk due to this large-scale industrialisation (Kachchh Camel Breeders Association 2013).

Kutch: a landscape in transition

Kutch is socially diverse and is home to several hundred ethnic groups with distinct customs, languages and identities (Mehta 2005). For much of its recorded history, emigration has been a way of life in Kutch and its geographical location on the western seaboard provided the required fillip to trade and mercantile activities, which, in part, led to the development of a multicultural and syncretic culture in this region (see also Chapter 3). Ibrahim (2007) locates the development in Kutch along two key axes: one, primarily emerging through the outward-looking trade and migration routes with other seafaring communities in East Africa, Bombay or the Persian Gulf, which she calls the *Vaniya-vegetarian-patidar* belt, and the other, hitherto neglected but equally important for the rise and sustenance of syncretism in Kutch, are the pastoral communities who were crucial to the overland trade routes through Pakistan, Afghanistan and Central Asia. Before the partition (1947), the Kutchis usually connected with Sindh more than Gujarat, which was often referred to as *pardes* (foreign land) in oral narratives (Ibrahim 2009; Interview, September 2016, Ahmedabad). *Maldharis* would often migrate to Sindh in times of drought. The land border after the partition severed these ties and successive India–Pakistan wars sealed the divide.

While irrigated agriculture and maritime development received significant attention after Independence in 1947, the contribution of the pastoral economy to Kutch and her people was both neglected and marginalised (Mehta and Srivastava 2019). State policies and programmes have systematically ignored the particular dynamics around variability, uncertainty and water scarcity in Kutch and the experiences and abilities of local communities, especially pastoralists, to deal with these, thus displaying "dryland blindness" (Mehta 2005). This "dryland blindness" and also the systematic denigration of pastoralism in policy discourses have accelerated with the rapid industrialisation processes that intensified after the 2001 earthquake.

Following the earthquake, Kutch became the symbol of reconstruction and development, a "new resource frontier" whereby the economy, nature and society were re-configured to create "spaces of capitalist transition" (Barney 2009: 146). Tax holidays, port development and the establishment of the SEZ have systematically altered the countryside and the coast leading to substantial changes in the demography, resource ownership and allocation in the region. In the name of development, the economy and social sector were opened to diverse actors, such as NGOs, business and corporate houses and other foundations (Kohli and Menon 2016). We now move on to show how uncertainty and transformation have played out in this altered landscape of Kutch.

Politics and perspective from "above", "middle" and "below"

Described in some government reports as a "museum of environmental hardship" (cited in Mehta 2005: 11), Kutch's geology, climate and topography make its resource endowments, especially water, crucial to the sustenance of life and livelihoods. The water endowments of the region vary considerably from place to place. They range from areas abundant in groundwater supplies (such as Mandvi) to vast desert-like saline tracts around the Rann. Different social actors in Kutch also have highly differentiated access to and control over water and land resources (Mehta 2005).

As a state falling in arid and semi-arid zones, Gujarat has traditionally had a drought cycle of five years, including two years of moderate rainfall, two years of low rainfall and one year of good rainfall (GUIDE 2014). Two or three consecutive years of low rainfall make it difficult for the local communities to sustain their livelihoods. In the period between 1958 and 2007, Kutch recorded the highest annual rainfall variability (57%) among the districts of Gujarat. Kutch, along with parts of Banaskantha, Patan, Surendranagar, Rajkot and Jamnagar districts, was also found prone to experience moderate to severe droughts in more than 30% of the years (Pandey *et al.* 1999, 2009). A 2014 study by the Gujarat Institute of Desert Ecology (GUIDE) also recorded an increase in the number of villages experiencing drought in Kutch over the past two decades (GUIDE 2014).

A long coastline also exposes the state to stressors such as cyclones, sea-level rise and salinity ingress. According to a coastal vulnerability assessment (2015), the Gulf of Khambat and north-western part of the Gulf of Kutch are classified under very high-risk category (Mahapatra *et al.* 2015). With the warming of the Arabian Sea, cyclonic activities are also likely to be amplified in this region given the recent trends in the incidence of extreme weather events in the Indian Ocean (Sarkar 2020).

Until a few decades ago, droughts and, to a lesser extent, cyclones were the major environmental challenges in the state as well as the district of Kutch. However, in recent times, increasing extreme events such as intense rainfall and heatwaves are adding to environmental vulnerabilities of the district. For instance, in August 2020, various parts of the district were flooded and the region recorded 32% higher rainfall than the season's average (The Hindu Business Line 2020). Like several other regions, Kutch also has a varied agro-climatic profile with different micro-climates in different regions, which require targeted adaptation strategies. So, how do policymakers and scientists understand climate-related uncertainties in Gujarat and more specifically in Kutch?

The bird's eye view: uncertainty from "above"

For the "above" in Gujarat, very few actors spoke of climate adaptation and mitigation strategies tailored for one specific region or district in the state. Instead, they largely referred to the aggregate state-level scenario where Kutch featured as one among the many districts of Gujarat which is vulnerable to climate change. This bird's eye view also meant that local perceptions and experiences of climate change rarely featured in policymaking on climate change.

For scientists in Gujarat, climate change is real and certain and is measured through key variables such as temperature, rainfall, sea-level rise and concentration of GHGs in the atmosphere. They concur that what is uncertain is the impact of climate change at the local and regional levels due to limitations of downscaling in the Global Circulation Models (GCMs) (Interviews, September 2016 and January 2018, Gandhinagar and Ahmedabad; Sarkar *et al.* (2015); see also Chapter 2). However, their position and emphasis on each of these variables varied where some tend to focus more on rainfall and adaptation, while others on temperature and atmospheric changes.

Almost all climate scientists that we interviewed agreed that climate change will have unprecedented effects on the social and economic life in Gujarat. Referring to these issues, the Director of IMD (Ahmedabad) stated: "there may be uncertainty about rainfall, but there is no uncertainty about maximum and minimum temperature in Gujarat as heatwaves will become more frequent and oppressive" (Interview January 2018, Ahmedabad).

Specifically for Kutch, a 2015 study on downscaling temperature and rainfall scenarios projects that Kutch is likely to get hotter and wetter by the end of this century. For instance, the study indicates that the daily maximum and minimum temperature would increase by at least 0.4 °C, 1.5 °C and 3.0 °C during 2011–2030, 2046–2065 and 2080–2099, respectively, compared to the baseline temperature (Sarkar *et al.* 2015). The study also concluded that rainfall projections were ridden with uncertainties and required further investigation.

For IMD rainfall had a higher margin of uncertainty because of reduced spells, delayed onset of monsoons (from June to October) and heavy rainfall in short spans which was bound to have a significant impact, especially on agriculture. Referring specifically to Kutch, the Director mentioned:

> In this area, the uncertainty will never decrease. It is an arid area, the south-west monsoon is not uniform, it comes in spells and pulse, sometimes we can have good rains and some time for twenty days, there will be no rains. In arid areas like Kutch, you will get very few spells, so you need to develop water storage capacity.
>
> *(Interview January 2018, Ahmedabad)*

For the scientist, in a government research institute who referred to being in a "privileged" position because of her existing networks with other scientists and policymakers, on the one hand, and vulnerable communities (through projects), on the other hand, uncertainty is not merely present in the models but embodied in the ways people perceive, respond and deal with climatic events. She argued that:

> Uncertainty does not exist merely at research levels but also in people's perception of the phenomenon i.e. how does it impact them. They [people] understand that things are changing and they would be able to relate with things like rainfall (rainy days have reduced) and temperature (the winters are not that cold). Uncertainty lies in the fact that we do not know how much is changing, whether this is real climate change or can be attributed to a local weather phenomenon.
>
> *(Interview September 2016, Gandhinagar)*

As discussed in Chapter 2, global projections on climate change are not particularly helpful when it comes to state or district-level planning. Policymakers usually rely on scientific expertise to understand climate change as a phenomenon, which is often limited to questions of changes in patterns such as the arrival of the monsoons, the severity of floods and the intensity of heatwaves, but this scientific input does not extend to policy planning or strategy development. Most of the scientists interviewed agreed that they faced challenges in communicating with policymakers, where they are often perceived more as "information providers" than substantive "policy shapers" because scientists find it hard to accurately predict local-level impacts given the uncertainties in the scenarios. Policymakers often downplay their advice since they only see the value in "hard" predictions.

In the past two decades, climate change has attracted significant policy attention in the state of Gujarat. In 2009, Gujarat became the first state in the country to establish the Climate Change Department (CCD). Announcing the initiative in the state assembly, Narendra Modi (then Chief Minister of Gujarat) said – "Gujarat government's separate department for climate change will act as a bridge between government and society to address the issues related to global warming" (cited in Business Standard 2013). Though introduced with a lot of fanfare, CCD has predominantly focused on mitigation rather than adaptation while devising the climate strategies of the state. Tasked with the role of mainstreaming climate change action into the state-wide policy of Gujarat, CCD's attempts to this day have been partial and this has been recognised by various policymakers (Roundtable dated January 2018, Gandhinagar). We conducted interviews with bureaucrats in this department who were not very aware of climate change issues but instead focused on the achievements of Gujarat in building the controversial Sardar Sarovar Dam, which was often packaged as a form of climate adaptation (Interview, May 2019, Gandhinagar). Although other departments have a diverse portfolio of projects on energy, agriculture, livestock and rural development that address the impacts of climate change, this often takes place through the route of poverty alleviation rather than deliberately targeting or framing these programmes around the language of climate adaptation.

While climate change is a definitive entry point of discussion with the policymakers, the use of uncertainty was at times met with scepticism. Largely, policymakers were uncomfortable with the use of the term and preferred to talk about climate change than about the "realms that cannot be known". This is explained by a former civil servant in Gujarat in the following way:

> The term uncertainty can create policy paralysis. Policymakers usually like to be certain about the course of action and they can work with likely scenarios but not with something that is highly uncertain. We need to justify our decisions […] uncertainty creates policy chaos, and decisions cannot be taken if the range of uncertainty is too high.
>
> *(Roundtable January 2018, Gandhinagar)*

Largely, the actors from "above" acknowledged that climate change impacts are most vigorously felt at the local level, especially in terms of the changes in water supply and resources, health, livelihoods, loss of forest and biodiversity. However, many considered the local level to be like a "blackbox" (Roundtable January 2018, Gandhinagar) where uncertainty is not articulated very clearly. They concurred that the everyday practices of people in terms of living and coping with climate change have not been documented or understood sufficiently, especially by the "above". Largely, there was a tendency to discredit these experiences as anecdotal evidence. This was evident at the roundtable organised in Gandhinagar which was very well attended by policymakers and officials from different departments of the state.

Very often, climate scientists and policymakers dismiss the everyday experiences of local people and situate them as "weather" as opposed to "climate", which has a longer-time horizon (see Chapter 2). However, as argued by Hulme (2017), there are overlaps between the two and it is the instantaneous experience of atmospheric conditions such as wind, temperature, cloudiness, pressure and so on, which averaged over a period of time becomes climate. There are also tensions about the visibility and invisibility of climate change where scientists contend that local people cannot "observe" climate change. However, local people "feel" the manifestations of climate change through changes in resource quantity and quality as well as in terms of impacts on their livelihoods (Rudiak-Gould 2013). Thus, a focus on the everyday practices shows how humans relate to nature encompassing socio-economic and demographic changes, conditions of political economy that impact patterns of resource use, social norms and cultural codes as well as the global flows of capital and labour (Leichenko and O'Brien 2008). We now turn to these experiences and their intersections in the next section.

Uncertainty from "below"

There is a great deal of regional variation across the sites and the experience of climate-related uncertainties is also differentiated by caste, class and gender. As with most drylands, rainfall is highly erratic and variable across Kutch. Farmers told us that over and above climatic variability, limited access to credit, lack of extension officers, the paucity of information and crop insurance, depletion of groundwater and salinity intrusion are the causes of their current vulnerability (GUIDE 2014).

For resource-dependent communities, who live close to nature, climate change is not a term they use. Rather, they speak of changes in the atmosphere, locally called the *havamaan*. Similar to the perceptions among the "above", temperature, erratic patterns of rainfall and drought, cyclones and sea-level rise also featured as key climate plots for the local people in Kutch although these were captured through the lens of changes in everyday routines and livelihoods (discussed below). For example, our photovoice initiative in Jimlivand revealed the gendered experiences of climate change among the *maldhari* women. It captured the more embodied, socially and culturally embedded experiences of uncertainty revealed through the powerful images of the "invisible" care economy that sustains the pastoral system on a day-to-day basis (Mehta and Srivastava 2020). Some examples include frequent trips to drying wells in the summer, picking fodder leaves, milking buffaloes and washing the calves, and the role of faith and religion in coping with climatic uncertainties (Mehta and Srivastava 2020). Across the sites, women and young girls reported spending more time in fetching water. For example, in Jalva, where wells are turning saline rapidly, young girls are dropping out of school to help with household chores.

Generally, when asked about the changes in the *havamaan*, oppressive heat and changes in seasonal calendars were a standard response to "feeling" the changes in the climate. These emerged as central themes during our discussions in both Merka and Jalva. Several interviews highlighted experiences of increased variability over long-term climate change. An ayurvedic doctor, who has lived in Jalva for most of his life, ruminated over the changes in this way:

> We have seen some changes after the earthquake [in 2001] but they have become more intense in the last 5–6 years, it is more variable. It is colder but for fewer days while the summers are getting hotter, and the heat lasts for more days. Seasons have also changed. Earlier rains would come at the end of June but now they come in September. Due to the changes in rainfall, crops are also changing.
>
> *(Interview February 2016, Jalva)*

Several studies have documented how communities that are highly exposed to climate variability adapt to uncertainty by drawing on local cosmologies and indigenous knowledge (IK) systems to predict, forecast and prepare for both immediate and distant futures (Scoones 2004; Mehta 2005; Naess 2013; Hastrup 2013). In the next section, we explore how local people in Merka and Jalva anticipate some of these changes and analyse the social and solidarity networks that they rely on. We also reveal how practices of anticipation are often not enough in conditions of radical uncertainty when ecological uncertainties intersect with wider changes.

Local cosmologies and uncertainty

Rama *Bappa*, a Rjput landowner in Merka, and his family own large tracts of land in Merka. He enjoys a lot of respect across different social groups, much to the envy of the Darbars. Farmers often approach him seeking advice for sowing and crop diseases. As we bite into *rotla* (local bread) smeared with butter, he narrates how farming has changed in the past few decades, with a higher incidence of pest infestation and that seasons have become much harder to predict. Similarly, other farmers also mentioned that their predictions based on lunar calculations were increasingly failing them and that nature was becoming hard to predict and prepare for.[3]

In Kutch, local people have historically drawn on IK to plan their livelihoods. They have used traditional methods to predict the arrival of the monsoons and the success and failure of crops. These range from observing seawater currents, animal and bird behaviour, the flowering of particular plants as well as planetary positions in the sky, with many preferring these "signs of nature" to scientific forecasts about rainfall (Mehta *et al.* 2019). The Rabaris look at the stars and perform certain rituals to make predictions about rainfall. Similarly, fishers in Jalva also rely on the movement of stars, the direction of the wind and the colour of the sea to make weather predictions.

In both Merka and Jalva, village elders are revered as repositories of knowledge. They read changes in the good and bad omens of nature. Binetkar *kaka* is a 70-year-old Jat, who many *Vaghers* in Jalva refer to as the "grandfather of fishing". In our conversations along the Jakhau coast, he talked about predictions, the colour of the sea and certain leaves which are only spotted before the onset of monsoons. He was confident that 2016 would be a year of good rainfall, but it did not turn out to be so.[4]

A 2014 GUIDE study reports that scientists found predictions based on IK to be 90–95% accurate in the 1995–2004 period, but after 2004, they acknowledge that local-level predictions of monsoon patterns have become more uncertain and difficult to predict for local people. A similar observation is made by a scientist, at a research institute in Kutch, who argued that "local people's forecasts are also based on observations but because long term climate and weather patterns are changing, these local forecasts are not working very well" (Interview June 2016; Kutch). In this way, traditions and practices of anticipation are faltering in the face of increased climate variability. Also, as we indicate below, the radical nature of these uncertainties becomes more apparent as they intersect with local livelihoods and resource insecurities.

Everyday practices and experiences around uncertainty are rarely conceptualised around climate change. Instead, they are usually felt and experienced in terms of access to livelihood opportunities which many local people referred to as *anishchit* (uncertain). In the following sections, we explore what *anishchit* means for the three predominant livelihoods in Kutch.

Livelihoods on the margins

Kutch receives the majority of its rainfall through the south-west monsoons between June and September. Although previously (between 1958 and 2001) July was the month of peak rainfall, in recent years that has shifted to September, with maximum rainfall now falling in this month (GUIDE 2014). The problem of salinity ingress is compounded by the indiscriminate invasion of *Prosopis juliflora*, locally referred to as *ganda bawal* (mad shrub), an invasive weed originally planted in Kutch to check desertification, but that eventually resulted in the loss of arable land. Extreme weather conditions in the form of droughts and floods have often wiped out crops, leaving farmers impoverished and helpless (GUIDE 2014). Since rainfall patterns have become more erratic, farmers find it difficult to plan their seasonal calendars. Rao *bhai*, a male Rjput farmer, explains how changing seasonal cycles have created challenges in agriculture:

> We are used to hot summers, but the temperature seems to be more extreme. Summers are oppressively hot, and winters are longer. Extreme heat and prolonged winters are not good for the crops. Winter rain is not unusual, but it seems to be increasing and is also not good for the crops.
>
> *(Interview June 2016, Merka)*

In Jalva, the compounded problem of *prosopis* juliflora along with increased salinity is pushing the farmers outside of agriculture. Several farming families that we spoke to had either abandoned farming or would only take crops after the monsoons. These families are also increasingly migrating to other livelihoods such as offering labour on the lands of other farmers or moving to other small-scale business. For example, Suli-*ben*,[5] a female farmer in Jalva who practices dryland farming lamented:

> I have spent a lot of money in digging wells and searching for sweet water but no luck so far. I do not think I can continue like this.
>
> *(Interview June 2016, Jalva)*

Poor agricultural yield has had cascading effects on other livelihoods, especially for the *maldharis* who graze their livestock in the farms and buy groundnut and wheat chaff as fodder from the farmers. With poor rains and lack of water and fodder/grass in the *simara*, the *maldharis* migrate to other parts of Kutch or Gujarat in search of food and water.

Although seasonal migration with animals in lean periods is a way of life for pastoralists, it is becoming increasingly difficult due to shrinking commons, lack of fallow fields to graze on due to perennial irrigation facilities, changing state policies and growing resentment towards pastoralists (Mehta 2005; Mehta and Srivastava 2019). Climate change leading to increased temperature, higher incidence of livestock diseases and shortage of water in summer has also influenced the milk yield of animals (GUIDE 2014). This has resulted in a dramatic increase of buffaloes in the livestock composition because they are better suited to the hot climate. An increase in the number of milk dairies and transportation facilities has also favoured this change (GEC 2011).

For example, the Jats of Jimlivand who once bred and reared camels have also moved onto a more sedentary lifestyle. Until a few decades ago, camels were used for farming, patrolling and transport. However, with changes in agricultural patterns and reduced access to grazing fields, the value of camels has declined and they are no longer an asset. Though buffaloes are more expensive than other livestock (cows, sheep or goats), their resistance to heat and higher tolerance to *prosopis juliflora* are cited as some of the reasons for this preference. They also have the advantages of better feed conversion efficiency, can sustain on poor feed and forage quality and provide higher returns from milk (buffalo milk across breeds has more than 8% fat) with a better nutritive value of milk (Balhara *et al.* 2017).

The Jats of Jimlivand comprise the big pastoralists who shift between fishing and livestock rearing. Small *maldharis* can only afford to keep a limited number of buffaloes and are largely reliant on small ruminants (i.e. sheep and goats) and hence face the brunt of ecological uncertainties. Since goats and sheep are more susceptible to livestock diseases, these *maldharis* are increasingly finding it difficult to continue with their traditional livelihood. Herders with small ruminants often fall outside of the drought mitigation schemes which largely target large livestock owners and farmers. For instance, Musa *bhai*, a small *maldhari* recounts:

> If we have good rainfall, then there is no problem but if the rainfall is not good, we are in loss, not profit. We are spending our money on purchasing drinking water, fodder grass, cotton and groundnut leaves and wheat. Livestock diseases have also increased. Now *maldharis* are migrating with animals in search of fodder and water. This year, there was no water in the *sim*, we gave the pipeline water to animals. In summer, we need to purchase more tankers. One tanker is 700 rupees. I do not think I can continue like this […] I do not want my grandson to struggle in the same way.
>
> *(Interview February 2016, Jalva)*

Similar to other livelihoods, it is estimated that climate changes will have profound effects on the marine ecosystem as warmer sea temperatures will lead to shifts in availability and adaptability of particular species (Harley *et al.* 2006). Fishing is both a major livelihood and a burgeoning business opportunity on the Kutchi coastline. It was the introduction of mechanised boats from 1981 onwards that led to the gradual development of Jalva as one of the major fishing harbours in the state (Gujarat Ecology Commission 2011).

Most fishers whom we interviewed said that they are now witnessing warmer sea temperatures and a decline in fish catch. Faiz *bhai*, the head of Jalva's fisher's association, narrates the changes in the following way:

> Due to warmer temperatures, there is a decrease in fish production. In the 1990s, the day temperature used to range from 7 to 10 degrees and the night temperature was around 2 degrees. But from 1995 onwards, heat has increased. The fish needs salt as well as freshwater. Industries and salt pan activities have also affected fish production. If the rains are late, the fish breeding period also changes accordingly. Jellyfish is food for the fish, but trawlers are catching this fish because of the high demand in China. The food shortage for fish may also be one of the reasons for the decline in fish production.
>
> *(Interview January 2016, Jalva harbour)*

Though several fishers spoke of oppressive heat and hot water, they rarely attributed these to climate change and blamed industrial activities for the problems instead. They were united in their anger towards large fishing trawlers who "break the rules" and go for the catch which is "rightfully theirs" (Interviews, February and June 2016, Jalva). They were also critical of the salt pans and industries, which discharged untreated toxic water into the sea, often killing the fish and destroying the mangroves, which are natural nurseries for fish breeding. Similar complaints were heard from the adjacent Mundra *taluka* regarding the harmful effects of industrial pollution on the marine and coastal ecosystem.

Across fishing communities in Mundra and Abdasa, fishers have noticed several changes in their habitats and attribute this loss to port activities, mangrove denudation and waste that is dumped into the sea (Srivastava and Mehta 2017). While the destruction of mangroves has resulted in the decline in fish catch, fishers' access to water channels is also blocked as the coastline is now populated by industries. Feroz *bhai*,[6] a veteran fisher, explained:

> Fishing is our livelihood. My father, my grandfather, all were fishers. We have been involved with fishing [for a long time]. For the past six to seven years it has been particularly bad [...] they [industries] draw water from the sea to cool their plants, small fish get stuck in the process and die. Then they release hot water. Fish go away[...] A lot of big projects come up on the coast [...] All these factors lead to less catch.
> *(Interview August 2016, Mundra).*

While the Vaghers and non-native fishers still manage to get some catch, it is the Kolis who have faced the brunt of these changes. The loss of mangrove cover and industrial pollution has also affected creek fishing. Referring to the fish trawlers, one Koli fisher lamented that "the big fish are eating the small fish [i.e. Kolis], and we have nowhere to go" (Group discussion February 2016, Jalva).

Thus, the experiences of uncertainty from "below" are mediated by relations of power within the "community" and asserted by more powerful actors such as the industries and the state. The livelihoods perspective underlines how climate change intersects with other political, social and economic factors for these marginalised communities as they continue to live with highly unfair and unequal conditions that have been imposed on them through social, historical and political arrangements.

The "above" takes an aggregate view of uncertainty, albeit realising the value of local experiences and the need for a more targeted approach, mostly in the form of technical interventions. The perceptions of the "below", by contrast, broaden the understanding of climate from an experience of an atmospheric phenomenon to lived realities as climate change intersects with various transitions in Kutch. These interactions are also facilitated by an alliance of actors within and outside of the state, bringing in the new constellations that emerged after the 2001 earthquake. We now turn to the role of some of these networks in the next section that this volume characterises as the "middle".

The "middle": intermediaries for transformation

After the 2001 earthquake, NGOs working on reconstruction and rehabilitation (R and R) rapidly developed expertise in disaster reconstruction while simultaneously addressing wider issues concerning Kutch's development trajectory. This became all the more crucial as corporates entered into Kutch in a big way after 2001. One NGO worker describes the changed context as follows: "We were so busy working on R and R that we hadn't realised that a corporate takeover had taken place" (Interview, October 2016, Bhuj).

We have already described the impacts of aggressive industrialisation on Kutch's coast and landscapes. Many NGOs have resisted these processes together with local communities. However, in some cases, new alliances between India's big corporate houses (Adanis, Ambanis, Tatas and others) and the NGOs have also emerged over the past two decades via the route of corporate social responsibility (CSR). Shrinking development funds from the state often leave CSR money as the only or predominant source of funding for many development NGOs and research organisations in Kutch (Srivastava and Mehta 2017). While some of the NGOs argue that this provides an opportunity "to bring about change from within by having a seat at the table", they also acknowledge that these relations are ridden with tensions (Interview October 2016, Bhuj).

Industries have also roped in scientists to support their compensatory afforestation and environmental assessment activities (Srivastava and Mehta 2017). Having worked in these areas for decades, these scientists not only bring along technical expertise but are also able to act as interlocutors between the industry and the local communities. Against the backdrop of shrinking development funding, these corporate-scientist and corporate-NGO alliances may have provided some legitimacy to the "development" discourse in Kutch as they are co-opted in the neoliberal project of development in Kutch (Srivastava and Mehta 2017). By contrast, more activist-oriented groups have challenged these top-down systems of intervention.

Thus, the "middle" is geographically varied, holds diverse positions and engages both with the community and the "above". As the "middle" often works within alliances, they often seamlessly merge into the "above" and "below" depending on the context and issue at hand. This also accounts for their heterogeneity and different strategies which include contestation, subversion and collaboration. For example, in the case of CSR, some scientists and NGOs tend to assume the role of the "above" dictating policies and programmes, while in other instances, they also identify themselves as the "middle" that brokers information from one group to the other.

Thus, torn between the "above" and "below", and recognising the deep divide, some NGOs compare their position to that of a *trishanku* (a state of limbo with conflicting aims and ambitions) (Interview June 2016, Rapar). For instance, a Gandhian social worker who has been working for tribal welfare in Rapar *taluka* states:

> Yes, there is uncertainty, but the uncertainty of the community is very different from the uncertainty of the "above". Their vocabularies are very different, and they speak in a different language. The "above" wants plans and strategies and the "below" is concerned about day-to-day food and work. Local communities often worry whether they will have food on the table for the next meal and if their kids would get education or jobs. And the "middle" is diverse and not united.
>
> *(Interview June 2016, Rapar)*

However, several NGOs are also working with communities to provide greater support to address these uncertainties. For example, an organisation working on groundwater issues in Kutch admits that the landscape of Kutch may have changed, but bridging this divide is crucial to navigating through this complex environment (Interview October 2016, Bhuj). They now train local people as *bhujal jankars* (those who have knowledge about groundwater) to understand groundwater ecology and to work on groundwater conservation in their communities. Several such bottom-up and transformative initiatives are currently underway in Kutch. One such case concerns the revival of camel rearing in Kutch, to which we now turn.

Restoring pastoral livelihoods

As discussed above, pastoral communities have been severely affected by industrial development on the Kutchi coastline. While local people bemoan the loss of their coastline to ports and industrial enclaves, it is the pastoralists who have lost access to grazing lands that are either destroyed, encroached upon or made off-bounds for them. A Kachchh Camel Pastoralists' Organisation study notes that camel grazing lands are shrinking due to widespread encroachment and degradation due to large-scale industrialisation in the coastal areas (KUUMS 2010). The report alleges that steel and thermal power plants have appropriated huge areas of mangroves, making them hard to access or useless for grazing. Being a border district, the threat of terrorism and international security is also often overplayed to deny common people access to the coast as well as coastal resources (Srivastava and Mehta 2017).

In Phuleri *vand*, the camel headcount has dipped from 10,000 to 80 camels over the past few decades. "We just can't get enough fodder, after a port and two thermal power plants took away much of the mangroves, and forest guards prevent entry to some other areas", laments Jarod-*bhai*. He states:

> With the company's arrival, people started selling their camels and some have migrated to other places in search of fodder. We are assuming that if this grazing land problem is not solved, in future no single camel will be available in this *vand*. We have to fight the company and the forest department.
>
> *(Interview August 2016, Mundra)*

The massive degradation of mangroves is also threatening the survival of an indigenous breed of camels, the celebrated *kharai* (salty) camels that can browse on land and also swim across to the *bets* (mangrove islands). Mangroves constitute about 70% of the *kharai*'s diet (Shrivastava 2013). In the monsoon, they swim to the *bets* and stay there for a few months getting the crucial nutrition required to make milk. However, their access to these mangroves is now very compromised, as explained by an ecologist at the NGO Sahjeevan:

> Mangroves [islands] are still there as per their [camel's] knowledge but they cannot access those mangrove islands due to all the industrial activities. So now they keep on migrating from one place to another. The herders are selling their animals. Earlier they had 500 to 600 camels in this particular area. Now they hardly have about 100 camels.
> *(Interview September 2016, Bhuj)*

Breeding of the *kharai* camel is the main source of livelihoods for many Jat and Rabari communities in several villages of Abdasa, Mundra, Lakhpat and Bhachau *talukas*. However, mainstream conservation debates within the state often blame herding and grazing practices for the denudation of mangroves (Srivastava and Mehta 2017). Scientists argue that overgrazing, "unscientific grazing patterns", that is, camels browsing on leaves and damaging the tree and cutting of leaves are responsible for the destruction of mangroves. By contrast, herders vehemently oppose this discourse and talk of the synergistic relationship between the camel and the mangroves. The Jats denounce the claim that camels could "ever be bad for mangroves because they share a natural relationship with the *cheria* (mangroves)" (BCP 2012; Srivastava and Mehta 2017). The *kharai* camels play an integral role in the pastoral landscape, and both men and women describe a deep connection with these camels. However, with aggressive industrialisation, their pastoral identity and landscape are now at risk. As a consequence, several Jat and Rabari herders have migrated to low-scale contractual jobs in the companies or left for towns and urban centres to work as security guards or taxi drivers (Mehta and Srivastava 2019).

Over the past few years, however, alliances have been made between civil society and local herders to preserve the pastoral identity and restore the landscape. The *kharai* camels have now been recognised in India as a distinct breed or "threatened" species that need protection. Sahjeevan is working closely with these marginal communities to revive their indigenous systems and restore the native habitats, food stocks and grazing routes of the *kharai*. The intervention is transformative in that it hopes to counter received wisdom regarding pastoralism on many fronts (particularly so on grounds of being unsustainable), while also using innovative methods and alliances to counter-arguments and pressures that threaten to disrupt pastoralist practices (Interview October 2016, Bhuj).

Compounded uncertainties under COVID-19

The first case of COVID-19 in Kutch was recorded in Lakhpat *taluka*, not far from where we are doing research.[7] Around 30 families with about 500 *kharai* camels use the tropical thorn forests and mangroves in these areas to graze their animals (Mehta *et al.* 2020). Several herders whom we spoke to over the phone narrated the problem of fodder and access to pastures in the early period of the lockdown. The lockdown coincided with the crucial summer months where sources of fodder and water have always been challenging. The immediate effect of the lockdown was felt acutely in terms of mobility restrictions, lack of food supplies and suspension of dairy activities. Since the villages are located in the remote border areas, access to hospitals, banks and shops was highly restricted. A Jat herder remarked: "food is a big problem, everything is closed and the shops and markets are also quite far" (Telephone interview August 2020). The easing of lockdown in May did not resolve the problem of mobility restrictions and suspension of livelihood activities. This meant that there was no liquid cash for purchasing essential commodities especially food items. In the months that followed, Kutch also experienced higher than average rainfall leading to flooded farms and waterlogging in various parts of the Abdasa taluka. This excess rainfall may have helped pastoralists but those who farm have been disproportionately hit by the devastation having lost their crops and agricultural income. These intersections of extreme climate variability and the health crises reveal the structural inequalities that have compounded the challenges faced by these marginal communities and cascaded into different livelihoods.

Discussion and conclusion

This chapter has argued that radical uncertainty, originating from the combination of changes in biophysical stressors, on the one hand, and socio-political changes such as marketisation and neoliberal trends, on the other hand, have exacerbated the vulnerabilities of the "below". Traditional methods of adapting to scarcity and droughts (e.g. temporary migration, change in cropping patterns, subsistence fishing) are struggling to deal with these radical uncertainties. Although traditional livelihoods around pastoralism, fishing and dryland agriculture are configured around ecological uncertainties, these have witnessed an almost tectonic shift in the wake of rapid industrialisation that has taken place in Kutch in the past two decades. These livelihoods are also interdependent, as uncertainty experienced in one sector cascade into the other (e.g. *maldharis* having to buy fodder when agriculture fails).

The "above" takes an aggregate view of uncertainty, albeit realising the value of local experiences and the need for a more targeted approach mostly in the form of technical interventions that seldom reflect the ecological and social diversity of this district. Furthermore, institutional silos and the mitigation/ energy focused bias in the climate strategy of Gujarat have meant that climate policy remains blind to the dryland dynamics of this ecologically diverse district (see Mehta 2005). This has hindered the mainstreaming of substantive pro-poor adaptation policies, which could include strengthening dryland agriculture and pastoralism rather than neglecting or denigrating them. This has often resulted in, for example, pastoralists giving up their livelihood in favour of casual labour.

Climate scientists, working within the remits of their discipline, certainly recognise the challenges of uncertainty and its associated limitations in modelling. Although integrating people's perceptions into climate science and modelling may be difficult, they are keen to "learn" how people cope with uncertainty and want to work towards providing information in real time to support livelihoods planning and diversification.

The perceptions of the "below", by contrast, broaden the understanding of climate from an experience of the atmospheric phenomenon to lived realities as climate variability intersects with various transitions in Kutch. Thus, the experiences of uncertainty from "below" are mediated by relations of power within the "community" and asserted by more powerful actors such as the industries and the state.

The "middle" comprises an assemblage of actors who have differing views and positions with regard to climate change and uncertainties. Most of the NGOs agree that industrialisation has aggravated the uncertainties faced by these marginalised communities, but they often find themselves tied to the political economy of aid and grants that limit the possibilities of working for transformative change. Through state- and corporate-funded projects, the "middle" acts as an intermediary when the communities are tied into relationships of patronage and dependency with either the state (through scientists) or the industries (through CSR projects) although these relationships are ridden with contradictions and internal tensions

In conclusion, this chapter has highlighted the various manifestations and perceptions of uncertainty amongst the "above", "middle" and "below" in Kutch. We have shown that changes in the wider political economy are depleting the adaptive capacity of people and, in most cases, accentuating their vulnerability. The experience of this radical uncertainty is often mediated by power relations between the "above", "middle" and "below" which shapes their interactions and responses to uncertainty. Alliances forged between different actors – state and corporate, CSOs and corporations and scientists and communities – have intensified the capitalist growth trajectories producing winners and losers. In parallel, new alliances are emerging which seek to challenge these incumbent neoliberal regimes. These initiatives demonstrate the beginnings of the unruly political re-alignments that are seeking to challenge incumbent power structures as well as top-down systems of knowledge and could potentially foster pathways to social transformation.

Acknowledgement

The authors would like to thank Fazilda Nabeel, Maxmillan Martin, Jagruti Sanghvi, Subir Dey and Rohit Jha for their research assistance.

Notes

1 These are areas demarcated in India to promote investment and trade. Business and tax laws are far more relaxed in the SEZs than in the rest of the country.
2 To respect anonymity, names of respondents have been changed and we have provided pseudonyms for the hamlets in Kutch.
3 Field Journal of Srivastava, 2016.
4 Field Journal of Srivastava, 2016.
5 Means sister; in Gujarati, women are often addressed as *ben* as a mark of respect.
6 Means brother; in Gujarati, men are often addressed as *bhai* as a mark of respect.
7 This section draws on our work in two ongoing projects: TAPESTRY https://steps-centre.org/project/tapestry/; ANTICIPATE: https://www.ids.ac.uk/projects/anticipating-futures-forecasting-and-climate-preparedness-for-co-located-hazards-in-india-anticipate/.

References

Asher, M. 2008. 'How Mundra Became India's Rotterdam'. Available at: http://bit.ly/2wUu2xC (accessed on 24 August 2016).

Balhara, A., V. Nayan, A. Dey, K.P. Singh, S.S. Dahiya and I. Singh. 2017. 'Climate Change and Buffalo Farming in Major Milk Producing States of India – Present Status and Need for Addressing Concerns'. *The Indian Journal of Animal Sciences*, 87(4): 403–411.

Barney, K. 2009. 'Laos and the Making of a 'Relational' Resource Frontier'. *The Geographical Journal,* 175(2): 146–159. https://doi.org/10.1111/j.1475-4959.2009.00323.x

Bharwada, C. and V. Mahajan. 2007. *Mangroves and Maldharis of Kutch: Understanding Coastal Pastoralists' Dependence on Mangroves.* Vadodara: Gujarat Ecology Commission.

Business Standard. 2013. 'Gujarat to Set up Asia's First Dept for Climate Change'. *Business Standard*, Mumbai, 19 January.

Eriksen, S.H., A.J. Nightingale and H. Eakin. 2015. 'Reframing Adaptation: The Political Nature of Climate Change Adaptation'. *Global Environmental Change*, 35: 523–533. https://doi.org/10.1016/j.gloenvcha.2015.09.014

Gajjar, S.P., C. Singh and T. Deshpande. 2018. 'Tracing Back to Move Ahead: A Review of Development Pathways that Constrain Adaptation Futures'. *Climate and Development*, 11(29): 1–15. https://doi.org/10.1080/17565529.2018.1442793

Government of Gujarat. 2020. 'Kachchh District Profile'. Available at: https://kachchh.nic.in/district-at-a-glance/ (accessed on 10 November 2020).

Government of India. 2011. 'Kachchh (Kutch) District: Census 2011 Data'. Available at: https://www.census2011.co.in/census/district/182-kachchh.html (accessed on 17 May 2018).

GUIDE. 2014. *Climate Change and Its Uncertainty: Dryland Scenario.* Bhuj: GUIDE.

Gujarat Ecology Commission. 2011. *Trends of Changing Climate and Effects of Eco-Environment of Kachchh District, Gujarat.* Vadodara: Gujarat Ecology Commission.

Haraway, D. 1988. 'Situated Knowledges: The Science Question in Feminism and the Privilege of Partial Perspective'. *Feminist Studies*, 14(3): 575–599. https://doi.org/10.2307/3178066

Harley, C.D.G., A. Randall Hughes, K.M. Hultgren, B.G. Miner, C.J.B. Sorte, C.S. Thornber, L.F. Rodriguez, L. Tomanek and S.L. Williams. 2006. 'The Impacts of Climate Change in Coastal Marine Systems'. *Ecology Letters*, 9(2): 228–241. doi:10.1111/j.1461-0248.2005.00871.x

Hastrup, K. 2013. 'Anthropological Contributions to the Study of Climate: Past, Present, Future'. *Wiley Interdisciplinary Reviews: Climate Change*, 4(4): 269–281. https://doi.org/10.1002/wcc.219

Hulme, M. 2017. *Weathered: Cultures of Climate.* London: SAGE Publications.

Ibrahim, F. 2007. 'Capitalism, Multiculturalism and Tolerance: A Perspective on 'Vibrant Gujarat''. *Economic and Political Weekly* 42(34): 3446–3449.

Ibrahim, F. 2009. *Settlers, Saints and Sovereigns: An Ethnography of State Formation in Western India.* New Delhi: Routledge.

Kachchh Camel Breeders Association. 2013. *Biocultural Community Protocol of the Camel Pastoralists of Kachchh.* Bhuj: Kachchh Camel Breeders Association.

Kay, J. and M. King. 2020. *Radical Uncertainty: Decision-Making for an Unknowable Future.* London: The Bridge Street Press.

Kohli, K. and M. Menon. 2016. 'The Tactics of Persuasion: Environmental Negotiations Over a Corporate Coal Project in Coastal India'. *Energy Policy*, 99: 270–276. https://doi.org/10.1016/j.enpol.2016.05.027

Lehmann, J., F. Mempel and D. Coumou. 2018. 'Increased Occurrence of Record-Wet and Record-Dry Months Reflect Changes in Mean Rainfall'. *Geophysical Research Letters*, 45(24): 13468–13476. https://doi.org/10.1029/2018GL079439

Leichenko, R. and K. O'Brien. 2008. *Environmental Change and Globalization: Double Exposures.* Oxford: Oxford University Press.

Mahapatra, M., R. Ramakrishnan and A. Rajawat. 2015. 'Coastal Vulnerability Assessment of Gujarat Coast to Sea Level Rise Using GIS Techniques: A Preliminary Study'. *Journal of Coastal Conservation*, 19: 241–256.

Mehta, L. 2000. 'Drought Diagnosis: Dryland Blindness of Planners'. *Economic and Political Weekly*, 35(27): 2439–2445.

Mehta, L. 2005. *The Politics and Poetics of Water: Naturalising Scarcity in Western India.* New Delhi: Orient Longman.

Mehta, L., P. Joshi, and M.R. Bhatt. 2020. 'How Pastoralists in Kutch Respond to Social and Environmental Uncertainty'. Available at: https://steps-centre.org/blog/how-do-pastoralists-in-kutch-respond-to-social-and-environmental-uncertainty/ (accessed on 8 January 21)

Mehta, L. and S. Srivastava. 2019. 'Pastoralists without Pasture: Water Scarcity, Marketisation and Resource Enclosures in Kutch, India'. *Nomadic Peoples*, 23(2): 195–217. https://doi.org/10.3197/np.2019.230203

Mehta, L. and S. Srivastava. (2020). 'Uncertainty in Modelling Change: The Possibilities of Co-production through Knowledge Pluralism', in Scoones, I. and Stirling, A. (eds.), *The Politics of Uncertainty: Challenges of Transformation.* Routledge, pp. 99–11.

Mehta, L., S. Srivastava, H.N. Adam, S. Bose, U. Ghosh and V.V. Kumar. 2019. 'Climate Change and Uncertainty from 'Above' and 'Below': Perspectives from India'. *Regional Environmental Change*, 19: 1533–1547. https://doi.org/10.1007/s10113-019-01479-7

Naess, L.O. 2013. 'The Role of Local Knowledge in Adaptation to Climate Change'. *Wiley Interdisciplinary Reviews: Climate Change*, 4(2): 99–106. https://doi.org/10.1002/wcc.204

Pandey, V., A. Shekh and R. Parmar. 1999. 'Occurrence of Droughts and Floods over Gujarat'. *Journal of Agrometeorology*, 1(2): 177–181.

Pandey, V., H. Patel and B. Karande. 2009. 'Impact Analysis of Climate Change on Different Crops in Gujarat, India'. Paper presented at the Impact of Climate Change on Agriculture Workshop, Anand Agricultural University, Ahmedabad, 17–18 December.

Pelling, M. 2011. *Adaptation to Climate Change: From Resilience to Transformation*. London: Routledge.
Ribot, J. 2014. 'Cause and Response: Vulnerability and Climate in the Anthropocene'. *Journal of Peasant Studies*, 41(5): 667–705. https://doi.org/10.1080/03066150.2014.894911
Rudiak-Gould, P. 2013. '"We Have Seen It with Our Own Eyes": Why We Disagree about Climate Change Visibility'. *Weather, Climate, and Society*, 5(2): 120–132. https://doi.org/10.1175/WCAS-D-12-00034.1
Sarkar, J., J. Chicholikar and L. Rathore. 2015. 'Predicting Future Changes in Temperature and Precipitation in Arid Climate of Kutch, Gujarat: Analyses Based on LARS-WG Model'. *Current Science*, 109(11): 2084.
Sarkar, S. 2020. 'Cyclones Rise as Climate Change Heats up Indian Ocean'. Available at: https://indiaclimatedialogue.net/2020/06/05/cyclones-rise-as-climate-change-heats-up-indian-ocean/ (accessed on 10 November 2020).
Scoones, I. 2004. 'Climate Change and the Challenge of Non-Equilibrium Thinking'. *IDS Bulletin*, 35: 114–119. https://doi.org/10.19088/1968-2020.116.
Scott, J.C. 1998. *Seeing Like a State: How Certain Schemes to Improve the Human Condition Have Failed*. New Haven: Yale University Press.
Shrivastava, K. S. 2013. The Sinking Ship'. Available at: http://www.downtoearth.org.in/coverage/the-sinking-ship-40705 (accessed on 24 September 2016).
Solecki, W., M. Pelling and M. Garschagen. 2017. 'Transitions between Risk Management Regimes in Cities'. *Ecology and Society*, 22(2): 38. https://doi.org/10.5751/ES-09102-220238
Soneji, V. 2017. 'The Camels and the Sea'. Available at: https://www.th ehindu.com/news/national/the-camels-and-the sea/article18190869.ece/p hoto/1/ (accessed on 12 August 2017).
Srivastava, S. and L. Mehta. 2017. *The Social Life of Mangroves: Resource Complexes and Contestations on the Industrial Coastline of Kutch, India*. Brighton: ESRC STEPS Centre.
Samerth Trust. 2013. 'XXX Village Watershed Plan: Internal NGO Report'. *Unpublished*.
Tschakert, P. 2007. 'Views from the Vulnerable: Understanding Climatic and Other Stressors in the Sahel'. *Global Environmental Change*, 17: 381–396. https://doi.org/10.1016/j.gloenvcha.2006.11.008
Walker, W., P.E. Harremoës, J. Rotmans, J.P. van der Sluijs, M.B.A. van Asselt, P. Janssen and M.P. Krayer von Kraus. 2003. 'Defining Uncertainty: A Conceptual Basis for Uncertainty Management in Model-Based Decision Support'. *Integrated Assessment*, (1): 5–17. https://doi.org/10.1076/iaij.4.1.5.16466

5
THE CERTAINTY OF UNCERTAINTY
Climate change realities of the Indian Sundarbans

Upasona Ghosh, Darley Jose Kjosavik and Shibaji Bose

FIGURE 5.1 Precarious fishing in the Indian Sundarbans (Photo credit: Shibaji Bose).

Introduction

While scientists and policymakers grapple with ways of understanding and framing climate-related uncertainty at macro-scales, people's everyday life is mired with uncertainties that are immediate. An understanding and appreciation

DOI: 10.4324/9781003257585-5

of these immediacies calls for studies from the grassroots that can build bridges with the macro-level framings thus informing substantive policymaking. Conway *et al.* (2019: 7) have argued for "the critical need to situate climate adaptation within the context of broader socio-economic, environmental and political processes; something that top-down approaches often fail to consider". "[T]he complexity of lived experiences" (ibid.: 7) provides the substratum for this chapter which seeks to understand the experiences of uncertainties as they unfold in the everyday lives of the people of the Indian Sundarbans, a marginal landscape and India's largest wetlands seemingly drifting out of mainland West Bengal in Eastern India. We focus on livelihood uncertainties and other uncertainties arising from climate, political economy and embankment politics, and the way the "above", "middle" and "below" (see Chapter 1) understand, perceive and respond to these (Figure 5.1).

We use elements of the livelihood framework (Scoones 1998; Ellis 1999, 2000) to understand the livelihood portfolio and the ongoing diversification process pursued by households in the study area. In the process, we coin the term "distress diversification", which we feel is more apt to describe what is going on in the Sundarbans. The term distress diversification captures the diversification of livelihood activities by households towards less profitable, more tedious, more risky, more dangerous, more fragile, more uncertain and marginal activities. It also includes diversification towards activities that are more labour and capital intensive, especially in eroded and marginal lands, which would require higher initial investments and incur higher cost of production than previous livelihood activities. While this distress diversification affects both women and men, the intensity is felt more by female-headed households. The term also captures the phenomenon of proletarianisation of agricultural and fishing households, when they are forced to work as part- or full-time wage labourers to contribute to the livelihood portfolio of the household. Households tend to engage in these activities under conditions of distress, as we elaborate later in this chapter.

The Sundarbans is a major climate hotspot and faces significant climatic and other ecological challenges such as degradation and disappearance of mangrove forests, erosion of islands due to rising sea levels, erratic rainfall and extreme whether events such as cyclones. While the delta has always been subject to climatic variations, recent changes have aggravated effects on the lives and livelihoods of the inhabitants. Although climate change impacts and related uncertainties have been well documented in the Sundarbans, this chapter tries to understand how actors at various levels understand, experience and respond to and/or cope with uncertainty and vulnerability. Our primary focus is on the two islands of Ghoramara and Mousuni in the Sundarbans, while also capturing the views and perceptions of "middle"-level actors involved in mediating policies of the "above".

The chapter is structured as follows: we first provide a brief overview of the Indian Sundarbans, contextualising the study, followed by a description of the study islands and methods. We then provide a historical overview of the political economic and ecological production of the Sundarbans and its uncertainties with an exposition of the general ecological and livelihood uncertainties and vulnerabilities. This is followed by an analysis of people's experiences of uncertainties with the two major livelihood options – agriculture and fisheries. The socio-political disturbances created by the embankment politics and conflicts and how these exacerbate livelihood uncertainties are then discussed. We discuss out-migration as the major coping strategy of the islanders and the attendant uncertainties. This is followed by an analysis of the pursuit of alternatives by the islanders and the crucial role of the "middle" in mediation. We then discuss the political economy of policymaking in the Sundarbans and provide some concluding remarks.

The Indian Sundarbans: a socio-ecological system in transition

The Sundarbans comprises an area of some 40,000 sq km that includes water, forested islands, inhabited islands, cultivable land and part of the mainland. This is the world's largest mangrove delta and is politically and administratively divided between India and Bangladesh. The whole land mass of the Indian part of the Sundarbans can be divided into two types of inhabited islands: areas closer to the mainland and areas on the fringes of the mangrove forest, reclaimed between 1900 and 1980. These two geographically distinct areas comprise the northern and western part, and the southern part of the Sundarbans, respectively. The north-west part is relatively elevated from the sea level and less vulnerable to storms and tidal inundations. This stable delta part has fertile soil and freshwater canal irrigation system. This part is also closer to West Bengal's capital city of Kolkata than its southern counterpart.

Islanders in the Sundarbans region have had to contend with shocks such as cyclones and floods, and variations in its deltaic ecology as well as socioeconomic marginalisation since the first settlements were established (for more historical context, see Chapter 3). In recent years, many scientific studies have shown that erratic climatic events (e.g. more intense rainfall, heatwaves and sea-level rise) are becoming more frequent and pronounced. These manifestations of climate change have added to the existing problems, including frequent embankment breaching; loss of land, homesteads and other assets and salinity ingress in agricultural land and freshwater ponds. All of these have placed huge stress on the traditional agro-fishing economy and strained the islanders' coping capacities. Households are forced to constantly change their livelihood patterns, for instance, undertake agro-fishing, wage labour, seasonal migration to other parts of West Bengal or other states of India and so on (WWF 2010; Hazra et al. 2012).

The literature on the Sundarbans (India and Bangladesh) and the Bay of Bengal delta depicts that prominent manifestations of climate change like sea level rise (SLR) is happening at an alarming scale making the life of the islanders increasingly vulnerable (see, e.g., Hazra et al. 2002, 2010; Ghosh et al. 2015). Incidences of harsh and extreme climatic events like floods and cyclones are predicted in the near future which would cause the disappearance of the landmass and subsequent displacement of the population. The Indian part of the Sundarbans is highly vulnerable to climate change manifestations like land erosion as it is losing its mangrove cover rapidly (Giri *et al.* 2007). Some of these changes, however, are attributed to the active geology of the delta and the several major rivers draining into the Bay of Bengal. For instance, Mukhopadhyay *et al.* (2015) suggest that the changes, especially in the islands of Sagar, Nayachar, Ghoramara and New Moore, are resulting from changing dynamics in the Bay of Bengal as well as its numerous rivers that play a major role in accretion and erosion dynamics of the delta. In a recent study on Ganga–Brahmaputra–Meghna (GBM) delta, Brown *et al.* (2018) found that GBM deltas are at high risk of long-term flooding, even if the global temperatures stabilise. Moreover, large-scale reclamation, deforestation and unsustainable exploitation of natural resources have contributed to changes in the physical and biological dynamics of the Sundarbans delta (Hazra *et al.* 2002; Ghosh *et al.* 2015; Hajra and Ghosh 2018).

Along with the changing climate, recent demographic trends (Census 2011) exhibit Sundarbans' marginality from a development point of view due to its mono-cropping-based agriculture and dwindling fishing economy despite being ahead of the state average in sex ratio (Sundarbans = 955, West Bengal = 950) and overall literacy (Sundarbans = 84.06%, West Bengal = 77.08%). At the same time, the impacts of globalisation have also led to changes for the islanders through the widespread uptake of mobile phones, television and satellite television and the consumption of packaged food and beverages. The problems that take centre stage in an ecologically challenged place like Sundarbans are heightened vulnerability to climatic events like floods and cyclones, which, in turn, exacerbates livelihood uncertainties.

Ethnographic exploration in Ghoramara and Mousuni

An ethnographic exploration was conducted in two islands, namely, Ghoramara and Mousuni, of the Indian Sundarbans between March 2015 and September 2018. These are among the ten sea-facing islands in the southern part of the Sundarbans and, therefore, most vulnerable to climate events (Hazra *et al.* 2010). Both these islands fall under the administration of Sagar and Namkhana Block of South 24 Parganas District and are the two most climate-affected islands within the Sundarbans (Hazra *et al.* 2002).

Ghoramara has already lost substantial land area due to climate change-induced land erosion and embankment breaching (Hazra *et al.* 2010). In 1975, the total area of this island was 8.51 sq km, which decreased to 4.43 sq km in 2012 (Ghosh *et al.* 2014), a reduction in size by half. This is an indication of the alarming rate of land erosion and the consequent loss of habitat and livelihoods. The situation has forced the islanders to out-migrate, causing a drop of 0.55% in the population growth per year compared to overall growth of the nearby Sagar islands (Census 2011; Hajra and Ghosh 2018). The Ghoramara Island has shifted laterally towards the east due to the extensive erosion of the western part and the acretion in the eastern part (Ghosh and Sengupta 1997). According to Ghosh et al. (2003) the eastern shore of the island is likely to merge with mainland India in two-three decades, while the western shore is likely to be totally washed away. Mousuni Island is situated near the river Hatania-Doania (a channel that connects India and Bangladesh). This island was severely affected when cyclone Aila hit the Sundarbans in 2009. Subsequently, a major flood in 2014 further breached the embankment and inundated huge tracts of land in the island. The island has lost 25% of its land area since 1969 and is projected to lose 15% more by 2020 (Hazra et al. 2010). Up to three-fourths of the island gets flooded each year.

The agricultural land area of Ghoramara is 1.2% and that of Mousuni is 17% of the total land area, respectively. The percentage of agricultural land is quite low in Ghoramara as this island has experienced the maximum land loss, including large extents of agricultural land over time (Hajra et al. 2016). The estimated erosion rates of agricultural land per year during the period from 1990 to 2015 were 0.02 sq.km in Ghoramara and 0.08 sq km in Mousuni (ibid.). Considerable changes have occurred in the shape and size of both islands due to processes of erosion or accretion (ibid.).

Interactions were conducted mainly with community members who faced climatic shocks directly or indirectly in the last five years (2015–2020). We had interactions with 86 persons, both women and men (including elders), who could describe climatic and related changes over the last 40 years, community leaders like Self-Help Group leaders, school teachers, political and religious leaders, local doctors and grass roots village health workers, local clubs and activists working with environmental issues, *Panchayat* (local administrative unit) members and local media personnel.

A participatory rural appraisal technique, namely, the Participatory Hazard Ranking exercise, was also undertaken as a visual means of enabling the respondents to construct and analyse their own uncertainty contexts in Mousuni and Ghoramara. These techniques were used after six months of the initial ethnographic observation and discussion with the community. The Participatory Hazard Ranking exercise was used to analyse the experiences of extreme climatic events after cyclone Aila. This is because many extreme events after Aila have not received the same attention because of their relatively low scale of impacts. Still they have contributed to the livelihood distress in the islands. The exception being cyclone Amphan of 2020, which we focus on briefly later in this chapter.

A total of 48 key-informant interviews were conducted with the "middle" of the Sundarbans, comprising actors starting from grass roots non-governmental organisations (NGOs), community-based organisations (CBOs) and journalists having an understanding of ground-level realities, to activists working in the Sundarbans for the past three decades and community leaders. We also focussed on the "above" of the Sundarbans, identified through snowballing and interviewed 30 representatives from several government departments, scientists working in universities and donor agencies funding different developmental projects. In-depth discussions were held with the "middle" and "above" regarding their perception on climate change in the Sundarbans and accompanying uncertainties in local people's livelihoods. We also relied on secondary literature ranging from journal articles, media reports, grey literature and vernacular writings and magazines.

Historical, political economic and ecological production of uncertainty in the Sundarbans

As discussed in Chapter 3, understanding the unique socio-ecological development of the Sundarbans has been a challenge to historians. According to Eaton (1990), the Sundarbans forest was a frontier zone for many centuries: from 1200 to 1750 AD, it was an economic frontier for wet rice farmers who came from further west of the region, a political frontier for the Delhi Sultanate (1204–1575) and the Mughal Empire (1575–1765). The wet rice farmers brought with them new technologies and forms of social organisation, and the state formation by the Islamic rulers played a major role in the intensification of rice cultivation and introduced new property rights systems. All these contributed to fundamental changes in the ecological system of the Sundarbans – the natural forested ecosystem began to undergo radical changes. The "process of clearing the forests preparatory for agricultural operations produced extremely complex tenure chains extending from the *zamindar* [landlord] at their upper end, down to the actual cultivator at the lower end" (Eaton 1990: 11) with numerous intermediaries in between. Land was leased to the zamindars, who sub-leased it to men who were, in turn, prepared to bring colonies of cultivators from the mainland to the Sundarbans islands. This system brought in countless intermediaries who were, in fact, capitalist speculators (Eaton 1990). Large tracts of natural forests were converted to paddy rice lands by the late 18th century when the British took over the governance of the region and the new colonisation of the area began. Some of the most remote forest tracts of the Sundarbans were transformed into fertile rice fields in the period between 1905 and 1920, by creating a class of small peasants who were forced to settle down permanently in the islands (Ascoli 2020). The extractive tenure systems and the tough ecological conditions of production resulted in the immiseration of the peasantry (Chatterjee 1990).

After independence, the Sundarbans was divided between India and (East) Pakistan (now Bangladesh). New borders were created across the rivers and water bodies, rendering the efforts to control the effects of floods, cyclones and other natural calamities a difficult task. The property rights regime and forest conservation policies continued along the colonial lines. Our discussions with the islanders revealed the complexity of the confused land tenure regimes they inherited through history (see also Chapter 3). A large number of households in our study area do not have land records, and this creates bureaucratic impediments to accessing services from the state including compensations for loss of land and crops due to floods, cyclones and other natural calamities. In this context, "middle"-level actors mainly the community leaders, NGO/CBO personnel and social science scholars working in the Sundarbans, highlighted that the islanders have to contend with the uncertainties imposed on them by history, geography and politics. Historically, their forefathers were forced to come to the islands by the *probashi zamindars* (absentee landlords) who got the right to the land as lease from the British, while some of the islanders are descendants of the *raiyats* (independent proprietors of land) who settled down in the Sundarbans when the *raiyatwari* system (a land tenure system where the registered land holder (raiyat) was recognized as the proprietor from whom revenue was collected directly by the government) was introduced. However, we also found that some households benefited during the massive land reforms implemented by the left-wing governments in the 1970s and 1980s in West Bengal, which included distribution of land to landless households and registration and regulation of tenancy contracts. The process of land reform was complex and protracted and eventually came to a standstill in the late 1980s (see Bardhan et al. 2014 for a discussion of land reforms in West Bengal). Hence, the process was not completed and a sizeable amount of households remained landless. In addition, due to unofficial in-migration in Sundarbans in the late 1980s and early 1990s, there has been a further increase in the number of landless people. However, a large part of the benefits from land reforms in Ghoramara and Mousuni have been lost to the sea, or rendered uncultivable due to salinity ingression, as explained by the informants.

According to experts and "middle"-level actors, climate-related uncertainties are caused by various factors including rising sea level, increase in sea current and increasing variability in the patterns around cyclones and floods. These are exacerbated by government apathy towards the maintenance of bunds, the construction of the Haldia port with total disregard for the islands which are nearest to the Bay of Bengal and insecurities around access to water, health and food. Due to the gendered division of labour, changing access to water, health and food particularly affect younger women and mothers who have caring responsibilities in the household. Ironically, globalisation and market forces have also increased vulnerabilities of local people, already dealing with the impacts of climate change. Take, for example, the advent of the fishing and the tourism lobby. One of the major tourist attractions – the sea beach of Bakkhali – was the temporary site for fish drying for local fishing families. The smell of the drying fish, however, was disliked by tourists and tourist operators. The strong political lobbying by the tourism industry resulted in mass evacuation of small-scale fishing families without providing them with alternatives. As pointed out by Ohdedar (2020), "This impoverishment [of the people of Sundarbans] is not a natural state or determined purely by the fragile ecology. Rather, it is the result of human agency, policies, laws and institutions".[1] Uncertainties and vulnerabilities of the local populations are, thus, produced through political economic and ecological processes, where the global and the local intersect through networks of power relations. Therefore, we need to go beyond the "schematic of external climatic threats and internal social exposures" (Taylor 2014: 4) in thinking about social transformation, as the internal and external are co-produced and intertwined in intricate ways.

Cascades of ecological vulnerabilities to livelihood uncertainties

Climate change in the Sundarbans is imposing uncertainty for different actors in diverse ways although this varies in pattern and magnitude. Among those, the most immediate and prioritised by the "below", "middle" and "above" is livelihood uncertainty. Our study shows that communities living in these islands face constant threats to their lives and livelihoods. Climate-induced changes have led to increased heat, unpredictable rainfall and delayed monsoon, whereas climate-induced geo-morphological changes like sea-level rise and increasing sea surface temperature have led to increases in flooding, cyclones, rapid erosion and salinity of land and freshwater sources. These changes have an increasing impact on the household income of the traditional agro-fishing communities. For example, a middle-aged male respondent from Mousuni Island narrates:

> In my childhood, the sea wasn't that rough, rain came on time for the seed sowing; we got good fish in ponds and grew vegetables plenty. God knows what happened in the last two decades, everything changes-the rain, the sea, the river, everything.
>
> *(Interview November 2016, Mousuni Island)*

Saline lands and ponds are rendered unsuitable for cultivation and pisciculture. Moreover, frequent flooding breaches the embankments and destroys household assets and crops, leaving the community in deep economic uncertainty. Consequently, households are compelled to change/modify/diversify their livelihood pattern constantly through multiple ways, viz., cropping pattern changes, wage labour, fishing, prawn seed collection, crab catching, seasonal migration and so on in order to secure income and resources. We discuss these in detail in the following sections.

To explore the frequency and intensity of extreme weather events and the extent of destruction, a Participatory Hazard Ranking exercise was conducted with a mixed group of community members in Ghoramara. The results are provided in Table 5.1. According to the group, except in 2013, every year after the 2009 cyclone Aila, there were natural hazards such as rapid land erosion, high water levels and relative inundation, embankment breaching and moderate cyclones that hampered the daily living and livelihood activities. The impacts were multi-pronged and multi-layered which created deep uncertainties for livelihoods and shelter. Salinity ingression in agricultural fields and fishing ponds; loss of standing crops; loss of other livelihoods; demolition of homestead; erosion of agricultural and non-agricultural lands were the major impacts of such consecutive climatic events. The respondents reported skin rashes, diarrhoea and other waterborne diseases during these periods. According to them, these small shocks cumulatively resulted in loss in fish catch, yearly loss of crops and large-scale out-migration of male family members from the island. Though communities received emergency support from the *Panchayats* and CBOs, they did not receive any long-term support or resources to rebuild their livelihoods or shelter.

TABLE 5.1 The climate shock history of Ghoramara Island. Compiled from the Participatory Hazard Ranking exercise in Ghoramara, 2016, by the authors

Year	Type of Extreme Event	Type of Destruction
2015	Flood and tidal inundations	• Water level increase • Breaching of embankment and Inundation initiated
2014	Moderate impact of cyclone Hudhud	• Inundation due to embankment breaching • Demolition of homesteads • Severe skin infection • Huge loss of agricultural crops • Loss of fish catch • Loss of cattle • Drinking water crisis due to salinity intrusion
2013	No significant climatic events	None
2012	Moderate impact of cyclone Phailin	• Households demolished • Livestock washed away • Children suffered from fever and diarrhoea for almost a month • Loss of agricultural crops and fish catch
2011	Severe Flood due to intense rainfall	• Huge loss of land to the sea • Households demolished • Livestock washed away • Children suffered from fever and diarrhoea for almost a month • Loss of agricultural crops and fish catch
2010	Moderate flooding and related inundation	• Water logging in households for months • Loss of pond fishing due to salinity intrusion • Loss of agricultural crops due to salinity intrusion

Mousuni Island too experienced similar consecutive impacts but being larger than Ghoramara Island, the manifestations were more localised and almost went unnoticed by even the local administration. As noted by a woman from Mousuni:

> This time only our hamlet got flooded during the annual high tide. The villagers kept an eye on the embankment the whole night and quickly fixed the embankment as and when it was breached, all on our own. The *Panchayat* did not help with anything as it was only a matter of few houses.
> *(Interview December 2016, Mousuni Island)*

The communities' experience shows that such localised events are gradually eroding the resources in a subtle manner which is often unrecognisable to outsiders and the bureaucracy but leading towards cumulative uncertainties in the Sundarbans.

Coping with livelihood uncertainties: towards distress diversification

The livelihood framework developed by Scoones (1998) is a common analytical tool especially in rural contexts to understand the resources and strategies available for households to earn a living. Households employ natural, economic, physical and human capital to pursue strategies such as agricultural intensification and/or extensification, diversification of activities, migration and so on. Ellis (1999, 2000) further developed the idea of livelihood diversification and discusses the idea of rural households' construction of livelihood portfolios. The livelihood framework focuses on what households already have and builds on that, where diversification is a strategy for expanding the livelihood portfolio to achieve sustainable livelihoods. Contrary to this, what we see in the Sundarbans is a constant erosion of the various livelihood capitals (natural, physical, financial and human capitals, cf. Scoones 1998), which places serious constraints on the possible strategies that could be pursued by households. Livelihood diversification is, indeed, ongoing in Mousuni and Ghoramara. This, as we elaborate in later sections, is a diversification towards less profitable, more dangerous, more fragile and more marginal livelihood activities such as switching from rice to betel leaf cultivation in unfertile eroded lands on the waters' edge, prawn seed collection, crab catching, fishing in dangerous waters and in the vicinity of the tiger reserve and so on. Therefore, we call this "distress diversification". In distress diversification, households have already lost the assets/capitals/resources they had and diversification is not a choice but a necessity for survival.

Households in Ghoramara and Mousuni are not only displaced to other locations within the islands for new shelter but are also forced to engage in diversified sources of income including wage labour and out-migration. A female farmer from Mousuni said, "We have to dig the earth; we have to work for others; we have to live life" (Interview September 2016, Mousuni Island).

Declining agricultural productivity

Most of the respondents reported loss of productivity of agricultural land due to salinity ingress after Aila and expressed concern that "at least five to six years would be needed to regain the productivity", as stated by a middle-aged male farmer from Mousuni Island (Interview November 2015 Mousuni Island). The experiential knowledge of respondents regarding increasing tidal inundations appears to be in concurrence with the scientific knowledge of sea-level rise in the region. As stated by a female villager from Mousuni:

> In my childhood we could not see the river bed from our village. We could see it only from a distance once we got to the top of the embankment. Now the river and the plain are at the same surface level, the river has come so near to us.
> *(Interview May 2016, Mousuni Island)*

It would also mean that the islanders continue to lose both natural and physical capital.

Other respondents added that these localised incidents lead to recurrent loss in agriculture, particularly rice crop and farmers succumb to the cycle of debt leading to gradual economic impoverishment by the loss of financial capital. Loss of agricultural land to the sea, that is, land erosion is also a common phenomenon, thereby losing both natural and physical capital. A farmer from Ghoramara stated:

> I had a plot of land until last year which was very near to the embankment. At the peak of harvesting time, the plot started sliding into the sea. It happened so rapidly that I could manage to harvest only a few kilos of paddy which was sufficient for household consumption only for a few months. The compensation given by the government was not applicable in my case as it was not related to floods or cyclone; hence I couldn't claim compensation for losing my land to the sea. Now I have to work as a labourer in my neighbour's field which is a bit centrally located within Ghoramara.
> *(Interview March 2017, Ghoramara Island)*

Moreover, as mentioned above, the loss of soil fertility leads to decrease in crop productivity. Rice is the primary crop and staple food of the study islands and the productivity of rice is an indicator of the regional economy (Hazra et al. 2002; Hajra and Ghosh 2016). About two-thirds of the population in these islands are dependent on rice monocropping (Aman crop) for their livelihoods (Census of India 2011; Hajra and Ghosh 2018). Islanders are trying to cope with livelihood uncertainties by changing cropping pattern – from food crops like rice and vegetables to cash crops like betel leaves, which, in turn, has implications for the food security of the islanders. A middle-aged betel leaf farmer from Ghoramara Island stated:

> In my childhood, I have seen Ghoramara producing sufficient amount of rice grains and vegetables like chilli and watermelon. The piece of land which was once fertile enough to produce 550–560 kg of paddy has reduced its production to 220–240 kg. We have now shifted from paddy cultivation to betel leaf cultivation. The continuous intrusion of saline sea water during tidal inundation has reduced the fertility of the land. It can hardly produce paddy and betel once in a year. Still we are struggling.
> *(Interview August 2016, Ghoramara Island)*

Switching to betel leaf cultivation is a form of distress diversification consequent to the loss of land fertility, that is, natural capital, as the land is unsuitable for rice cultivation, which is the preferred crop. These lands are perched on the water's edge and could be rendered unviable or vanish into the sea any time by tidal surges and inundations. Construction of betel leaf garden incurs high costs and only a few can afford to do that. Most of the islanders build the structures necessary for betel leaf garden by taking loans from the local money lenders at high interest rates. As mentioned by respondents, this is a risky strategy. If and when there is a crop loss, due to flooding or erosion of the plot, the farmers are unable to repay the loan and they get caught in a debt trap. Some of the islanders who have already lost their lands work as wage labourers in the betel gardens.

Women farmers are more vulnerable in this regard. We were informed that women who previously had lands used to work their own fields. But after losing their land to the sea, they ended up working as agricultural labourers in the betel leaf gardens of others. From the discussions, it became apparent that this is still a "comfortable" option for them to work within the island as the owners of the gardens are either their close neighbours or fellow villagers. The women we spoke to mentioned that there are limited options left for them to sustain livelihoods like kitchen garden and livestock rearing, due to the loss of land. "As paddy cultivation is depleting, our livestock is getting less amount of fodder. In many cases we have to sell them, though we know that we are losing another source of income", stated a female villager during an all-female discussion in Mousuni (Interview November 2016, Mousuni Island). Increasing proletarianisation of both women and men is, thus, ongoing in Ghoramara and Mousuni, in the wake of loss of land and other income earning on-farm activities such as animal husbandry. The islanders are increasingly adding wage labour to their livelihood portfolio as a distress diversification strategy.

Agricultural livelihoods are, thus, characterised by continuous loss of natural, physical and financial capitals and distress diversification to other crops as well as wage labour. Although there is no specific intervention targeted at small, marginal or landless farmers to address the aforementioned challenges, there are a few initiatives taken by the "middle" – the CBOs/NGOs with scientific support from agricultural scientists ("above") of various Universities of West Bengal are supporting the depleting agriculture to adapt in the face of climate change. Discussions with the CBOs revealed that there are attempts to bring back salinity-resistant rice varieties to the marginal farmers especially those who lost productivity of their agricultural land due to salinity ingression. These are contributing to processes of reintroducing local knowledge and practices that existed in the region. These practices had almost been lost due to the Green Revolution agricultural practices promoted by the government of India, where the focus was on the adoption of high-yielding varieties (HYV) of crops and use of chemical fertilisers and pesticides. Of late, the collaboration between agricultural scientists, local CBOs and farmers has led to the development of farmers' associations in large parts of the affected areas which are attempting to revive traditional and local agricultural practices alongside general awareness programmes of organic farming. Model farms have been selected by a few leading NGOs, mostly concentrated within the project implementation areas. However, there is not much uptake either by the government or by the community outside the implementation areas. These interventions, if scaled up, could contribute to the revival of livelihoods and perhaps slow down the process of distress diversification to the high-risk betel leaf cultivation as well as diversification out of agriculture to wage labour and other marginal and risky activities such as fishing and crab catching, as discussed below.

Between the tiger and the deep sea: fishing in uncertain waters

Fishing is a traditional livelihood activity in the Sundarbans. One of the traditional inland fishing activity – *meendhar* (prawn seed collection) – was associated with the women fishers of the Sundarbans. This small-scale fishing was considered to be mainly a "women's job" as it was less risky than deep-sea fishing. Women fishers could contribute to the livelihood portfolio of the household through their *meen* catch. Prawn seed collection, though deemed less risky, is, indeed, a tedious process, which demands standing long in waist deep salt water, leading to health consequences like vaginal infection and body ache.

Deep-sea fishing in coastal waters was another significant source of livelihood for majority of the people in the Sundarbans. Many of their local belief systems and social structure are also built around this livelihood activity. Climate change along with globalisation is now driving this traditional livelihood towards extinction. According to the local fisherfolk, the amount of fish caught in the past two decades is much less than their previous experience. According to the respondents, both climatic and non-climatic factors have caused the declining fish catch. For instance, the extinction of a few fish species due to extreme climate events and the increasing number of fishing trawlers from other states active in the waters of the Sundarbans have caused a decline in the quantity and quality of the fish catch of the islanders. They are also concerned that the waters have become more unfriendly to the traditional ways of fishing. According to them, fishing has now become a professional activity undertaken commercially by outsiders rather than a traditional livelihood activity of the islanders. A middle-aged fisher of Mousuni Island said:

> It is not at all a profitable option anymore. The nature of the water has changed; it became rough and wavy along the coast. We-the fisher folk of the village took a collective decision to leave fishing and take up wage labour to sustain livelihood.
>
> *(Interview April 2016, Mousuni Island)*

The respondents mentioned that the amount of fish catch around the coast is declining. Now they have to go far out into the sea for longer number of days to catch a desirable quantity. "We are not getting good fish catch along the coast. My sons have to go for 7–10 days in the deep sea to catch fish now. I have discontinued going with them as my health is not permitting the stress of journey into the sea", stated an elderly fisherman from Ghoramara (Interview January 2017, Ghoramara Island). The islanders also referred to the menace caused by the increased intrusion of mechanised trawlers, leaving chemical pollutants in the water, which has led to degradation of river water and disappearance of some fish species. The diminution of natural capital – the fish population, fish species and the quality of coastal waters, signals increased uncertainties within the fishery-based livelihoods.

Fishers' experiences and observations correspond to the scientific explanation (Hazra et al. 2010; WWF 2011) that rising sea surface temperature is impacting the costal marine life and forcing the species to move into the deep sea. "The coastal marine life has changed especially after Aila. Some of the species have changed their habitat due to the increasing sea surface temperature and migrated to the deep sea", stated the Principal Scientist of Central Institute of Brackishwater Aquaculture, Kakdwip Research Centre (Interview, January 2017 Kakdwip).

The declining fish catch and increasing operational cost make the condition difficult for the fishers in the Sundarbans to continue with this once most viable livelihood option. Available credit facilities are now declining and fishers find it difficult to meet the operational expenses. Inland small fishing, which used to be a prominent livelihood option in Sundarbans, is also decreasing, especially after Aila. Salinity intrusion into the fisheries has made them unsuitable for freshwater fishing and unusable especially for *meendhara* (prawn seed collection). Moreover, *Meen* has always been in controversy because of biodiversity conservation in the Sundarbans as this traditional practice is considered a threat to the conservation of marine species (see also Jalais 2010; Sen and Pattanaik 2017). According to the Biodiversity Conservation Act, prawn seed collection from the fringes of the river is now illegal. From a livelihood perspective, the ban on *meen* collection has resulted in the loss of this natural capital for the households in general and women in particular. This has forced them to engage in distress diversification to crab catching, as discussed "below".

The islanders mentioned that, given the increasing constraints in coastal fishing, inland fishing and prawn seed collection, most of the fishers have switched to crab catching. However, this activity entails more physical stress and is riskier as crabs are mostly found around the tiger reserves, inhabited by the fierce Bengal Tiger. The waters are also home to a large number of crocodile populations. While "tiger widow" is a common phenomenon in the Sundarbans due to a large number of men losing their lives to the tiger in pursuit of livelihoods (collection of minor forest produce, crab catching, fishing, etc.), now women themselves and children are increasingly at risk. This is, indeed, the epitome of distress diversification, especially by the most vulnerable groups – women and children. As told by the respondents, it is mostly women and children who are engaged in crab catching as men are compelled to out-migrate seasonally to work elsewhere for cash incomes. However, as the demand for crab in the market is relatively low compared to prawn and in the absence of commercial market regulations for crab selling, crabs fetch lower prices than the actual market price. This is a reflection of the patriarchal social norms, which undervalue the labour of women and children.

Although crab catching is pursued by many islanders as it is a relatively profitable option, respondents from the "middle" (NGOs/CBOs) reflect on two main challenges that make commercial crab catching not so viable for the community. One, crab is not considered to be a nutritious food in Bengali food culture; hence, it is not very popular in the daily diet. Second, quite related to the first, there is a lack of marketing strategies to sell the collected crabs in an organised way. The respondents maintained that there is a steady demand for Sundarbans' crab in the Chinese market. However, due to the lack of formalised regulations and influence of the middlemen, the catchers who are risking their lives do not receive adequate payments. According to the "middle", crab catching can be an alternative for the people if marketised well in combination with risk reduction measures. While crab catching is a potentially viable livelihood activity, it risks the loss of human capital, including human lives.

The above discussion highlights the different forms and dimensions of the distress diversification of livelihoods the people of the study islands are engaged in. They constantly incur loss of natural capital, physical capital, economic/financial capital and human capital due to the extreme weather events, which compel them to engage in distress diversification to marginal, more dangerous and precarious livelihood activities, which, in turn, might result in further loss of human capital and human life itself. In the Sundarbans context, therefore, it may not be fruitful to focus on what households already have, as envisaged in the livelihood framework, but focus should be on the erosion of the various capitals and support alternative less precarious livelihood strategies.

Socio-political uncertainties: embankment politics and conflicts

Embankment failures during extreme events are a common phenomenon in the study islands. These often contribute to the vulnerabilities faced by the islanders due to the loss of homesteads, land and livelihoods and sometimes life itself. The repeatedly breached and continuously eroding embankments in the study islands starkly highlight the ongoing uncertainties faced by the islanders and serve as a foreboding of the disasters-in-waiting. The scale of displacement this has generated and continues to generate is huge. In Ghoramara, after the disappearance of a significant part of the island Khasimara, 30,000 households had been resettled to Jibantala in Kakdwip Block 40 years ago. Since then, there has been no official rehabilitation programmes by the government, although breaching of embankments is a recurrent phenomenon along the coastline of the island. We were told that households from the eroded hamlets keep moving towards the interior of the islands in a centrifugal fashion and live in make-shift houses almost every year. This has, in turn, increased the population density in the interior parts of the island and has led to further pressures on vital resources like drinking water, homestead and cultivable lands. The embankment breaches have led to a gradual stratification of the island societies with the livelihoods of the households living in the periphery taking a direct hit compared to their fellow islanders living on higher grounds or towards the central part of the affected islands. The loss of homesteads and habitats, agricultural lands, salination of ponds, loss of drinking water sources, etc. are far greater for the people living close to the embankments. This has resulted in livelihood inequities leading to variable uncertainties vis-á-vis the geography within the islands.

Embankments are a highly contested technology in the context of the Sundarbans. Historically, mud embankments began to be erected in the 1770s during the British colonial period in order to facilitate the reclamation and settlement of people and to protect the agricultural lands from tidal waves (Sarkhel 2013; also see Chapter 3). Though continuously maintained by the Public Works Department, the repeated extreme weather events, sea level rise and tidal surges have led to the collapse of large sections of the embankments. In the period between 1961 and 2000, the Sundarbans region experienced 31 severe cyclones. The cyclone Aila in 2009 was an extreme weather event that had catastrophic effects and resulted in the destruction of about 500 kilometres of embankments (Sarkhel 2013). Following this, with the financial assistance of the World Bank, the Sundarbans Embankment Reconstruction Project has been initiated to build "modern" concrete embankments (Mehtta and Bhattacharyya 2020).

While some hail this as a technological breakthrough in the protection of the Sundarbans against climate change, others are critical and ask if this is a sustainable approach to the problem. For example, the title of a National Geographic article reads "Building tomorrow in the Sundarbans: How an inspiring project is rebuilding the lives of an endangered community facing the threat of rising sea levels" (National Geographic 2019).[2] This project employing "modern" technology is expected to "turn the tide" according to the article. Mehtta and Bhattacharyya (2020), on the other hand, ask, "Is concrete the way forward in rebuilding the Sunderbans?" "During Cyclone Amphan, these modern embankments, with their whopping budgets and their supposed state-of-the-art material, developed cracks, broke and collapsed".[3] Rudra (2010) has discussed extensively the socio-ecological consequences of concrete embankment building in the Sundarbans in the aftermath of Aila.

A scientific expert and senior bureaucrat, in an interview, pointed out: "The World Bank sanctioned INR 5,000 Crores for building concrete embankments in the Sundarbans, out of which only INR 149 crores has been utilised in the last seven years". Embankment – the life line of the Sundarbans – has not been planned according to the scientific inputs provided to the relevant departments, as stated by several "above" and "middle"-level respondents. According to the website of State Irrigation Department (updated in January 2018), after the devastating cyclone Aila in 2009, which broke at least 400 km of embankments,[4] a task force on "Restoration of Sundarbans Embankments damaged by the cyclone Aila" was formed by the Union Ministry of Water Resources. Concrete embankments were proposed by the Department of Irrigation, which was recommended by the task force and approved by the Ministry of Water Resources as well as the Planning Commission.

According to Irrigation Department officials in the Blocks to which the study islands belong and the website of the same department, this new embankment is going to be higher than it was previously, which would need more lands from the islands thus making the land mass smaller. It is planned to slant towards the coast covered by mangroves as first line of defence against storms or cyclones. In line with scientific expertise from the Irrigation Department, incorporation of geo-tubes has been proposed in more erosion-prone zones. However, the rest of the embankments is going to be earthen. Ground-level staff of Irrigation Department, a crucial actor for implementation who are mainly working at Block level, pointed out the gap between knowledge and implementation in the construction of embankments in eroded parts of the region. According to the irrigation officer of one of the studied Blocks:

> We are not giving enough time to the land to be mature geomorphologically to hold the dense population. More so, building embankment on one side create pressure on the river to erode the land on the side where the homesteads are situated. This faulty design of embankment along with cutting down of mangroves catalysed the rapid erosion of the Sundarbans.
>
> *(Interview May 2016, Kakdwip)*

The embankment is a bone of contention among various actors. Amidst the pressures and compulsions of competitive electoral politics, the politicians are compelled to act, in forms that are "visible" to their constituencies. The technocrats are always already prepared for technological solutions, while the bureaucrats seem ever ready to push any solution that comes to the table. The voices that arise from the amphibian landscape of the Sundarbans get drowned even before they leave the islands.

According to "below" respondents, breaching of embankments is almost a regular phenomenon now, especially during the monsoons. Local people expect that every year the necessary maintenance and repair works be done before the monsoon in a pro-active manner. However, according to local communities, the Irrigation Department officials and contractors responsible for building or repairing embankments fail to deliver work on time; hence, submergence and temporary displacement occur repeatedly every year. Previously, there was ground-level staff from Irrigation Department (called *beldaar* in Bengali) posted in each island to monitor the status of the embankments. Eventually, these posts were abolished or remained vacant due to the negligence on the part of the Panchayat. At the time of our fieldwork, Ghoramara had only one *beldar* who was close to retirement age (60 years) and without the required equipment to repair the embankments, and Mousuni did not have such a post. The *beldar* of Ghoramara stated that the private contractors appointed by the *Panchayat* have become more powerful as they are generating wage labour opportunities for the islanders amidst the uncertainties related to traditional livelihoods.

The highly politicised nature of the embankments became obvious during the discussions with the islanders. They mentioned the complexities created by the partisan politics that prevails in the islands, a reflection of wider patron/client nature of West Bengal and Indian village politics which has resulted in prioritising repair work for selective households that support the elected representative. A community leader from Mousuni stated:

> The embankment building in the present political context is just to earn some more money. Nothing else. The situation has changed completely. Now we are not making a proper embankment; we are using low quality materials; we often pluck the bricks from the embankment and allow the water to come in; we even break the portion at night which has been built during the day. The political parties are earning benefits out of this embankment breaching.
>
> *(Interview February 2017, Mousuni Island)*

Embankments are thus not merely physical structures of uncertainty to be breached by the waters but contested political structures to be repeatedly breached and repaired in an effort to sustain livelihoods and negotiate political power at the margins.

The role of out-migration

Migration has emerged as the most popular and accepted way of coping with the ever-present difficulties and vulnerabilities on the islands. The Sundarbans is currently experiencing permanent out-migration as well as seasonal out-migration. Permanent out-migration means that islanders leave Sundarbans and settle down permanently elsewhere, mainly in a nearby city or town. This has been historically attributed to the pull factors (Todaro 1969). Of late, climate change uncertainties and vulnerabilities, that is, push factors are also contributing to permanent out-migration. The northern and the southern parts of the Sundarbans are only about 4–5 and 5–6 hours, respectively, by road from the mega city Kolkata and are experiencing the impact of globalisation and increasing urbanisation. These act as pull factors especially for the educated rural elite of Sundarbans to settle down near Kolkata where they have access to better education opportunities for their children (e.g. English-medium schools) and healthcare facilities (e.g. multi-speciality hospitals). However, they usually leave their parental home under the care of their relatives or elderly parents, sometimes, a piece of agricultural land in these islands as a symbol of their roots. The educated youth are often able to find off-farm employment in the towns and cities. The discussions we had with the educated elite youth revealed that they wanted to leave the Sundarbans because they are worried about the extreme weather events and are not prepared to face another Aila or Amphan (the cyclone which struck in 2020). "It has now become a land of fury, cyclones, floods, no facilities. I do not want my daughter to be here anymore. I have bought a house in Sonarpur. My daughter got admission in a good school in Kolkata. At least she will have a good life", stated a young man from Mousuni (Interview August, 2016, Jaynagar, South 24 Parganas).

Seasonal out-migration especially by men has also emerged as a widely accepted coping strategy. Male members migrate to the cities and towns of West Bengal or to other states in India for certain periods of the year and engage in unskilled work like wage labour, as restaurant waiters, working in cold storages, construction sector and so on. The uneducated rural poor mostly opt for seasonal migration. Respondents stated that it is quite difficult for them to cope with this livelihood transition as they often lack even the basic level of skills required for the jobs and they do not have opportunities for acquiring the new skills in the Sundarbans. Hence, physical wage labour is the only option. Most of the households in Mousuni and Ghoramara have at least one family member who has migrated either to other states like Haryana, Kerala, etc., or cities like Delhi, Mumbai, Chennai, or to cities within West Bengal such as Kolkata, Hooghly and Burdwan. During fieldwork, we met with some migrants who had returned home from other states for a certain period of the year and were waiting to travel back to their host regions. In the absence of men, women assume the responsibility as head of the household. When they do not receive remittance in time, they are compelled to borrow from money lenders at high interest rates to meet household expenses. Women in a group interaction in Mousuni stated:

> Mahajans increase the rate of interest as per his wish any time. But still we have to take loans from them, if husbands fail to send money on time. Earning options are becoming less and less here. How can we run the show?
>
> *(Interview May 2017, Mousuni Island)*

It would seem that for a number of island households incomes from seasonal migration of family members are uncertain as well. Therefore, the coping strategy of seasonal migration adds another dimension to the uncertainties.

Searching for alternatives and the crucial role of the "middle"

As the traditional livelihood opportunities are depleting, there is a growing need to build new skills for livelihood and address the problems they face regarding the existing livelihood options. With growing demand from the community, a section of the "middle" is trying to fill the gap by implementing various alternatives by creating alliances. Personnel from NGOs and CBOs widely acknowledged the funding apathy for long-term climate change programmes and went on saying that the big donor agencies are more interested in short-term disaster reliefs whose impacts are rapid and visible. The Chief Secretary of a local NGO stated:

> The international agencies rushed with aid and disaster relief to partially ameliorate the sufferings of the people in the immediate aftermath of cyclone Aila. But little has been done with an eye to provide sustainable solutions that address the basic necessities of the islanders for preparing them to handle climate change impacts.
>
> *(Interview January 2017, Kolkata)*

For them, skill or capacity development of the community to take up new livelihood options is the priority amidst uncertainties. NGOs working in the Sundarbans have taken a few initiatives in developing capacities of the local youth. Some NGOs run vocational training courses like nursing, beautician or electrical works for youth who successfully completed 12th grade in school. Alongside they are also organising computer training for women through Self-Help Groups (SHGs)-based women's cooperatives, specifically to understand banking processes. This is a timely intervention as most women in the islands receive money from their husbands who are seasonal migrants.

However, according to the members of the civil society organisations we spoke with, their initiatives have been adversely affected by erratic funding cycles from the "above", be it government or the big donor agencies and, in most cases, failed to address the core issues of sustainability. The "above" seems to be more keen to invest in building and construction work or activities that are easily visible rather than on human resource development. This points to the eagerness of the "above" to show off to the islanders, the outsiders and the media, the development activities that happened/are happening through their benevolence and funding. The sinking islands of the Sundarbans including Ghoramara and Mousuni are hotspots of media activities – both domestic and international media. Harms (2018) provides an insightful account of the social consequences of media encounters with the islands and islanders. Film crews that regularly visit these sinking islands produce captivating footage on climate change for global audiences, while at the same time rework the memories of the displaced islanders and often producing new memories by staging acts of remembering in front of the camera. "In both instances, particular pasts are prioritised and imbued with a sense of urgency and relevance to foreign film teams and global audiences" (Harms 2018: 1).

The media, thus, is an important "middle"-level actor in the Sundarbans. The print, electronic and of late several online pages and forums in social media play an active role both as a watch dog and reporting about this deltaic region. In the period before cyclone Aila in 2009, the occasional stories that dotted the pages of the mainstream media were mainly on the Bengal Tigers and projecting the region as a World Heritage site. A senior journalist mentioned in discussions that, cyclone Aila, with its devastating consequences, stunned the media into realising the vulnerability of the delta region, the climate shocks and the precarious nature of the islanders of the Sundarbans. The media played a major role in highlighting the devastation in the islands, pressured the government into providing immediate relief to the islanders as well as plan for the building and repairing of embankments. However, with time, both media's attention and the state government's attention towards fast tracking of the projects waned. The more recent cyclones Amphan in 2020 and Yash in 2021 have once again brought the media's attention back to the Sundarbans. It could be surmised that media's role and attention as a "middle"-level actor is largely seasonal and waxes and wanes in tandem with the extreme events.

A senior member of the media fraternity who has reported extensively on the region for a long period sums up media's attention on the region in the following words:

> Like the government and most other institutions working in the region, the media too is fickle in terms of how to report about the region. The media has somewhat failed in communicating the voices from the region and instead has limited itself to reporting calamities and climate change warnings.
>
> *(Interview March 2017, Kolkata)*

One could say that the opinion pieces, expert columns and the editorials of the print media have mostly lacked the coherency and consistency of a narrative that would make the decision-makers and decision influencers to give a policy direction to deal with the short- and long-term developments in the Indian Sundarbans. Based on a study of the role of media in the health system of the Sundarbans, Ghosh et al. (2016) argue for the need of sensitisation and awareness raising of the local media so that they can support integration and translation for wider awareness and dissemination related to locally led cooperatives and women's Self-Help Group initiatives.

The Political economy of climate policymaking in the Sundarbans: the disconnected "above"

"Sundarbans as a region is not homogenous in terms of characteristics, dimensions and climate change impacts. Hence a one-size-fits-all approach cannot resolve challenges of the Sundarbans". This was raised by a leading health economist working on the health system of Sundarbans for more than a decade. According to him, one needs to understand that there are "many Sundarbans within the one" (Interview January 2018, Kolkata). A leading NGO person reminded us of the interlinked socio-ecological system of the islands: "Climate change in Sundarbans cannot be separated from its geology, geo-morphology and society". She continued, "Social evolution is unique in Sundarbans which was always centered on its environment. The socio-political institutions have a crucial role to play now in the present day social transition in Sundarbans accelerated by climate change impacts" (Interview January 2018, Kolkata). A noted ex-bureaucrat of West Bengal said, "Within this perplexing transition, implementers often miss to hit core factors and end up with messy, unsustainable strategies. Policymaking too, is a subject of this differentials" (Interview January 2018, Kolkata).

The above narratives reflect a significant gap in knowledge while making policies for the Sundarbans keeping the dimensions of "many Sundarbans" in mind. "Many Sundarbans" refers to various geographical locations – (a) the coastal pockets; (b) the deltaic Sundarbans and (c) the mainland, each of which is subject to varied impacts of climate change. "In each location climate change impacts are manifested differently and people are responding in the way they are facing it. This knowledge has to be incorporated in the policy making", stated a senior climate scientist working for decades in the Indian Sundarbans (Interview January 2018, Kolkata).

Evidence suggests that there seems to be a disconnect between scientific knowledge from environmental experts and policymakers. Though both belong to the "above" in our heuristics, they have failed to draw up a coordinated plan for tackling climate change in the Sundarbans. From our discussions with the "above", it became clear that this has been exacerbated by the lack of motivation and interest in getting connected with each other and build bridges between concerned departments and academia so that they could act in tandem rather than in an isolated manner. "We are more interested to get connected with the community. We have relations with a few bureaucrats but that's more on a personal note", stated one leading climate scientist working on the Sundarbans (Interview September, 2017, Kolkata).

The responses from the donor agencies – a part of the "above" – indicate that they too are not keen to get connected with the policymakers. This concerns the overpowering political influence on the development programmes in the state. Almost all the respondents from donor agencies stated that the state government shows little interest in receiving financial and technical support from them despite their repeated facilitation and advocacy.

> I am heading the Sundarbans programmes in my organisation; I never took a single penny either from the past Left Front government or from the present government. If I take money from the government then I have to listen to them who do not have any people-centric approach. And if they listen to us, they cannot build bridges, roads and other infrastructural development which is adding to the people's sufferings, stated a senior programme officer from an international donor agency.
>
> *(Interview December, 2017, Kolkata)*

The donor agencies are well connected with the "middle"-level NGOs/CBOs for implementing their development programmes. Nevertheless, this parallel implementation by donor agencies and NGOs appears to be a patch work which is benefitting only a miniscule portion of the people. For example, a local-level NGO working in a particular region in the Sundarbans is the partner for different donor agencies. They use the funds received from different donor agencies for implementing programmes in that particular region where they operate. Other regions in the Sundarbans with similar development challenges remain ignored.

A lacuna has been observed in the short- and long-term planning and preparedness by the government and civil society who are mainly focusing on disaster response. Following the lessons learnt after cyclone Aila in 2009, the state and local administrations seem to be confident that large shocks can be managed through emergency responses. Yet, despite the consensus between the scientists that concrete embankments are not a permanent solution to coastal erosion/ storm water surges, there has been a dominant focus on concrete embankments in the policies for the Sundarbans, as discussed in an earlier section. Ground-level implementation of schemes, such as land acquisition for embankments, mangrove conservation and compensation for crop loss due to natural calamities as well as employment of rural youth under livelihood schemes severely lack community knowledge and participation. For example, the people in Ghoramara told us that after severe flood damage, people from some parts of the island affected with land erosion could not claim compensation for crop loss as the affected agricultural land simply disappeared into the sea. Mostly being tenants and due to lack of knowledge regarding legal/formal formalities, the farmers could not produce the required land documents to the government officials. Consequently, the claims for compensation were rejected. One is reminded of the rendering of the "Anti-Politics Machine" by Ferguson, where development actors construct the object of development in order to deliver development (Ferguson 1990). When the "object" of development, in this case, the land with crops on it, vanishes into the deep waters without leaving a trace, the bureaucracy is at a loss to grapple with it and, consequently, compensation is denied to the farmers as they are unable to document the object of development. It would seem that the certainty of citizenship itself is linked to *terra firma* – firm grounds on which people can stand on and make claims on the state. Discussing the case of the island Lohachara in the Sundarbans, which was subject to large-scale erosion and disappearance of villages, Harms (2017) has pointed to the uncertain citizenship rights and entitlements due to coastal erosions. "Environmental degradations involve" (ibid.: 70), what he calls "corrosion of citizenship at the margins" (ibid.: 70).

Concluding remarks

The findings bring to the fore the experiences and understandings of climate-related uncertainties and other vulnerabilities from the standpoint of different actors. The people at the grassroots ("below") have a clear perception about changes in weather patterns that have occurred over the last five to ten years. Local perceptions of changes in the climate include increased heat, overall colder winters, reduced and erratic rainfall and frequent floods and cyclones. The "below" is also experiencing negative effects of climatic change on the various livelihood capitals, so much so their livelihood portfolio is characterised by distress diversification – engaging in more risky, more fragile, more capital intensive and less profitable livelihood activities. The local perceptions of climate change were consistent with scientific evidence regarding climate change impacts in the Sundarbans.

The islanders perceive that their current problems are certainly human induced at least in large part. Nature makes their life uncertain but, paradoxically, also had added an element of certainty through their livelihood activities centred on agriculture, fishing and collecting minor forest produce. As discussed in this chapter, islanders are now increasingly forced into distress livelihood diversification due to the diminution of their livelihood capitals. The increasing imposition of restrictions by the government on fishing, prawn-catching and other livelihood activities in the name of "conservation" is also intensifying and reinforcing climate-induced uncertainties.

As we understand from this study, marginalised environments like the Sundarbans call for radical–critical adaptation as well as the strengthening and protection of local ecosystems and biodiversity in a people-friendly and locally appropriate way. We use the term radical–critical adaptation to flag the structural dimensions and the necessity for radical restructuring of the capitalist relations of production towards a more equitable and socio-ecologically just production and distribution system. Vulnerabilities and uncertainties emanate not merely from an externally imposed climate threat but primarily from the historical–political economic–institutional power relations, which engender differentiated experiences and responses to climate change. We have discussed how the socio-ecological marginalities and uncertainties have been historically produced in the Sundarbans at the confluence of the incorporation of the island's resources into the circuit of global capital and the twin imperatives of conservation and late globalisation. As argued by Taylor (2014), we need to produce ourselves and our environments differently. This calls for a transformation of the current capitalist relations of production. We would argue that, for this to happen, an ideological shift is warranted.

Postscript

Our last field visit to the Sundarbans was in September 2018. Since then, the islanders have faced four catastrophic events – cyclone Bulbul in 2019, COVID-19 and associated lockdowns since early 2020, supercyclone Amphan in May 2020 and cyclone Yash in 2021. In addition to the loss of lives and infrastructure, these have further exacerbated the livelihood uncertainties of the islanders. Livelihood losses include hundreds of livestock and the agricultural produce of nearly half a million farmers. Amphan hit at a time when the communities were already subject to the impact of COVID-19 in terms of lives and livelihoods (see Ghosh et al. 2020). The lockdown has hindered even the "distress diversification" activities including crab catching and fishing around tiger reserves (see Basu 2020). Seasonal migration, the major coping strategy of the islanders, has all but stopped due to the COVID-19 pandemic. Moreover "there has been a steady stream of migrant islanders who are now being forced to return to the delta from different parts of India" (Ghosh et al. 2020).[5] The intersecting nature of these disastrous events are, indeed, devastating for the lives and livelihoods of the Sundarbans islanders, which need further research to unravel the short- and long-term effects.

Notes

1 https://www.thethirdpole.net/en/climate/opinion-to-rebuild-the-sundarbans-india-needs-to-rethink-its-laws/ (accessed on 20.05.2021)
2 https://www.nationalgeographic.com/environment/2019/02/partner-content-transforming-sundarbans/ (accessed on 12.01.2021)
3 Mehtta and Bhattacharyya (2020) The Telegraph online, dated 01.07.20, https://www.telegraphindia.com/opinion/is-concrete-the-way-forward-in-rebuilding-the-sundarbans/cid/1784882 (accessed on 12.01.2021).
4 A study of embanked landscapes in the Bangladesh Sundarbans found that the islands enclosed by embankments in the 1960s have lost an elevation of 1.0–1.5 m; and as a consequence when there was large scale breaching of embankments during hurricane Aila, the islands lay inundated for more than two years until the embankments were restored (Auerbach et al. 2014).
5 Ghosh et al. (2020) https://steps-centre.org/blog/rebuilding-same-or-rebuilding-different-critical-questions-in-the-aftermath-of-cyclone-amphan/ (accessed on 05.02.2021).

References

Ascoli, F.D. 2020. *A Revenue History of the Sundarbans: From 1870 to 1920*. New York: Routledge.
Auerbach, L.W., S.L. Goodbred Jr., D.R. Mondal, C.A. Wilson, K.R. Ahmed, K. Roy, M.S. Steckler, C. Small, J.M. Gilligan, and B.A. Ackerly. 2014. 'Flood Risk of Natural and Embanked Landscapes on the Ganges-Brahmaputra Tidal Delta Plain'. *Nature Climate Change*, 5: 153–157. https://doi.org/10.1038/nclimate2472
Bardhan, P., M. Luca, D. Mookherjee, and F. Pino. 2014. 'Evolution of Land Distribution in West Bengal 1967–2004: Role of Land Reform and Demographic Changes'. *Journal of Development Economics,* 110: 171–190. https://doi.org/10.1016/j.jdeveco.2014.02.001
Basu, J. 2020. 'Indigenous Peoples in Sundarbans Ruined by Lockdown, Cyclone'. Available at: https://www.thethirdpole.net/en/livelihoods/indigenous-peoples-in-sundarbans-ruined-by-lockdown-cyclone/ (accessed on 05 February 2021).
Brown, S., R. Nicholls, N.A. Lázár, D. Hornby, C. Hill, S. Hazra, K.S. Addo, A. Haque, J. Caesar, and E. Tompkins. 2018. 'What Are the Implications of Sea-Level Rise for a 1.5, 2 and 3°C Rise in Global Mean Temperatures in the Ganges-Brahmaputra-Meghna and Other Vulnerable Deltas?'. *Regional Environmental Change*, 18: 1829–1842. https://doi.org/10.1007/s10113-018-1311-0
Chatterjee, S. 1990. 'Land Reclamation in the Sundarbans – An Overview'. *Proceedings of the Indian History Congress*, 51: 440–446.

Conway, D., R. Nicholls, S. Brown, M.G.L. Tebboth, W.N. Adger, B. Ahmad, H. Biemans, F. Crick, A. Lutz, R. De Campos, M. Said, C. Singh, M.A.H. Zaroug, E. Ludi, M. New, and P. Wester. 2019. 'The Need for Bottom-up Assessments of Climate Risks and Adaptation in Climate-Sensitive Regions'. *Nature Climate Change*, 9: 503–511. https://doi.org/10.1038/s41558-019-0502-0

Eaton, R. 1990. 'Human Settlement and Colonization in the Sundarbans, 1200–1750'. *Agriculture and Human Values*, 2(3): 6–16. https://doi.org/10.1007/BF01530432

Ellis, F. 1999. 'Rural Livelihood Diversity in Developing Countries: Evidence and Policy Implications'. *ODI Natural Resource Perspectives*, 40.

Ellis, F. 2000. *Rural Livelihoods and Diversity in Developing Countries*. London: Oxford University Press.

Ferguson, J. 1990. *The Anti-Politics Machine: Development, Depoliticization, and Bureaucratic Power in Lesotho*. Cambridge: Cambridge University Press.

Ghosh, A., S. Schmidt, T. Fickert, and M. Nüsser. 2015. 'The Indian Sundarban Mangrove Forests: History, Utilization, Conservation Strategies and Local Perception'. *Diversity*, 7: 149–169. https://doi.org/10.3390/d7020149

Ghosh, T. and S.K. Sengupta. 1997. 'Morphological Changes of Ghoramara Island, West Bengal: A Documentation'. *Indian Geographical Environment*, 2: 64–65.

Ghosh, T., G. Bhandari, and S. Hazra. 2003. 'Application of a 'Bio-Engineering' Technique to Protect Ghoramara Island (Bay of Bengal) from Severe Erosion'. *Journal of Coastal Conservation*, 9(2): 171–178.

Ghosh, T., R. Hajra, and A. Mukhopadhyay. 2014. 'Island Erosion and Afflicted Population: Crisis and Policies to Handle Climate Change'. In *International Perspectives on Climate Change: Latin America and Beyond*, edited by F. Leal, F. Alves, S. Caeiro, and U. Azeiteiro, 217–226. Cham: Springer.

Ghosh, U., S. Bose, and D. Chakraborty. 2020. 'Rebuilding Same or Rebuilding Different? Critical Questions in the Aftermath of Cyclone Amphan'. Available at: https://steps-centre.org/blog/rebuilding-same-or-rebuilding-different-critical-questions-in-the-aftermath-of-cyclone-amphan/ (accessed on 05 February 2021).

Ghosh, U., S. Bose, R. Bramhachari, and S. Mondol. 2016. 'Building Capacity of Local Media to Facilitate Intersectoral Action for Health in the Sundarbans, West Bengal'. *BMJ Glob Health*, 1(1): A2–A43. http://dx.doi.org/10.1136/bmjgh-2016-EPHPabstracts.38

Giri, C., B. Pengra, Z. Zhu, A. Singh, and L. Tieszen. 2007. 'Monitoring Mangrove Forest Dynamics of the Sundarbans in Bangladesh and India Using Multi-Temporal Satellite Data from 1973 to 2000'. *Estuarine, Coastal and Shelf Science*, 73: 91–100. https://doi.org/10.1016/j.ecss.2006.12.019

Hajra, R., A. Ghosh, and T. Ghosh. 2016. 'Comparative Assessment of Morphological and Landuse/Landcover Change Pattern of Sagar, Ghoramara, and Mousani Island of Indian Sundarban Delta through Remote Sensing'. In *Environment and Earth Observation: Case Studies in India*, edited by S. Hazra, A. Mukhopadhyay, A.R. Ghosh, D. Mitra, and V.K. Dadhwal. Cham: Springer.

Hajra, R. and T. Ghosh. 2016. 'Migration Pattern of Ghoramara Island of Indian Sundarbans: Identification of Push and Pull Factors'. *Asian Academic Research Journal of Social Sciences & Humanities*, 3(6): 47–55.

Hajra, R. and T. Ghosh. 2018. 'Agricultural Productivity, Household Poverty and Migration in the Indian Sundarban Delta'. *Elementa Science of the Anthroposcene*, 6(3). https://doi.org/10.1525/elementa.196

Harms, A. 2017. 'Citizenship at Sea: Environmental Displacement and State Relations in the Indian Sundarbans'. *Economic and Political Weekly*, 52(33): 69–76.

Harms, A. 2018. 'Filming Sea-Level Rise: Media Encounters and Memory Work in the Indian Sundarbans'. *Journal of the Royal Anthropological Institute*, 24(3): 475–492. https://doi.org/10.1111/1467-9655.12856

Hazra, S., T. Ghosh, R. DasGupta, and G. Sen. 2002. 'Sea Level and Associated Changes in the Sundarbans'. *Science and Culture* 68(9–12): 309–321.

Hazra, S., K. Samanta, A. Mukhopadhyay, and A. Akhand. 2010. *Temporal Change Detection (2001–2008) Study of Sundarban*. Kolkata: School of Oceanographic Studies, Kolkatta: Jadavpur University. Available at: https://doi.org/10.1002/2017EF000732 (accessed on 04.02.2021).

Jalais, A. 2010a. *Forest of Tigers: People, Politics and Environment in the Sundarbans*. London: Routledge.

Jalais, A. 2010b. 'Braving the Crocodiles with Kali: Being a Prawn Seed Collector and a Modern Woman in the 21st Century Sundarbans'. *Socio-Legal Review*, 6: 1–23.

Mehtta, M. and D. Bhattacharyya. 2020. 'Shifting Lives in the Mangroves: Is Concrete the Way Forward in Rebuilding the Sunderbans?'. *The Telegraph*, London, 17 July.

Mukhopadhyay, A., P. Mondal, J. Barik, S.M. Chowdhury, T. Ghosh, and S. Hazra. 2015. 'Changes in Mangrove Species Assemblages and Future Prediction of the Bangladesh Sundarbans using Markov Chain Model and Cellular Automata'. *Environmental Science: Processes & Impacts,* 17(6): 1111–1117. https://doi.org/10.1039/c4em00611a

National Geographic. 2019. 'Building Tomorrow in the Sundarbans: How an Inspiring Project Is Rebuilding the Lives of an Endangered Community Facing the Threat of Rising Sea Levels'. *National Geographic*, USA, 22 February.

Ohdedar, B. 2020. 'Opinion: To Rebuild the Sundarbans, India Needs to Rethink its Laws'. Available at: https://www.thethirdpole.net/en/climate/opinion-to-rebuild-the-sundarbans-india-needs-to-rethink-its-laws/ (accessed on 05 February 2021).

Rudra, K. 2010. 'The Proposal of Strengthening Embankment in Sundarban: Myth and Reality'. *Refugee Watch*, 35: 86–92.

Sarkhel, P. 2013. 'Examining Private Participation in Embankment Maintenance in the Indian Sundarbans'. SANDEE Working Paper, No. 75-12, SANDEE, Kathmandu.

Scoones, I. 1998. 'Sustainable Rural Livelihoods: A Framework for Analysis'. IDS Working Paper, No. 72, Institute of Development Studies, Brighton.

Sen, A. and S. Pattanaik. 2017. 'How can Traditional Livelihoods Find a Place in Contemporary Conservation Politics Debates in India? Understanding Community Perspectives in Sundarban West Bengal'. *Journal of Political Ecology*, 24(1). https://doi.org/10.2458/v24i1.20971

Taylor, M. 2014. *The Political Ecology of Climate Change Adaptation: Livelihoods, Agrarian Change and the Conflicts of Development*. London: Routledge.

Todaro, M.P. 1969. 'A Model of Labor Migration and Urban Unemployment in Less Developed Countries'. *American Economic Review*, 59(1): 138–148.

6
CLIMATE CHANGE AND UNCERTAINTY IN INDIA'S MAXIMUM CITY, MUMBAI

Hans Nicolai Adam, Synne Movik, D. Parthasarathy, Alankar, N.C. Narayanan and Lyla Mehta

> *It is said that Bombay never sleeps*
> *Never stops*
> *Never tires*
> *But brother, on Tuesday 26 July*
> *Bombay stopped*
> *Bombay tired*
> *Every mobile phone went silent*
> *When the cloudburst struck Bombay*
> *Darkness prevailed when the power went out*
> —A Bhojpuri music video called 'Museebat mein Bambai'[1] describing Mumbai's mood following the 26th July 2005 flooding

Introduction

In this chapter, we explore how climate change and uncertainty shape the urban landscape of Mumbai – a megalopolis whose land was largely reclaimed from the sea and that faces ever-increasing threats from climate change, environmental deterioration and development pressures (Figure 6.1). Globally, the city consistently ranks as one of the most threatened megacities from the effects of climate change (Hanson *et al.* 2011; Abadie *et al.* 2020), with flooding arguably one of the most formidable natural hazards it faces. In 2005, Mumbai experienced a traumatic and devastating flood event, the so-called Mithi deluge, which claimed more than 1,000 lives, in addition to causing enormous economic and property damage (Bhagat *et al.* 2006). Despite promises and efforts by urban authorities to transform Mumbai and prioritise flood mitigation in the aftermath of the 2005 event, flooding remains chronic with regular disruption, economic damage and loss of human lives occurring every year in pockets or affecting the

FIGURE 6.1 Koli fishers and urban expansion in Mumbai (Photo credit: Hans Nicolai Adam).

entire city. Multiple flood events continue to wreak havoc and have brought the central and suburban districts to a standstill for intermittent periods over the past years (see Kumar 2019; Singh 2020).

Flooding is, however, not a "natural" phenomenon attributable to climate change and rainfall alone. It also relates to the physical characteristics of the city's landmass, its built environment, urban governance as well as socio-economic characteristics – and the growing uncertainties that accompany these interlinked issues. We explore these aspects by examining the nexus between urban development, political economy and the science–policy interface through the perspectives of the "above", "middle" and "below".

Flooding is not new to Mumbai. It is expected and "normal" to experience waterlogging, localised inundation and disruption to transport services on a seasonal basis – especially with the onset of monsoon rains. Flooding and climate-related uncertainties in the monsoon season are usually experienced within normal bounds, and as we document in this chapter, residents of the city have devised coping and adaptation strategies accordingly. Yet, rare "outlier" events have increased since 2005 – ranging from cyclone threats to droughts or extreme rainfall variations. For example, in July 2020, the city recorded its wettest month on record (Chatterjee 2020) with threats of the "worst cyclone in decades", Cyclone Nisarga in the same year, prompting the evacuation of tens of thousands of people (BBC 2020). Every year appears to bring about new climatic challenges, and in 2020, the pandemic was added to the mix. Thus, a new type of radical uncertainty is emerging that lies outside the bounds of what is regularly experienced – straining tried and tested coping and adaptation mechanisms, with implications for future urban policy and development.

What makes Mumbai so vulnerable? The coastal megalopolis is a complex urban landscape that represents a microcosm of the conflicts, threats, opportunities and uncertainties that global integration, economic growth, demographic transition and climate change bring forth. It is the financial capital of India and one of its largest urban agglomerations with a population of over 12 million people in its municipality (Census of India 2011) and an estimated 20 million plus in the metropolitan region. The increasingly dense built-up space in central and suburban Mumbai has diminished scarce open spaces that act as flood plains, limiting water percolation and leaving central areas of the city highly flood prone. Disappearing coastal wetlands, flood plains and poor disaster governance (Revi 2005, 2008) further heighten Mumbai's vulnerability to already chronic flooding. The destruction of mangroves in the city and its periphery has aggravated livelihood threats to the thousands of Koli fishers, the original inhabitants of the city, along the east and west coast (Chouhan et al. 2016). Nearly half of Mumbai's residents live in informal and temporary dwellings with limited provision of basic services such as clean water, education, sanitation and healthcare (de Wit 2016). Across the city, the most severely affected residents from flooding, and displaced by infrastructure projects tend to be poorer, socially excluded and are forced to live on marginal, low-lying land. Inadequate sanitation, solid waste management, poor governance and illegal construction activities compound threats from regular rainfall events and climate change to leave the city and its residents highly vulnerable (Revi 2005; Hallegatte et al. 2010; Ranger et al. 2011; Parthasarathy 2018).

In this chapter, we explore this vulnerability context and tease out the politics and perspectives around the (changing) nature and impacts from climate change and uncertainty in Mumbai. Our focus is particularly on the city's most vulnerable residents, who make up a heterogeneous mix of migrants, castes and religious minorities living largely in informality and threatened by the intersection of climate change, flooding and iniquitous development interventions. We argue that the dominant pathways of dealing with climate- and flood-related uncertainties are exclusionary in nature and vie for control through structural measures, while not integrating alternative planning ideas or evolving climate change threats into urban governance and policy. The chapter proceeds as follows: we first briefly sketch out our conceptual framework, proceed to describe Mumbai's socio-economic profile, before engaging with the narratives, understandings and approaches from the "below", "middle" and "above" – informed by our ethnographic fieldwork – and end with a concluding discussion that presents our main findings.

Conceptual framework: uncertainty in urban Mumbai

Climate mitigation and adaptation concern much of contemporary urban development planning and policy. Urban centres in the global South play a vital role in achieving climate targets because of their importance as population centres, drivers of economic growth, vulnerability to climate impacts and also sources of greenhouse gas emissions (While and Whitehead 2013; Heynen 2014; Kumar *et al.* 2020). The "mainstreaming" of climate priorities into development planning, urban governance and policy has concomitantly accelerated, albeit with mixed results that heighten the possibility of maladaptive action (Eriksen *et al.* 2021) and long-term climate risk integration into planning falling short in India's urban centres (Singh *et al.* 2021). How do we conceptualise our research in Mumbai with respect to these issues? Vulnerability studies underpin much of existing work on climate adaptation (Adger 2006), with different interpretations of vulnerability having implications for the way adaptation action is framed and practised (O'Brien *et al.* 2007). We go beyond understanding adaptation merely as a response to climate stimuli in a separated human–environment system. Instead, we understand adaptation as part of an existing vulnerability context that is premediated by socio-historic and scaled economic, cultural and ecological factors. We also respond to Ribot's critique of "locating causality within the hazard" (2014: 667), and the undue focus in the risk-hazard literature on proximate causes for vulnerability, which pays little attention to causality by sidestepping interacting socio-ecological processes that leave people vulnerable in the first place. In contrast, a more technically, natural science-informed framing of adaptation concentrates disproportionately on homogeneous, quantifiable limits and costs and benefits. Responses here concentrate on techno-managerial solutions that leave little space for differentiation and political contestation (O'Brien and Barnett 2013; Eriksen *et al.* 2021). As discussed in the Introduction and Chapter 2, despite the apparent limitations of dominant, quantitative methodologies and their efforts to vie for "control" through static, deterministic approaches (van de Sluijs 2005), they remain at the forefront. This is demonstrated by the disproportionate attention that technical measures receive in adaptation and resilience projects as well as "universalist" urban planning approaches (UNEP 2014; Zeiderman *et al.* 2015) that rely on centrally designed "master plans" as instruments to achieve a set of economic, social and political goals (Watson 2009).

Uncertainty, as we conceptualise in this book, is becoming an ever more important feature in climate and development debates in urban areas. Urban agglomerations form "cluster points" for various uncertainties to meet in a turbulent age of globalisation, migration, environmental change and technological upheaval (Zeiderman *et al.* 2015). These uncertainties fall into ontological and/or epistemological categories (Walker *et al.* 2003) and as we distinguish in the Introduction, fall into ecological, knowledge/epistemic and political economy domains (see also Mehta *et al.* 2019). As discussed in the Introduction, uncertainty in climate change projections compound the problem for urban policymakers to formulate strategic responses in adaptation or mitigation realms. For example, to what height should storm surge barriers be built, based on what projections and at what location? Ecological uncertainties extend to those found in the knowledge realm. In the case of Mumbai, as we show, a pertinent example of aforementioned "knowledge politics" is the approach to "control" or "tame" flooding through the construction of boundary walls along the Mithi river and other drainage channels – prejudicing one knowledge regime over alternatives that might be anchored on local peoples experience but are deemed "unscientific". Uncertainties also extend to the political economy realm where they may be a product of social differentiation (gender, caste, class or ethnicity), historical or political arrangements. These warrant an exploration of the diverse range of institutions, processes and structures (climate-related and otherwise) that "modernist" urban planning approaches have so far largely bypassed (Watson 2009). Urban governance itself emerges here as a source of uncertainty, in conjunction with a confluence of social, political and economic uncertainties that intersect with ecological ones in intricate ways (see also Parthasarathy 2018). The location, origin and nature of uncertainty also differ depending on the kind of climate-induced impact one is studying and on the social actors that are the subject of interest.

We understand a transformation of this vulnerability context in broad terms according to Few et al. (2017), in the sense as adaptation that generates transformation as outlined in Chapter 1. In the urban context of Mumbai, this implies that social and environmental justice goals (equality, inclusiveness and participation), a co-production of knowledge that acknowledges plurality and incorporation of environmental values in planning and a departure from "business as usual development", would emerge as priorities. At the core of transformation lies a re-configuration of relative power dynamics that address the factors which enable vulnerability in the first place (lack of housing, gender and caste discrimination) and goes beyond strengthening of resilience, technical measures or disproportionate attention towards incentivising coping action (Ribot 2014).

Methodology

We used methodological tools and approaches that were ethnographic and qualitative in nature. These included transect walks, key informant interviews, group discussions, structured, semi-structured interviews and key event analysis. Snowballing was used extensively to locate key informants. Interview guides developed over the heuristics of the "above", "middle" and "below" were used to identify respondents, pose research questions and follow up on analysis. A cross section of respondents that are reflective of gender, class, polity, academia and bureaucracy was subsequently interviewed. These included several key government officials with the Mumbai Metropolitan Region Development Authority (MMRDA), Mithi River Development and Protection Authority (MRDPA), Brihanmumbai Municipal Corporation (BMC) – including its disaster management cell, Maharashtra Forest Department and Maharashtra Pollution Control Board (MSPCB) working on disaster and urban governance issues. In addition, professors and scientists from the IIT-B, Tata Institute of Social Sciences (TISS) and National Environmental Engineering Research Institute (NEERI) who have been involved in water, flood, development and disaster management planning were interviewed, as well as civil society figures from leading think tanks, environmental non-governmental organisations (NGOs) and civil society organisations (including Vanashakti, Observer Research Foundation [ORF], Mithi Sansad, fisher and residential associations). To protect the identity of respondents, their names and designation have been anonymised. In addition, a literature review covering policy documents, scientific articles, newspaper coverage, reports and other sources was conducted. Data collection by the research group took place during multiple field visits in the period from 2015 to 2020 covering different seasons. In total, more than 130 interviews were conducted, providing a rich data set. Where possible, interviews were recorded and transcribed; otherwise, detailed field notes were taken. Government reports, newspaper clippings as well as transect walks over the duration of different study periods were consulted in efforts to identify sites.

Study sites

Maximum city Mumbai

Mumbai, formerly Bombay, sits mostly on reclaimed land, in building efforts that date back to the 18th century. The first settlers in this area were fishers belonging to the Koli community who now reside in 45 Koliwadas (fishing villages) spread across the nooks and corners of the greater metropolitan area. Bombay city itself grew out of seven islets, Colaba, Old Woman's Island, Bombay, Mazgaon, Parel, Mahim and Worli, which were connected over the years from inter-tidal zones to lay the physical foundation stone for the city. This process continued over two centuries and ended with the last major official land reclamation in the 1970s at the southern tip of Mumbai at Nariman point (Perur 2016) with unofficial reclamation continuing even now. Today, the city is composed of a contiguous 438 km^2 landmass surrounded by the Arabian Sea, Harbour Bay and Thane creek on three sides. Administratively, Mumbai is composed of two parts, the island district to the south with the downtown area hosting the most densely populated parts and the suburban district reaching towards the inland.

Most of the city's landmass lies between 2 and 5 m "above" sea level, with some areas lying "below" the high tide mark (Hallegatte et al. 2010; Pramanik 2017). The most visible, "hard" manifestation of exponential, unregulated growth is the mushrooming of high-rise residential towers, transport infrastructure (e.g. flyovers, metro) which stand in contrast to poor public facilities, housing and deteriorating air and water quality – interspersed with spots of affluence found in malls and iconic public infrastructure projects such as the gleaming Mumbai international airport or the state-of-the-art Bandra–Worli sea link. Real estate in densely populated central Mumbai belongs to the most expensive in the world. An estimated 220 billion USD investment volume in civic infrastructure is required in the metropolitan area over the next 20 years alone to accommodate the needs of this growing city, according to global consultancy firm McKinsey (Thomas 2018). Many mega projects including the Mumbai metro, Navi Mumbai airport, the trans-harbour link and coastal road project are already being constructed in fits and starts despite legal obstacles.

Migration has historically played an important role in shaping the city's burgeoning informal economy, which provides for the bulk of employment. Migration has also traditionally been a source of inexpensive labour and contributes to the heterogeneous character of its population, attracting people from all states of India and beyond. In recent years, however, population growth in the central parts of the city has slowed, in part, because of overcrowding and higher rental prices but also because of employment opportunities in the suburban areas and changing demand for skills in response to established industries (such as tanning or textiles) either becoming defunct or relocating (de Wit 2016). Economic prowess combined with the diverse migrant community, relatively liberal culture and colonial history has produced a uniquely wealthy and cosmopolitan city boasting of the richest municipal body in India (de Wit 2016).

Mumbai is a city of stark contradictions and inequality with immense wealth, corporate power and poverty co-existing side by side, with slums and modern high-rises jostling for space just a few metres apart. The intense mix of people, economics and politics over a confined, dense and contested space led to the popularised label of "maximum city" (Mehta 2004). The city also has the dubious distinction of having the highest proportion of slum dwellers relative to the total city population in India with an estimated 40–55% of the population residing in such areas (Census of India 2011; Alexander and Bhatia 2020).

Population growth, land reclamation and economic development contributed to extensive alterations of the metropolitan region's biophysical environment. Mangroves play a role in reducing wave strength, soil erosion and provide ecosystem services important to reduce the effects from climate extremes and sea-level rise. They also play a crucial role in the livelihood strategies of vulnerable fishing communities in and around Mumbai, by providing safe sanctuaries and a breeding ground for fish. According to Vijay *et al.* (2005: 310), 50,000 Koli fishers are active in the region. There is competing demand on mangroves for various land uses in the city, and this has led to a 40% decline in mangrove cover between 1990 and 2005, despite protective legislation (Vijay *et al.* 2005: 310; Singhi 2015).

Climate change in Mumbai

Climate change is affecting the city in profound ways. As a low-lying coastal city built on reclaimed land, sea-level rise is one of the most notable threats and is estimated to lie between 2.5 and 3 mm annually at present (Pramanik 2017).

Projections expect a further average rise of 30–80 cm by 2100 (TERI 2014) with a study (Larour et al. 2017) finding that glacial melt alone could account for a 15 cm rise in sea levels over the next century. Mangroves are specifically vulnerable to sea-level rise because of their location at the interface of the sea as "between 0.4–0.9 m 'above' mean sea level" (Ellison 1989 cf. Jagtap and Nagle 2007: 331; Vivekanandan 2011: 17). A recent study by McKinsey found that up to three million people will be severely threatened by a combination from sea-level rise, flooding and high tides by 2050 (Woetzel *et al.* 2020). Sea surface temperatures off the Arabian coast have already registered an increase of 0.32 °C per decade from 1985 to 1998 (Khan *et al.* 2004). Likewise, mean atmospheric temperatures have risen by 2.4 °C (from 1881 to 2015; NASA 2015) and are projected to rise to 1.5–1.8 °C by 2050 (TERI 2014). Heavy rainfall is a regular occurrence in this region during the south-west monsoon from June to September, with an average precipitation of 2420 mm per year. Changing climatic configurations will likely intensify rainfall variability (18% rise in minimum and maximum precipitation) and tropical cyclones are expected to become more frequent (TERI 2014; D'Monte 2017). The occurrence of health effects ranging from an increase in vector-borne and communicable diseases to those related to heatwaves is also set to increase (TERI 2014).

Politics and perspectives from the "above", "middle" and "below"

Mumbai's population is highly heterogeneous and comprised of varied, oftentimes competing interest groups. As one of the most densely populated cities in the world and with a high concentration of wealth and extreme poverty in the central and flood-prone areas interspersed with fishing villages, the politics of the city are complex – even by the standards of a megacity. In the following section, we tease out some of the key experiences, perceptions and responses that respondents from the "above", "middle" and "below" have voiced with regard to climate change, urban development and flooding in relation to intersecting uncertainties.

Climate change and uncertainty from "below"

"Climate change" emerges as a multifaceted term among the residents of Mumbai. Its link to a global phenomenon is not always straightforward, with considerable uncertainty regarding attribution in an urban environment. For some respondents, it relates mostly to weather changes at a local level. According to a taxi driver in Bandra: "Earlier there was a familiar pattern of rainfall in Mumbai, but now it has become very erratic, for the last couple of years there has been very poor rainfall" (Interview December 2017, Mumbai). As discussed in Chapter 2, instead of perceiving climate change as a long-term phenomenon with distinct implications, local residents often perceive even wide-ranging temperature and precipitation changes as a local outcome of development activities. Growing population, urban mismanagement, a densely built-up environment, depletion of natural resources or vehicular pollution are often reference points to attribute environmental changes. Interviewed residents in most colonies along the Mithi riverbank and closely adjacent areas perceive the weather to have become hotter and less predictable. The intensity of monsoon showers was also observed to have changed when we interviewed residents in the commercial hub of Saki Naka (near the international airport). Additionally, people noted that ambient temperatures increased alongside a reduction of cooling sea breeze. In other densely populated and built-up areas, with few open spaces like Dharavi, these perceptions on experiencing increasing heat were particularly pertinent. A female shopkeeper in Dharavi highlighted how oppressive the heat has become alongside a reduction in "cooling winds". Yet, daily livelihood uncertainties usually eclipse those from climate change. These include inflation rates, access to affordable housing, water and other basic services, job security and the threat of communal conflict.

For upper-middle-class residents such as an elderly couple in Bhandra (West), the scientific and global dimensions of climate change are more relatable. Climate change is perceived here as a distinct phenomenon. Temperature and precipitation changes, glacial melting, flash floods, urban heat island impact and the spread of diseases find recognition. Climate change is, thus, part of an established, global discourse in addition to local environmental changes. On the other hand, a stronger emphasis hinges upon divinity and less on "pollution" with other sections of society when discussing climatic changes, including with the Koli community. The role of different climatic patterns and extreme weather (e.g. thunderstorms, cyclones) is also associated with supernatural phenomenon, over which there is little or no human control and influence.

Koli fishers interviewed in Mahim, Versova and Cuff Parade are intimately dependent on marine and coastal ecological systems and articulate a nuanced understanding of environmental changes. According to the Koli respondents, climate change manifests itself in the form of depleting fish catch and increasing uncertainty in interpreting weather signs. Nevertheless, the main reason cited for their livelihood uncertainty lies in Mumbai's unbridled and expansive growth where Kolis and Koliwadas (urban fishing villages) are turning into sites of conflict between powerful interests, including commercial trawlers, real-estate developers and conniving state actors. In addition, the immediate coast is suffering from pollution and depleting fish stocks on account of the double stresses of ecological changes and overexploitation (Chouhan et al. 2016). Kolis dominantly fish within an exclusive 12 km radius from the coastline, a zone reserved for small/artisanal fishers. Altered weather patterns and changed seasonal patterns have led to decline in the quantity of fish available in this radius although it is not a uniform opinion across sites. Yet, unusual changes in temperature over the land surface impact wind patterns and most respondents insist that there is a direct connection between weather conditions and fish stocks. The older generation reported that they had a good understanding of time and location of fish breeds – without technological aids like modern GPS/sonar systems. These traditional knowledge systems rely on reading weather signals, where not only wind but also astronomic signals such as a star constellation or the moon position help in predicting weather patterns. However, environmental changes have considerably reduced predictability, contributing to a new type of radical uncertainty. Fish movements have changed, and some species entirely disappeared or are reduced to negligible numbers. Rainfall intensity and patterns have also shifted. Prolonged periods of rain lasting up to two weeks were regular earlier, but this has reduced to intense downpours within a shorter span of time – to days/hours – with reduced wind speeds. Over the last 15 years, the cooling effects from monsoon showers and wind have also decreased according to a fisher in Cuff Parade who reported that extreme and memorable weather events such as cyclones are becoming more frequent.

The certainty of flooding and uncertainty from development planning

As discussed earlier in this chapter, flooding is a common occurrence in the city during the monsoon. However, one event stands out. The massive rains and floods in the last week of July 2005 (*bada paani* in local slang and also referred to as the 26/7 event) that killed more than a thousand residents with nearly an entire years rainfall descended on the city within 24 hours. All respondents – cutting across class lines – who lived in Mumbai during that time, remember it as a traumatic event and as an "outlier". While the livelihood loss was much more pronounced with poorer residents who lived in shacks and lost their entire livelihood, middle-class residents remember it as an event where they lost access to power, remained stuck in traffic, had to wade through water or escape from dangerous flood waves and faced health hazards. Yet, beyond this "extreme event", there exists a certainty around annual flooding and it is perceived as a not unusual event – despite damages and interruptions caused every year. In terms of impact, there is a differentiation between wealthier/middle-class residents who live in flat complexes (on higher ground or in higher stories) versus those who live directly adjacent to Channels/along the Mithi river and in shacks that can get washed away.

At the same time, while monsoonal rainfall is viewed to be natural and "certain", waterlogging is socially, politically and economically constructed. Haphazard urban development – building over water bodies, failure to increase the capacity of stormwater drains, changes to nallahs and streams/creeks and poor solid waste management practices were cited as key reasons in addition to inequalities in social and economic status. As a result, not all people or localities face similar levels or impacts from flooding – the intensity and effect is usually a function of a differentiated socio-economic status and location. Geography and terrain, municipal attention as well as people's collective involvement and power in maintaining or improving their immediate residential areas explain differential experiences. There is more certainty in avoiding flooding in areas that are on higher ground, for instance – but are also more expensive to live in.

In areas that experience regular inundation (e.g. in Saki Naka, Kurla or Dharavi), the chronic nature of flooding has prompted residents to resort to opportunistic coping measures. They told us that accumulated knowledge and the drawing on "lived memory" helps tide over regular flood events, with several anticipatory steps taken to manage and limit uncertainty. Following the 26/7 event, interviewed residents along the Mithi and its tributaries display a higher level of sensitivity to the river flow following heavy rainfall and undertake control exercises themselves. Disaster preparedness and warning systems are community-based. Once a visible danger mark is exceeded (marked through drawn lines along walls or the flooding of key structures), residents quickly disseminate information through informal networks and take precautionary steps. Adaptation measures, that is, those that go beyond short-term coping, include the construction of double-storied (popularly referred to as 1+1) structures – wherein valuables are stored and sleeping spaces are made available on the upper stories of a building – including for neighbours living in lower storied structures as documented in Indira pipeline colony. The normal flooding level is defined by marks on walls that lie within pre-defined uncertainty bounds. But were an "abnormal" flooding to re-occur outside these bounds, the only option is temporary relocation or evacuation. There exists little faith and expectation in early warning to have changed by state agencies: "in the 2005 flooding we saw the police running away shouting for others to follow…this was disaster warning at that time" (Interview March 2016, Mumbai). Residents also mention that some structural measures including higher boundary walls and the widening of channels have increased drainage capacities but not enough to stave off heavy monsoonal rainfall. Similarly, it was reported that increasing the boundary wall height in one area simply pushes the flooding onwards to other low-lying locations.

How do other residential areas fare? In pockets of middle-class and relatively wealthier areas, within Bandra (East) and adjoining Kurla Pipeline Road localities, low-lying areas are also flood prone and interspersed by densely populated slums, where prolonged waterlogging is not unusual. Places like Airlines Colony in Kalina are not as prone to floods over regular rainfall periods because structural measures like concretisation such as boundary walls and small steps prevent flooding. Similarly, in Kherwadi locality of Bandra (East), flooding is more of a concern because it is densely populated with slums and middle-class residential flats lying adjacent. Many residents from posh Bandra (West) mentioned that post-2005, residential complexes took up concretisation autonomously around compounds and roads within their premises. We were shown around different stretches with new concretisation to prevent even minor water accumulation, where wealthier compounds attempted to insulate themselves from waterlogging. A side effect of these uncoordinated and autonomous activities was to increase uncertainty, vulnerability and flood proneness for other colonies that might not have resources to institute similar measures or are even lower lying. This effort also showcases the extent to which a lack of municipal involvement (from ward level upwards), co-ordination and structural socio-economic inequality increase uncertainties for some while reducing them for others. Concretisation efforts are in addition blamed to contribute to the urban heat island effect and limit groundwater percolation (Fernandes 2019). The failure to undertake similar interventions in other public spaces within Bandra (West) is problematic, but not exclusive to this area. In affluent south Mumbai, rare waterlogging was experienced in 2020 after intense rainfalls. A respondent mentioned that "At this point, even people in South Bombay know what flooding is like now after all this" (Interview October 2020, Mumbai) and attributed it to misguided and intrusive infrastructure development in connection with the metro and coastal road project, in addition to climatic changes.

The contestation between mitigation and adaptation priorities, with the former dominating the city discourse, was evident during our fieldwork in the poorer localities. The prospect of forced dislocation of unregulated residential colonies along the Mithi river – in the name of flood mitigation – looms large and is one of the greatest uncertainties poorer residents face. Inextricably related to flooding is drainage and solid waste management, which is of common concern for all respondents. Respondents state that poorly managed drainage and callous mismanagement of solid waste creates serious problems for drainage flow, in addition to numerous health hazards. Muslim residents in colonies where they are in the majority expressed frustration that despite promises, the BMC does not collect garbage and they are in effect forced to use drainage channels to dispose of waste material/sewage – forcing the clogging up of channels as a result of neglect. In some of these areas, the household waste relates to the livelihoods they are involved in which are home based – for example, garment sweat shops. There is also uncertainty on which of these belong to household/industrial waste.

The flooding of 2005 and Mithi river have a clear relationship in the minds of Mumbai's residents. Yet, there is little uptake among those we interviewed (especially the middle-class) to stark warnings of academics and environmental activists with respect to the state's plans and actions of concretising and taming the river. Respondents expressed that city authorities need to ensure that issues like desilting, preventing sewage and pollution from entering the river, channelising and widening of natural rivulets like the Mithi are a must to prepare for future extreme flooding events. For some wealthier interviewees, who have travelled widely, examples of other large, flood-prone cities that draw on other solutions to mitigate flood risk are used to contrast what is happening in Mumbai. The same respondents insist that mangroves must be preserved to bear with cyclone events in the future and also improve the air quality of the city.

Flooding did not emerge as a main concern for the Koli fishers. Instead, their main livelihood uncertainties stem largely from the infrastructure projects that have encroached upon the coast, fishing grounds and mangrove land. At present, the coastal road project is the most important intervention around which Kolis are protesting against and which causes livelihood and ecological uncertainties. The project to construct a 29.2 km long freeway from north-south Mumbai on its eastern coastline has been mired in legal conflicts and temporarily stalled before resuming work in 2020. A fisher we met at a public hearing on the project in Khar Dhanda in 2020 called the project out for "finally putting an end to the remaining fishing in our Koliwada" (Interview January 2020, Mumbai) because of the land reclamation along the coast, destruction of boat landing and fish breeding grounds as well as effects on coastal currents through the building of giant stilts that support the freeway. At the same public hearing we attended, the coastal road project and its planning were cited by a group of female activist's as emblematic of the lack of acknowledgement of Koli livelihood rights, sensitivities for coastal ecology and the top-down nature of project implementation. Despite petitions, protests and promises to take action on their behalf, construction on another mega project – the coastal road continues on core harbour and fishing grounds of the fishers along the eastern coast – creating immense livelihood uncertainties and also having implications for the city's ecology. There is also a clear gender bias in the impacts and uncertainties, with women from the fishing community loosing space and income for their shore-based livelihood activities that include pre- and post-harvest preparations.

Views from the "middle"

No uncertainty here: the flood-prone city

Considerable uncertainty exists regarding why exactly the city is so flood prone, how far climate change is responsible and what the way forward is. Many of the interviewees agree that cause and effect here are subject to complex interactions that include climate change but are not limited to it. One commentator employed at a prestigious social science institute when prompted on the uncertainty of flooding stated that:

> Mumbai is a city of seven islands, with 66 villages on either side. Mumbai was marshy land and all surrounded by water. Lot of land has been reclaimed. It was certain that flooding was going to happen, and it's not an unexpected event.
>
> *(Interview May 2016, Mumbai)*

The commentator elaborated, in line with other respondents, that activities to stem flooding are mired in controversy, delayed and suffer from planning uncertainties. Over the past 20 years, most planned activities (88% according to the respondent) have never been implemented, which partly explains the city's vulnerability to flooding. The research director of an institute asserted that "basically the State itself, in the case of Mumbai, gave up on the idea of planned development" (Interview May 2016, Mumbai). Recommendations from comprehensive studies and committees like the Chitale committee report[2] (2005) have barely seen any or only piecemeal implementation. Similarly, the BRIMSTOWAD (Brihanmumbai Storm Water Drain System) project has seen the completion of only 38 out of 58 planned projects in the past 14 years (Singh 2020). Several interviewed academics attribute the lack of resolution in completing construction activities to the lack of resolve on the part of the bureaucracy, red-tape, corruption and "vote bank" politics that protect illegal settlements and structures, thereby obstructing water discharge from stormwater drains and the Mithi river. The solutions to stem flooding and uncertainty by controlling it through engineering mean, for example, retainer walls, pump stations and the deepening of the Mithi river, are not perceived as problematic, especially by academics who are influential in proposing and designing policy solutions.

An academic working on disaster management mentioned that since the 2005 deluge, capacities to deal with flooding have increased and improved. The expert noted that from 225 mm of rainfall that could be drained, the capacity has now increased to 450 mm, increasing the uncertainty bounds – but not sufficient for extreme events on the scale of 26 July 2005, where 946 mm of rainfall was recorded over 24 hours. Disaster response mechanisms underwent similar reform by improving response time, co-ordination between civic agencies and expanded emergency capacities. The NDRF (National Disaster Response Force) controls equipment (e.g. boats), manpower and other resources located in Goregaon (suburb in Mumbai) that can be quickly deployed to respond to severe flooding or other disaster events. Engineering solutions themselves are not perceived as problematic by a section of "middle" respondents. However, another expert, when prompted on the solution lying in techno-centric measures emphasised with respect to giant pump stations being constructed at multiple locations (e.g. Juhu) that "Pump stations...where do you take the water and where do you put it? Tides push the water back into land!" (Interview May 2016, Mumbai). A recent study (Fernandes 2019) confirmed this assessment which noted that only six of the 186 drainage outfalls to the sea are "above" the high tide mark, which is when the worst flooding occurs. Mumbai's geographic features are not suitable and sustainable for this kind of intervention of forcing drainage out to the sea.

The conflict between removing informal settlements – being a key livelihood uncertainty for the "below" – and "reclaiming" natural drainage space along the Mithi river as weak as other drainage channels and spaces is acknowledged but proves to be a contentious issue. What about these underlying root causes related to "encroachments"? The historic influx of poorer migrants and pressure on already scarce land is a reason cited for the proliferation of obstructive settlements and flooding. In contrast, a social scientist elaborated here that housing and the multi-generational nature of family units which requires long-term planning is totally ignored and contributes to the constitution of officially labelled "slums" or "encroachments", including in sensitive wetland areas. Most people from the "below" in Mumbai work in the informal sector and provide low-cost labour, with their location in the central areas essential to provide low-cost services. This is largely unacknowledged in the mainstream discourse.

> The middle class is reacting to an informalised settlement, with which they are not in sync. Their aspirations of the city is basically in terms of a city which services them... The middle class today, in a city like Mumbai survives on the poor.
>
> *(Interview May 2016, Mumbai)*

The lack of concern to provide safe and affordable housing for economically marginalised people is an important but often ignored factor in flood proofing and adaptation. Here, social justice and equality tie in with livelihood- and flood-related uncertainties. From an urban perspective, the "invisibility" of the informal sector became "visible" in the aftermath of the COVID-19 outbreak in 2020 when many migrants left urban areas. In the aftermath of this distress migration, labour for various services was lacking (from domestic workers to factory workers) and caused temporary supply chain disruptions. An environmental activist substantiated that while there are often complaints about informal settlements, residential towers for middle-class and upper-middle-class sections are aggressively built and encroach on fragile lands, including mangroves or wetlands and face much less opposition vis a vis informal settlements.

Regarding the iniquitous development approach, the state has also reneged on its obligation to allow for participatory planning and delimited opportunity structures for shaping development discourses and imaginaries. Planning horizons of government and state agencies tend to follow short cycles and are influenced by electoral considerations – creating significant institutional uncertainties (Interview May 2016, Mumbai), in the words of a researcher in a leading academic institution.

> ...since the 90s the government has really been engaged with project planning and keeping things away from the public, plan the way which was public but not participatory and in doing projects one is basically taking them out of the public space.[3]

This stands contrary to the devolution of localised planning directives under the 73rd constitutional amendment (1992/1993). Another prominent activist working on environmental issue for more than two decades substantiated that the proposals by the respondent and likeminded people have been met with neglect and largely ignored.

> They call me anti-development... on every issue I have protested and raised awareness [waste dumping, mangrove destruction] I have provided an alternative solution...but no one listens or incorporates the alternatives. Instead, politicians and bureaucrats are influenced by the building mafia and money power
>
> *(Interview April 2016, Mumbai)*

The view of being labelled anti-development for providing alternative solutions or questioning certain projects was frequently cited by other social and environmental activists as well as critical academia.

On institutional uncertainties and mangroves

The lack of addressing basic, civic issues like sewage discharge figures prominently in the discourse around flood uncertainties. As a respondent noted, "Sixty per cent of the populations sewage comes straight into the river" (Interview May 2016, Mumbai). Therefore, drainage channels are chocked up and prevent discharge of excess surface water. While efforts to clear possible chocking points exist, institutional infighting and uncertain jurisdiction pose challenges. "Contractors are only given contract to remove silt. There is an institutional issue as to who is responsible for clearing the nallahs. The Indian railways says that it is the BMC [Brihanmumbai Municipal Corporation] and vice versa" (Interview May 2016, Mumbai). This does not mean that no efforts have been undertaken, but jurisdictional overlaps and boundaries complicate planning and sustainable outcomes. As a governance researcher from a think tank noted:

> MMRDA [Mumbai Metropolitan Region Development Authority] makes one plan, BMC makes another plan. MMRDA is with state and BMC with city…if there is different political parties in power with MMRDA/BMC blame game ensues. Other important stakeholders in the planning process that have confused co-ordination are Indian railways, Port trust, CPWD [Central Public Works Department].
>
> *(Interview May 2016, Mumbai)*

A simple measure like cleaning drainage channel does not happen regularly, what could and should be done every 15 days happens only once a year according to the same respondent.

The responsibility for mangroves is characterised by a similar process of institutional uncertainty with several departments involved in their management (e.g. fisheries, forests, revenue). Some of this uncertainty ensues because of ecological uncertainties related to the dynamic nature of mangrove growth and expansion into areas where they were not found previously. Ecological knowledge and political-economic uncertainty intersect here at multiple scales and provide a backdrop for contentious debates. Most "middle" respondents agreed that mangroves play an important role in flood mitigation and climate change adaptation. However, an engineering expert highlighted that mangroves are a controversial topic and questioned their role in flood mitigation "they are more useful in protection against tsunamis…but obstruct tidal movement and water outflow". Other respondents across academia and think tanks opposed this view and pointed towards the protective qualities they provide against a range of natural hazards. It is precisely for these properties (pollution control, coastal erosion, tidal buffers, ecosystem services) that they require conservation and protection. Mangrove conservation is also interlinked with questions around livelihoods and housing.

Migrants and poorer sections of society settle on "open" wetlands because of the lack of alternative cheap housing. Mangroves are subsequently destroyed and displaced. As a social science researcher highlighted: "policy for low-cost housing should be implemented. Delhi has shelters, why not Mumbai? Also protects the forested/protected area". Effective social policy becomes a harbinger of better ecosystem protection and flood mitigation in this narrative.

Some environmentalists tend to take a different view. For them, preserving mangrove ecosystems is essential if Mumbai is to survive in the long term. They emphasise the ecological value of mangroves and importance for climate change mitigation and adaptation, citing scientific studies for the same and see in it a struggle of "environment vs people". The best flood control measure is then to restore the Mithi river and surrounding wetlands to a "natural state" with inherent self-healing and regulating properties.

> The Mithi is the most important flood control in the city and if the river is to be saved it needs restoration. look at it now and you don't even recognize it as such' and 'walling the river is a nonsensical solution.
>
> *(Interview April 2016, Mumbai))*

What the environmental activists lament is a dilution of protective law and insufficient enforcement of existing statutory wetland regulations. Quite contrary to the way, other actors perceive the "biopolitical" creation/use of law and its anchoring in a politics for control. Another prominent environmentalist substantiated that the BMC, MMRDA and CIDCO (City and Industrial Development Corporation)[4] instrumentalise scientific and institutional uncertainties around mangroves by claiming that they are a cause of flooding and justify land conversion exercises accordingly. Money power and greed are the driving forces for the strategic capture of fragile lands according to many interviewed "middle" actors. Fighting court cases to steer/shape development outcomes – especially by NGOs appears in the short term to be the main avenue of resistance according to respondents.

Transformative pathways and climate change

How has the city so far dealt with the issue of climate change? Most respondents, especially NGO members, paint a rather stark picture of apathy and missed opportunities. According to a prominent social activist:

> I was part of the first panel discussion on climate change… if we were to run through some of the key decisions of the government in the past few years, they do not align themselves with either adaptation or mitigation at all.
>
> *(Interview May 2016, Mumbai)*

An NGO leader and lawyer, when talking about the Mumbai metro project, questioned whether it will be able to operate once flooding aggravates due to higher sea levels and more intense rain. Mega infrastructure projects of this nature are also considered to contribute to flooding by obstructing the outflow of water to drainage channels and the sea. Other interviewees did not see evidence of an integrated planning approach that is climate friendly and integrate climate risk into planning decisions. For instance, instead of expanding a pedestrian and cycle friendly city with more green and public spaces, the emphasis appears to promote mostly personalised, motorised transport. A leading urban planning and transport expert, in the context of the coastal road project, stated that there is a strategic effort to silence legitimate concerns by affected communities, while increasing ecological uncertainties of its fragile coast and accentuating socio-economic inequalities by promoting transport for the wealthier middle-class (Interview January 2020, Mumbai). All respondents perceive adaptation activities following the 2005 flooding as "incremental" and don't see evidence of any kind of transformation. "In 2016 if we're still seeing fires, still seeing the same amount of waste going to dumping grounds, clearly the system has not learned anything" (Interview May 2016, Mumbai). However, the identification of causality for this vulnerability differs. For one, underlying problems appear to lie in fundamentally skewed growth trajectories that are at the heart of carbon-centric industrialisation, neo-liberal growth paradigms and the climate crisis – all generating massive uncertainties that the city is finding increasingly difficult to manage "industrialisation and urbanisation are false concepts…climate change is a symptom and we need to return to a nature friendly, community based lifestyle" (Interview October 2017, Mumbai). This is a rather extreme view but supported by a person employed in a major multinational company and active in the same NGO. Other environmentalists also hinted at the same issue. Respondents said that some climate change impacts are obvious and not so uncertain. Mumbai is a sinking city, with climate change-induced sea-level rises likely to swallow parts of it in future. Not acknowledging this "scientific fact" and longer time horizons in planning will be disastrous. A lawyer and activist at the forefront of many legal struggles in the city added that a relocation of parts of Mumbai further inland is a necessary transformative option in the long run and must be explored. At present, however, few respondents saw transformative changes on the anvil. Recourse to judicial mechanisms was, in contrast, often quoted by respondents as more realistic option to galvanise or restrict projects, and there is a need for "judicially related reports to be fully implemented".

The head of a fisher's co-operative society in Versova painted a stark picture of the prospects for the fishing community. According to him "in 10 years' time, there will be no fishing community here" (Interview April 2016, Mumbai). The pressures from ecological (including climatic changes) and political economy uncertainties, such as climatic changes and changing aspirations among young people pose excessive stress and don't leave enough opportunities for the continued existence of the Kolis in the heart of Mumbai. Already today, out of 600 members in the co-operative, only 50–60 fishers regularly use their 12 boats. Another fisher representative from Cuffe Parade provided a more complex narrative. He mentioned that while young people face livelihood uncertainties and struggle for gainful employment in the fisheries sector, they are interested to take up rights and economic issues through new media and technology. Livelihood uncertainties stem mostly from development projects like the Shivaji statue, coastal road project and large trawlers that compete on unequal terms with local fishers. Within the dynamics of the city, the fishers have a sense of powerlessness against large corporate entities and conniving state power. Despite promises and protests, their concerns regarding infrastructure interventions have not been heard. Young people, because of the multiple uncertainties in traditional professions, seek alternative employment in the service sector that provide a more certain income…but still retain a "fisher identity".

Views from "above"

Climate change is a certainty

All the respondents from the "above" acknowledged that climate change is a reality, albeit with contested ideas on the influence and role that climate science and modelling has at the local level and especially in a built-up urban space such as Mumbai. More details on the views of scientists interviewed will be covered in detail in Chapter 2. A senior official with the MMRDA and MRDPA was clear in his assessment that today's urbanisation and climate change pose unique challenges but added that the government is already taking responsive steps, especially on the mitigation side. Mitigation policy options that focus on reducing carbon intensity in industries, increasing energy efficiency (e.g. LED lamps) and planting more trees on the lines of the "smart city" narrative was emphasised. The MMRDA is active in promoting green building codes and transport options, be it the new metro project, solar roofs on government, private buildings or water harvesting technologies. However, the "government can only do so much", community-level involvement and behavioural change are key aspects to change in addition to private initiatives. Educational institutions are important to reach younger people, build awareness and motivate participation, that is, through cleaning their neighbourhoods and not throwing garbage into channels. This ties in with the need to anchor climate issues within an everyday context "everyday living is a priority not global change". Another senior official with the disaster management cell added that in response to a variety of natural hazard threats the government has initiated steps to increase disaster response capacities, including those stemming from global climatic changes. Low-cost technological options were also emphasised by a MSPCB official as being pivotal to achieve mitigation targets. Specifically, technology transfers from the developed world are required in the absence of resources and know-how.

Controlling floods and the role of mangroves

How does the "above" relate to uncertainties surrounding flood control and mangroves management? With respect to flooding, a senior official from the MRDPA added that "flooding in Mumbai is not an uncertainty, it is a certainty" (Interview April 2016, Mumbai). However, attributing rainfall as a causality is a key problem when framing the planning discourse around flood proofing. It acts as a diversion from addressing real issues by a host of actors. Flooding "is a result of high tides, rainfall, encroachments, sedimentation, concretisation and the urban heat island affect as well as infrastructure projects such as the Mumbai airport" (Interview April 2016, Mumbai). However, the official substantiated that since 2005, the BMC and MMRDA have undertaken a number of steps to protect the Mithi river and allow for greater flood proofing. It was conceded that despite marginal improvements no transformative change has taken place. What solutions exist? There are "no soft solutions for hard problems, hard solutions are required". This implied freeing adjacent land around the Mithi from illegal encroachments and strictly enforcing legal regulations around land usage. In connection, it was acknowledged that dilemmas and uncertainties exist; especially with trade-offs that revolve around housing and jobs. Solutions need to be found nevertheless in conjunction with rehabilitation, and this can only be achieved with civil society participation. It was also noted that environmental variables still do not figure actively in planning narratives, including with climate change policy, a point that needs improvement and a change in governance procedures. Actionable steps on how this can be achieved were, however, not forwarded.

According to a respondent who was a senior engineering consultant to flood mitigation projects in Mumbai, "The Mithi flood wall is based on experiences from other cities", pointing out that such interventions have worked elsewhere (i.e. in Singapore). The consultant added that the "government comes to us [scientific institution] to seek advice on flood mitigation however there is no continuity in governance". He added that "science itself is not at fault, however it is not used for the people, we need good science and good scientists" (Interview April 2016, Mumbai). As to the ineffectiveness of the engineering solutions to prevent regularly occurring inundation, the engineering expert substantiated that "our science is not at fault and the engineering structures work" (Interview April 2016, Mumbai). Instead, the onus with respect to the lack of proper implementation and outcomes is placed on governance and political uncertainties that prevent a translation of knowledge into practice. Based on political exigencies (e.g. bureaucratic appointment to key positions being a highly sensitive exercise), key personnel in the urban planning sections of the BMC or MMRDA are shunted out from office before their terms expire or are replaced by bureaucrats with very different expertise and approaches. In turn, this prevents continuity in governance and harms the implementation of flood control and mitigation projects.

An interviewee at the BMC disaster management cell highlighted that "response capacities to flooding have considerably improved and we can react now within a very short time". While flooding on the scale of 2005 is not preventable, regular flooding does not pose a major hurdle in terms of disruptive potential.[5] The BMC disaster management cell is well networked and makes extensive use of technology to quickly receive information, for example, from the IMD (Indian Metrological Institute), which is then processed, civic agencies alerted and response activities quickly levied to address any physical disruptions (fallen trees, electric shutdowns, rescue, etc.). These capacities did not exist in 2005 and signify a transformation within disaster management, combined with a better management of uncertainty. The use of modern information and communications technology, like smart phone apps also provide early warning and helpful tips to every citizen on how to behave during a disaster event. The caveat being that the respective app has been downloaded only a few thousand times. The official also pointed out how important it is to be quick and efficient in disaster response in a city such as Mumbai.

"If there is disruption in services it creates a political storm, even regular maintenance disruptions is a major issue". He, however, conceded that flood mitigation itself has not been very successful. "There is priority towards actionable, immediate interventions that allow the city to function [without any long term planning] ... Mumbai is so complex, with so many interests it is very difficult to...take right steps" (Interview January 2017, Mumbai).

On the matter of sewage and obstruction to the Mithi river flow, an official from the MSPCB asserted that "The cleaning up of the river doesn't require any rocket technology, it's a very simple one, to prevent the sources, that is the minimum requirement" (Interview April 2016, Mumbai). He also asserted that most of the polluting industries have been shifted away and "Mumbai it doesn't have a problem of the industry, it's the problem of the residential solid waste". This is on account of traditional industries such as textiles increasingly having shifted outside of central Mumbai.

A departmental engineer at the BMC described the steps taking to install pumps, barriers and construct concrete walls in areas that were flood prone. The engineer stated that these interventions were designed according to rainfall data, inundation areas and vulnerability maps and prevent recurrent flooding. All interviewed actors agreed that collaborative efforts at the community level are required for successful adaptation and better disaster preparedness to be achieved but did not provide concrete steps on how such participation and collaboration can be achieved that will improve on existing processes. The Mumbai Development Plan 2034 was referenced by some "above" and "middle" actors as a positive initiative, receiving widespread input from various civil society groups and citizens, yet it was also criticised by activists who pointed to the lack of location-specific flood planning, a focus of the plan on maximising construction heavy built-up environments and ignoring climate change concerns (Joshi 2019).

A bureaucrat with the mangrove cell explains that the strategic capture of mangroves by the building mafia and "slumlords" remains an issue. Also, debris from construction activities and dumping are problems. However, the department has been active to fulfil its mandate to prevent encroachments and "4000 illegal hutments in Mumbai were demolished on encroached land" (Interview January 2017, Mumbai). The mangrove cell, constituted in 2012 to consolidate governance among different departments (forest, revenue, fisheries), has emerged as a model for combining livelihood/community and conservation activities according to the respondent. In the Mumbai region, 5,400 hectares alone are classified as mangroves and they have increased in coverage over the past few years. In the Thane creek (around Uran), there is no threat to mangroves, and in general, "the situation is better than reported now a days", with increased public education, awareness and protection. Only 12 hectares of mangrove patches are under imminent threat. In Navi Mumbai (airport development) and the trans-harbour link in Mumbai, where mangroves had to make way for development projects, "blood money" had to be paid by the actors involved, those funds (186 INR crore) flowed into the establishment of a mangrove trust that pays for compensation, conservation and rehabilitation of people and forests across the region. Similarly, for small farmers, "mangroves are a curse", as their land become valueless, don't allow for agrarian activities and invite state involvement. This private–public partnership could be a model for the future. At the same time, the official remains sceptical of other infrastructure interventions and expresses a sense of powerlessness against interests that push giant infrastructure projects like the coastal road project.

Concluding thoughts

In this chapter, we engaged with the narratives, understandings and approaches of the "below", "middle" and "above" in the urban context of Mumbai and the various interlinked uncertainties that the city and its people confront. As we illustrate, substantial differences exist in the way that actors from the different heuristic categories (and sometimes within) understand, experience and respond to uncertainties arising from flooding, climate change and development interventions. We uncovered the deeply unequal nature in which these uncertainties are distributed, with poorer and marginalised sections of the "below" being the worst affected people in the city, having to confront a confluence of livelihood and ecological uncertainties. These include, in particular, Koli fishers facing existential threats from the construction of exclusionary development projects such as the coastal road zone project and suffering from dwindling fish stocks as well as migrants and poorer people residing in informality along the Mithi river and similar areas living in constant fear of eventual displacement and flooding. We also highlighted the complexities and uncertainties that exist in Mumbai when tackling issues of flooding and climatic change.

Climate change as well as issues around its attribution emerge as a nuanced and socio-economically differentiated phenomenon. For most interviewed respondents, climate change manifests itself through changing rainfall patterns, increasing heatwaves and powerful winds. While for the middle-class, there is a tenuous connection to the scientific conceptualisation of "climate change", this is not so much the case for poorer residents living in informal settlements in central Mumbai. They also point to pollution, the built-up environment, loss of green spaces and divinity for the more extreme weather and climate shifts. For marginalised Koli fishers, on the other hand, the effects are most pronounced with their traditional knowledge systems increasingly becoming obsolete, unable to adapt within short time spans to climatic and ecological alterations. Fish grounds have also shifted or are depleted although this is mostly linked with pollution, damage to marine ecology and unsustainable fishing practices by large trawlers.

Repeat flooding events over recent years illustrate how endemic the nature of flooding remains and is likely to aggravate in future with climatic change becoming ever more pronounced – be it through sea-level rise or extreme variations in rainfall. In 2020, even the wealthiest parts in south Mumbai, which mostly escapes flooding, were hit. Flooding in low-lying areas around the Mithi river has come to be expected and normal, especially during the monsoon season, but constitutes a source of episodic uncertainty for the "below", which has been met with local and autonomous adaptation action that is usually not coordinated with state planners or institutions (e.g. concretisation around flat complexes) and hits the poorest people the hardest. While disaster response efficiency appears to have improved, little progress has been made on flood mitigation. Much of this lack of progress was also attributed to insufficient long-term planning, where climate and flood risks are actively considered in planning prerogatives and incorporate local realities (geographic and socio-economic). The increasing incidence of extreme weather events also signals the emergence of an era of radical uncertainties that urban planners will have to confront. Existing policy frameworks, including the Maharashtra State Action Plan on Climate Change, Mumbai's National Disaster Management Plan or Mumbai's Development Plan 2034, have fallen short to incorporate long-term climate risks, focusing instead on mitigation action, short-term responses or economic growth maximisation.

Adaptation interventions are heavily informed by "above" actors and overwhelmingly directed at structural improvements that are more amenable to dominant pathways of decision-making, embedded in the political economy of the city, its governance regime and rely on technical measures. These are interventions that seek to control flooding through concretisation and various engineering solutions. The "middle", civil society activists and some academics feel sidelined in deliberations around flood control planning and highlight how their alternative suggestions are routinely bypassed. This does not mean that no improvements have taken place. Retainer walls have been built, drainage capacity increased and pump stations built. Yet, all these interventions fall only within the coping realm, in fact, often creating new spots for flood uncertainties to emerge as "below" respondents reported. Structural interventions, including the construction of pump stations, also fail to take into consideration Mumbai's unique geography with respondents from the "middle" highlighting the tenuous physiography, low-lying city and sensitive ecology that surrounds Mumbai. Governance approaches in Mumbai remain fractured with central, state, urban and local agencies unable to effectively coordinate, network or jointly create more inclusive and long-term planning alternatives. This institutional uncertainty was pointed out by all heuristic categories as a key issue that prevents planning and proper execution of urban development projects, including for flood mitigation.

We, thus, see that urban governance and development modes in Mumbai are driven by a desire to control and follow universalist planning modes, with insufficient capacities to acknowledge and incorporate uncertainties, plural perspectives or incorporate the concerns of its most vulnerable residents. What could be a way forward? A shift towards a plural perspective is a precondition for the city to transform from its current state of vulnerability and address multiple, intersecting uncertainties in a more sustainable and equitable manner. This would also allow for more communicative planning that draws on multiple knowledge regimes and actors, involves participatory planning exercises, better integrated and coordinated city and regional planning, a prioritising of public goods and services, and a continued sensitising of the public and officials towards ecological and civic realities. As Edelenbos *et al.* (2017: 15) observe, urban development "cannot be controlled and steered from one point ... and needs efforts to collaborate rather than efforts to control". A shift in Mumbai's exclusionary approach of urban governance and development is, thus, much needed and key when addressing the multiple, intersecting uncertainties, including from climate change, that confront the city and its most vulnerable residents.

Acknowledgements

The authors would like to thank the IIT research assistants and scholars Abhiram Sarahsabude, Sagat, Nandankumar, Suddhawati and Hemant Chouhan for sharing their expertise, time and patience. We would also like to thank the anonymous respondents for their active participation, insights and time when carrying out this research.

Notes

1. See: https://www.youtube.com/watch?v=-RM_Kh4NbSg&ab_channel=Ultra Cinema.
2. The Chitale committee report, accepted by the government, pointed towards encroachments along riverbeds and basins, land use conversion and waste dumping for flood proneness.
3. Agency formed by the Government of Maharashtra tasked with urban development duties
4. Interview conducted before 2 major flood events in autumn 2017.
5. In 2016, before the monsoon, these were promised to prevent substantive inundation. However, on visiting these areas during the monsoon they were heavily inundated.

References

Abadie, L.M., L.P. Jackson, E.S. de Murieta, S. Jevrejeva, and I. Galarraga. 2020. 'Comparing Urban Coastal Flood Risk in 136 Cities Under two Alternative Sea-Level Projections: RCP 8.5 and an Expert Opinion-Based High-End Scenario'. *Ocean & Coastal Management*, 193: 105249. https://doi.org/10.1016/j.ocecoaman.2020.105249

Adger, W.N. 2006. 'Vulnerability'. *Global Environmental Change*, 16(3): 268–281. http://dx.doi.org/10.1016/j.gloenvcha.2006.02.006

Alexander, S. and S. Bhatia. 2020. 'Mapping Mumbai's Slum Challenge in Coronavirus Battle'. *The Live Mint*, New Delhi, 9 April 2020.

BBC. 2020. 'Cyclone Nisarga: India's Mumbai Escapes Worst Cyclone in Decades'. *BBC*, London, 3 June 2020.

Bhagat, R. B., M. Guha, and A. Chattopadhyay. 2006. 'Mumbai after 26/7 Deluge: Issues and Concerns in Urban Planning'. *Population and Environment*, 27(4): 337–349 https://doi.org/10.1076/iaij.4.1.5.16466

Census of India. 2011. 'Cities Having Population of 1 Lakh and Above'. Available at: http://censusindia.gov.in/2011-provresults/paper2/data_files/India2/ Table_2_PR_Cities_1Lakh_and_Above.pdf (accessed on 5 March 2019).

Chatterjee, B. 2020. '2020 Monsoon is Mumbai's Second Wettest in 10 Years'. *Hindustan Times*, New Delhi, 13 September 2020.

Chouhan, H.A., D. Parthasarathy, and S. Pattanaik. 2016. 'Coastal Ecology and Fishing Community in Mumbai'. *Economic and Political Weekly*, 51(39): 48–57.

D'Monte, D. 2017. 'Cyclones will Cause More Cyclones in Arabian Sea'. Available at: http://indiaclimatedialogue.net/2017/12/20/climate-change-will-cause-more-cyclones-on-arabian-sea/ (accessed on 9 June 2018).

De Wit, J. 2016. *Urban Poverty, Local Governance and Everyday Politics in Mumbai*. New Delhi: Routledge.

Eriksen, S., E.L.F. Schipper, M. Scoville-Simonds, K. Vincent, H.N. Adam, N. Brooks, ... and J.J. West. 2021. 'Adaptation Interventions and Their Effect on Vulnerability in Developing Countries: Help, Hindrance or Irrelevance?'. *World Development*, 141: 105383. https://doi.org/10.1016/j.worlddev.2020.105383

Fernandes, S. 2019. '70% Rise in Concretised Surfaces Increased Flooding in Mumbai: Report'. *Hindustan Times*, New Delhi, 25 September 2019.

Few, R., D. Morchain, D. Spear, A. Mensah, and R. Bendapudi. 2017. 'Transformation, Adaptation and Development: Relating Concepts to Practice'. *Palgrave Communications*, 3. https://doi.org/10.1057/palcomms.2017.92

Hallegatte, S., and J. Corfee-Morlot. 2011. 'Understanding Climate Change Impacts, Vulnerability and Adaptation at City Scale: An Introduction'. *Climatic Change*, 104: 1–12. https://doi.org/10.1007/s10584-010-9981-8

Hallegatte, S., N. Ranger, S. Bhattacharya, M. Bachu, S. Priya, K. Dhore, F. Rafique, P. Mathur, N. Naville, F. Henriet, and A. Patwardhan, K. Narayanan, S. Ghosh, S. Karmakar, U. Patnaik, A. Abhayankar, S. Pohit, J. Corfee – Morlot, and C. Herwijer. 2010. 'Flood Risks, Climate Change Impacts and Adaptation Benefits in Mumbai'. Environment Working Paper, No. 27, Organisation for Economic Co-Operation and Development, Paris.

Hanson, S., R. Nicholls, N. Ranger, S. Hallegatte, J. Corfee-Morlot, C. Herweijer, and J. Chateau. 2011. 'A Global Ranking of Port Cities with High Exposure to Climate Extremes'. *Climatic Change*, 104(1): 89–111. https://doi.org/10.1007/s10584-010-9977-4

Heynen, N. 2014. 'Urban Political Ecology I: The Urban Century'. *Progress in Human Geography*, 38(4): 598–604. https://doi.org/10.1177/0309132513500443

Jagtap, T.G. and Nagle, V.L., 2007. Response and Adaptability of Mangrove Habitats from the Indian Subcontinent to Changing Climate. *AMBIO: A Journal of the Human Environment*, 36(4): 328–334.

Joshi, P., 2019. 'Expert View: Poor Planning Destroying Lives and Property'. *Daily News Analysis India*, Mumbai, 8 July 2019.

Khan, T.M., D.A. Quadir, T.S, Murty, and M.A. Sarker. 2004. 'Seasonal and Interannual Sea Surface Temperature Variability in the Coastal Cities of Arabian Sea and Bay of Bengal'. *Natural Hazards*, 31(2): 549–560. https://doi.org/10.1023/B:NHAZ.0000023367.66009.1d

Kumar, H. 2019. '32 Dead as Worst Flooding in a Decade Hits Booming Mumbai'. *The New York Times*, New York, 02 July 2019.

Kumar, A., A.C. Pandey, and M.L. Khan. 2020. Urban Risk and Resilience to Climate Change and Natural Hazards: A Perspective from Million-Plus Cities on the Indian Subcontinent. *Techniques for Disaster Risk Management and Mitigation*, 33–46. DOI:10.1002/9781119359203.ch3

Larour, E., E.R. Ivins, and S. Adhikari. 2017. Should coastal planners have concern over where land ice is melting? *Science Advances*, 3(11): e1700537.

Mehta, L., S. Srivastava, H.N. Adam, S. Bose, U. Ghosh, and V.V. Kumar. 2019. 'Climate Change and Uncertainty from 'Above' and 'Below': Perspectives from India'. *Regional Environmental Change* 19(6): 1533–1547. https://doi.org/10.1007/s10113-019-01479-7

Mehta, S. 2004. *Maximum City: Bombay Lost and Found*. New York: Vintage.

NASA. 2015. 'GISS Surface Temperature Analysis (v4)'. Available at: https://data.giss.nasa.gov/gistemp/station_data/ (accessed on 9 November 2017)

O'Brien, K. and J. Barnett. 2013. 'Global Environmental Change and Human Security'. *Annual Review of Environment and Resources*, 38: 373–391. https://doi.org/10.1007/978-3-540-75977-5_24

O'Brien, K., S. Eriksen, L.P. Nygaard, and A.N.E. Schjolden. 2007. 'Why Different Interpretations of Vulnerability Matter in Climate Change Discourses'. *Climate Policy*, 7(1): 73–88.

Parthasarathy, D. 2018. 'Inequality, Uncertainty, and Vulnerability: Rethinking Governance from a Disaster Justice Perspective'. *Environment and Planning E: Nature and Space*, 1(3): 422–442. https://doi.org/10.1177%2F2514848618802554

Perur, S. 2016. 'Story of Cities #11: The Reclamation of Mumbai – from the Sea, and Its People?'. *The Guardian*, London, 30 March 2016.

Pramanik, M.K. 2017. 'Impacts of Predicted Sea Level Rise on Land Use/Land Cover Categories of the Adjacent Coastal Areas of Mumbai Megacity, India'. *Environment, Development and Sustainability*, 19: 1343–1366. https://doi.org/10.1007/s10668-016-9804-9

Ranger, N., S. Hallegatte, S. Bhattacharya, M. Bachu, S. Priya, K. Dhore, F. Rafique, P. Mathur, N. Naville, F. Henriet, and C. Herweijer. 2011. 'An Assessment of the Potential Impact of Climate Change on Flood Risk in Mumbai'. *Climatic Change*, 104: 139–167. https://doi.org/10.1007/s10584-010-9979-2

Revi, A. 2005. 'Lessons from the Deluge: Priorities for Multi-Hazard Risk Mitigation'. *Economic and Political Weekly*, 40(36): 3911–3916.

Revi, A. 2008. 'Climate Change Risk: An Adaptation and Mitigation Agenda for Indian Cities'. *Environment and Urbanization*, 20(1): 207–229. https://doi.org/10.1177/0956247808089157

Ribot, J. 2014. 'Cause and Response: Vulnerability and Climate in the Anthropocene'. *Journal of Peasant Studies*, 41(5): 667–705. https://doi.org/10.1080/03066150.2014.894911

Singh, C., M. Madhavan, J. Arvind, and A. Bazaz. 2021. 'Climate Change Adaptation in Indian Cities: A Review of Existing Actions and Spaces for Triple Wins'. *Urban Climate*, 36: 100783. https://doi.org/10.1016/j.uclim.2021.100783

Singh, L. 2020. '140-Year-Old Drainage System, Highest Rain Since '74 – Why South Mumbai Flooded'. *The Indian Express*, Mumbai, 7 August 2020.

Singhi, V. 2015. 'Despite Court Orders, Mumbai and Nearby Areas Lost 15–20% Mangroves, Wetlands in 5 Years'. *The Times of India*, Haryana, 11 November 2015.

The Energy Research Institute (TERI). 2014. *Assessing Climate Change Vulnerability and Adaptation Strategies for Maharashtra: Maharashtra State Adaptation Action Plan on Climate Change (MSAAPC)*. New Delhi: The Energy and Resources Institute.

Thomas, T., 2018. 'Mumbai Needs About $220 Billion for City Infrastructure over 20 Years: Report'. *The Live Mint*, New Delhi, 25 June 2018.

UNEP, 2014. *The Adaptation Gap Report 2014*. Nairobi: United Nations Environment Programme (UNEP).

Van der Sluijs, J. 2005. 'Uncertainty as a Monster in the Science–Policy Interface: Four Coping Strategies'. *Water Science and Technology*, 52(6): 87–92.

Vijay, V., R.S. Biradar, A.B. Inamdar, G. Deshmukhe, S. Baji, and M. Pikle. 2005. 'Mangrove Mapping and Change Detection around Mumbai (Bombay) Using Remotely Sensed Data'. *Indian Journal of Marine Sciences*, 34(3): 310–315.

Vivekanandan, E., 2011. Marine Fisheries Policy Brief-3; Climate Change and Indian Marine Fisheries. *CMFRI special publication*, 105: 1–97.

Walker, W. E., P. Harremoës, J. Rotmans, J.P. Van Der Sluijs, M.B. Van Asselt, P. Janssen, and M.P. Krayer von Krauss. 2003. 'Defining Uncertainty: A Conceptual Basis for Uncertainty Management in Model-Based Decision Support'. *Integrated Assessment*, 4(1): 5–17. https://doi.org/10.1076/iaij.4.1.5.16466

Watson, V. 2009. 'Seeing from the South: Refocusing Urban Planning on the Globe's Central Urban Issues'. *Urban Studies*, 46(11): 2259–2275. https://doi.org/10.1177%2F0042098009342598

While, A. and M. Whitehead. 2013. 'Cities, Urbanisation and Climate Change'. *Urban Studies*, 50(7): 1325–1331. https://doi.org/10.1177%2F0042098013480963

Woetzel, J., D. Pinner, H. Samandari, H. Engel, M. Krishnan, B. Boland, and C. Powis. 2020. *Climate Risk and Response: Physical Hazards and Socioeconomic Impacts*. London: McKinsey Global Institute.

Zeiderman, A., S.A. Kaker, J. Silver, and A. Wood. 2015. 'Uncertainty and Urban Life'. *Public Culture*, 27(2): 281–304. http://dx.doi.org/10.1215/08992363-2841868

7
BRIDGING GAPS IN UNDERSTANDINGS OF CLIMATE CHANGE AND UNCERTAINTY

Synne Movik, Mihir R. Bhatt, Lyla Mehta, Hans Nicolai Adam, Shilpi Srivastava, D. Parthasarathy, Espen Sjaastad, Shibaji Bose, Upasona Ghosh and Lars Otto Naess

FIGURE 7.1 Roundtable engagement in Gujarat, 2018 (Photo credit: All India Disaster Management Institute).

Introduction

There is a "globalising instinct" in knowledge-making about environmental change, in general, and climate change more specifically (Hulme, 2010: 559). As discussed in Chapter 2, climate change as an object of research and action is structured globally – measurements such as temperature, precipitation and carbon dioxide concentrations are fed into models that produce global patterns

DOI: 10.4324/9781003257585-7

and projections (see e.g. Edwards, 2010; Hastrup & Skrydstrup, 2012; Schneider & Walsh, 2019). At the same time, the impacts of climate change are largely felt locally and understandings of climate change and climate change-related uncertainties are shaped by local contexts and experiences (Heymann, 2019; Hulme, 2012). However, it has been argued that this global synoptic, which could be likened to a "God's eye view" of climate change, is so ingrained that local perspectives and historical contingencies are easily sidelined (see e.g. Dyson, 2015). Moreover, this tendency towards global abstraction can serve to marginalise and exclude the experiences of those living with climate change, in what is described as the "loss of the human scale" (Heymann, 2019: 1549).

How, then, can we build bridges between the ways in which climate change and climate-related uncertainties – both epistemic and ontological (cf. Walker et al., 2003; Walker, Lempert, & Kwakkel, 2012) – are understood and perceived at the global and local levels? Chapter 2 in this volume explored how uncertainty is understood by scientists and policymakers, collectively referred to as the "above". This chapter puts emphasis on how diverse actors perceive and relate to each other's understandings and knowledges and how bridging gaps in understandings and perceptions can be used to inform policymaking to better reflect how realities are understood and experienced on the ground. When we talk about "bridging gaps", we are not merely talking about translating knowledges from "above" for those "below" or vice versa, rather the notion of bridging covers a more comprehensive confluence of understandings between the "above", "middle" and "below".

To address this question, we focus on the various actors who are involved in bridging knowledges as well as the spaces and practices used for experimenting with bridging, such as roundtables and techniques for co-producing knowledge, such as participatory methodologies, including photovoice. We explore how stakeholder dialogues and roundtables that seek to break down political power and disciplinary divides can provide diverse actors with opportunities to engage with and learn from different perspectives (AIDMI, 2018; Bhatt et al., 2018). Such emerging dialogues stress the importance of bringing to the fore often hidden and varied perspectives and solutions, while highlighting the need to address epistemic diversity and the power imbalances that suppress alternative knowledges and ways of valuing. To facilitate the experiment of bridging through roundtables, we organised four distinct roundtables in three different socio-ecological settings in India (Mumbai, Kolkata, Gandhinagar, all organised by the All India Disaster Mitigation Institute) and one in Norway (Oslo, organised by the Norwegian Institute for Water Research).[1] The purpose was to bring together government officials, academics, scientists, practitioners and activists to share their perspectives and experiences and to explore how discourses on uncertainty from "below" and "above" are contested, accommodated and/or hybridised in these politically charged spaces.

As discussed in Chapter 2, the often abstract and supposedly "objective" knowledge on climate change is commonly represented by quantitative methodologies and more specifically, climate modelling, which tends to neglect the subjective and political dimensions of uncertainty (cf. Jasanoff, 2010). The global/local paradigm is, moreover, characterised by a distinctive difference in ways of viewing suggests the anthropologist Tim Ingold (Ingold, 2003; see also Schneider & Walsh, 2019). Global, two-dimensional views tend to be opaque, massive, objective, detached and distant, to mention a few distinguishing features, whereas what Ingold terms spherical views are transparent, soft, subjective, close and experienced. All living beings, due to their sensory limitations, experience their environments – including climate change – in a spherical fashion. This spherical view is retained in many traditional societies and the knowledge and experience that these societies possess about aspects of environmental change have come to be increasingly appreciated and recognised (see e.g. Mahony & Hulme, 2016; Rudiak-Gould, 2013).

The practice of bridging should involve an understanding of how knowledge and climate-related uncertainty are conceived at the different levels of "below", "middle", and "above". The experiences, knowledges and effects of climate change are local, felt by people in their daily lives, through the effects of increasing frequency of extreme weather events such as storms and cyclones, heatwaves, droughts, floods and sea-level rise (see e.g. Mehta, Adam, & Srivastava, 2019). The globalising instincts towards knowledge-making are, therefore, "psychologically sterile" as it is beyond the horizon of people's individual experience (Hulme, 2010: 560). Local people have developed practices and strategies to deal with variability in weather and ecological uncertainty, such as seasonal migration and crop diversification (Hastrup & Skrydstrup, 2012). Climate change radically reinforces these uncertainties. While there may be clear differential power relations between the "above", "middle" and "below", as shown in the previous chapters, we do, however, need to tease out how conceptions and understandings are translated across different domains, to explore the potential for negotiating and bridging knowledge practices (see e.g. Hulme, 2010; also Mehta *et al.*, 2019).

For example, through his anthropological work on how climate change is experienced on the Marshall Islands, Rudiak-Gould (2012) points to the need to appreciate how climate change is being translated. He notes that

> public knowledge of global warming depends on the translation of climate science from specialist communities to citizens and from scientific language to the vernacular; yet, no two cultures or languages being perfectly commensurable, this process of translation necessarily entails a transformation of the climate change concept

and teases out the implications for local understandings of climate change (Rudiak-Gould, 2012: 46). Further, as argued in the Introduction, the ways in which the "above" and "below" conceptualise uncertainty differ markedly in terms of the spatial and temporal emphases. Uncertainty from "below" and uncertainty from "above" are culturally and socially embedded in local institutions, practices and power relations. While various forms of climate-related uncertainty have been identified and explored within the context of science (e.g. Smith & Stern, 2011; Stirling, 2010), differences in the sources and culture of knowledge across perspectives will entail forms of uncertainty not captured by scientific terminology. Understanding and reducing these forms of meta-uncertainty, arising from the interaction of perspective-specific uncertainties, must be one of the goals of the bridging discussed here.

Gaps in knowledge and understanding between science and local perspectives are also linked to communication within the "above". The history of modern science has pointed out the dangers of extending isolated lessons across both time and space and the folly of letting elegant but inappropriate scientific ideas take root in bureaucracies and extension services (Barrett & Wittgenstein, 1978; Li, 2007). The interrelated models of ecology, resource management and property rights used to stigmatise mobile pastoralism as inherently inefficient and environmentally destructive represent a widespread and persistent example (e.g. Fairhead & Leach, 1996; also see Chapters 3 and 4, this volume). The conflicts and abuse that attend such panaceas are attributable to the failure of science to sufficiently absorb local feedback but also to the complexity of the science–policy interface (see Chapter 2); and they thus serve to undermine faith in both policymaking and the science that informs it. Climate change science, with its globalising tendency and reliance on educated guesswork, is surely not immune to these hazards.

In this chapter, we highlight how, in historical terms, subjective accounts, stories and narratives formed important parts of scientific practices more generally, later to be eclipsed by approaches that focused more narrowly on models and objectivity. While practices of knowledge-making are again opening up more generally, with calls for more democratised ways of knowledge-making (e.g. Lidskog, 2008; Stirling, 2006) and with traditional or indigenous knowledge gaining greater appreciation (see e.g. Huntington, 2011; Masinde, 2012; Masinde, 2014; Nakashima, Krupnik, & Rubis, 2018; Nakashima, McLean, Thulstrup, Castillo, & Rubis, 2012; Nyong, Adesina, & Elasha, 2007; Speranza, Kiteme, Ambenje, Wiesmann, & Makali, 2010; Williams & Hardison, 2013), there are issues of how climate change science is being framed, translated and understood. While co-production offers a potentially fruitful basis on which to bridge knowledge gaps, the concept and how it is employed needs careful consideration. We then go on to describe attempts at bridging in the Indian context in more detail, relating how roundtables that sought to bring together experts and laypeople, representatives from the "above", "middle" and "below", engaged with one another in dialogues and exchanges of ideas and perspectives in efforts to bridge the gaps in understandings and perceptions across the different domains. We discuss these experiences, before rounding off with some concluding reflections.

Climate change and the practices of knowledge-making

The ebbs and flows of opening and closing down plural practices of knowledge-making

The tendency towards abstractions and generalisations in current climate science is, in part, intrinsic. As scientists working with big data are the only ones "able to identify, define and characterise climate change", they indirectly shape what counts as the human dimensions of climate change (Goldman, Turner, & Daly, 2018: 2). Another aspect relates to the fact that climate science is intrinsically transdisciplinary, drawing from atmospheric physics and chemistry, environmental science, chemical engineering, chemistry, mechanical engineering and hydrology, among other fields and sub-disciplines. Many scholars have criticised such abstractions, calling for more nuanced approaches and understandings of what counts as climate change, how it is known and unevenly experienced and highlighting the power dynamics at play (Eriksen, Nightingale, & Eakin, 2015; Nightingale, 2016; Watts *et al.*, 2017).

This tendency towards abstraction manifests itself in other fields of scientific inquiry too, as reflected in the work of Mazel-Cabasse (2017: 343) for seismology:

> Yet, in seismology, like in many other scientific domains, progress of research over the last century has favoured the movement from *subjective accounts to instrument-produced data, allowing for the development of predictive models and probabilistic conceptions* of earthquake risk. In the process, earthquakes have become more abstract objects of science, defined mainly by complex mathematical operations and modelling.

The historian Deborah Coen (2012) relates how, in the 19th century, "scientific description of an earthquake was built of stories – stories from as many people, in as many different situations, as possible". Coen examines seismology's history as a form of "citizen science". In the 19th century, standing networks of seismic observers transformed earthquakes into natural experiments at the nexus of human behaviour and planetary physics (ibid.). There are similar experiences from volcanology, for example, how the eruptions of Krakatoa and its effects on global climate have been studied through paintings of clouds.[2] In another example of historical analysis of knowledge practices, Carey (2010) provides an account of glacial melting in the Peruvian Andes, elucidating the complex climate–society interactions underlying glacier environmental change and emphasising how economics, power relations and cultural perceptions all form part of the story. Further, the spatial turn (Agar & Smith, 2016; Ophir & Shapin, 1991) invited geographers into the discussion of scientific knowledge-making about the environment, which emphasised taking "place" and "space" seriously in environmental knowledge-making and appreciating the complexity of social–ecological interactions (Grevsmühl, 2016). The scientific discipline at the forefront of the global scientific effort to document climate change – climatology – has undergone an evolution from one of a "clearly on humans-oriented climatology" (Flohn, 1954: 11) towards "globalising reductionism" that operates only at scales (global) outside the graspable human realm (Heymann, 2019).

Such historical accounts and the more recent efforts to pay attention to space and place bring to the fore the role of subjectivity, political economy and power in shaping knowledge production practices that help inform understandings of society–nature relations. This demonstrates how the contemporary call to open up for a broader understanding of knowledge production practices is not necessarily novel, as past practices of scientific inquiry encompassed more comprehensive conceptions of what constituted knowledge.

Constructing bridges – appreciating plural practices of knowledge-making and valuation

Thinking about bridges between the "below", "middle" and "above" involves thinking about multiple forms of "local" knowledges and understandings of uncertainty and change and how these can speak to scientists and policymakers – and vice versa. The notion of bridging, then, does not merely refer to a simple construct between one set of knowledges or epistemologies and another, but rather refers to the fluid and dynamic linkages across disciplinary and sectoral boundaries and across multiple scales and actors at the "above", "middle" and "below" or "local". What, then, is "local" knowledge? One definition of local knowledge, drawn from the policy sciences, states that local knowledge is "knowledge that does not owe its origin, testing, degree of verification, truth, status, or currency to distinctive professional techniques, but rather to common sense, casual empiricism, or thoughtful speculation and analysis" (Lindblom and Cohen, 1979: 12, cited in Corburn, 2003: 421). The anthropologist Clifford Geertz defined local knowledge as "practical, collective and strongly rooted in a particular place", which constitutes an "organised body of thought based on immediacy of experience" (Geertz, 1983: 75, cited in Corburn, 2003, p. 421). There is, however, a need to avoid reifying local and expert, or professional, knowledge as monolithic entities (Agrawal, 1995; Wynne, 1996; cited in Corburn, 2003). Further, local knowledge is often "held by members of a community that can be both geographically located and contextual to specific identity groups" (ibid.: 421).

One issue that emerges when discussing different types of knowledge at different levels is what might be termed the politics of valuation. A certain politics of knowledge and valuation results in particular domains (especially so-called hard science) gaining authority over the others. Yet, all forms of knowledge (including so-called expert knowledge) are culturally and socially embedded and moulded by particular social, power and gender relations. Models are also embedded in narratives and storylines about a future based on certain assumptions (Hajer, 1995; Roe, 1994) but through a range of political practices and boundary-ordering devices gain authority over other forms of knowledge (Heymann, 2019; Shackley & Wynne, 1996; Wynne, 1996).

Framings of climate change and the question of visibility and attribution

As alluded to above, the gap between expert and local knowledge stems, in part, from the fact that climate change is understood predominantly as an intrinsically global and long-term phenomenon. The "gulf between brute, visible reality and climate change is crowded with arcane mathematics, high-tech measuring devices and inhumanly large temporal and spatial scales" (Rudiak-Gould, 2014: 121). However, if one instead labels it "long-term weather change", this is not inaccurate and it narrows down the gap, as "weather" is something everyone can relate to, as we noted in the chapter on Kutch (Chapter 4). As argued by Rudiak-Gould "the words 'long-term' and 'change' spread the word 'weather' out over a period of time, rendering the climate/weather distinction moot" (Rudiak-Gould, 2013: 123). Moreover, one could have considered using concepts such as "pervasive" or "multi-sited" to substitute for the "global" (Rudiak-Gould, 2013: 123). The tendency has been towards understanding climate as a globalised, abstract, invisible phenomenon – a statistical and technical concept described by distributions of variables as temperature and precipitation – in contrast to weather, which is immediate, visible and subjectively experienced. Another reason for globalised conceptions of climate is also the interconnectedness of, and interactions between, regional weather phenomena such as El Niño and the Indian Summer Monsoon (as discussed in chapter 2). The issue of whether climate change is visible brings to the fore the deep divisions between different disciplinary fields (Rudiak-Gould, 2013). The "invisibility" camp argues that "anthropogenic tampering with the atmosphere does not result in specific weather events but merely 'loads the dice' in a stochastic system; no individual (visible) event can be attributed with certainty to climate change" (Allen, 2011; quoted in Rudiak-Gould, 2013: 121). While some have softened their stance somewhat, conceding that individual events can, indeed, be attributed to climate change, the conflict stems from a larger battle of authority and politics. Scientists' "insistence on describing the phenomenon with the terms 'global' and 'climate' does not stem merely from a desire for terminological exactitude but from a particular political outlook in which scientific authority is central" (Rudiak-Gould, 2013: 121).

There are challenges with visibility too, though, for example, that climate change is what Rudiak-Gould terms a "promiscuously corroborable" concept, it can be used to explain all sorts of phenomena experienced by local communities (Rudiak-Gould, 2012: 52). "A middle way between understanding climate change as abstract and invisible and as local and visible, is to render it visible through translating from the useable realm of climatological abstraction into the (seeable) realm of local narratives" (Marx, 2017; cited in Rudiak-Gould, 2013: 128) and vice versa: "sensory experience on the ground breathes life and urgency into desiccated expert assessments, while scientific generality serves to unite disparate communities around the travelable concept of climate change and methodological scepticism provides a cautionary counterpoint to over-exuberant local attribution" (Rudiak-Gould, 2013: 129). This tension also came out in our roundtables where policymakers often characterise these sensory experiences as anecdotal and not something that is driven by generalisable facts (see Chapter 3).

Co-production and bridging

Thus, there is a need to bring together these sensory experiences and scientific generality. One promising avenue is the concept of co-production. The increasing appreciation of the existence of multiple epistemologies has led to efforts that aim towards co-producing knowledge (e.g. Goldman *et al.*, 2018; Jasanoff, 2004b; Lane *et al.*, 2011) which plays an essential part in efforts to bridge knowledge gaps. The concept of co-production emerged from diverse theoretical and disciplinary perspectives across the social sciences and humanities (Bremer & Meisch, 2017). One way of defining co-production, espoused by many science and technology studies scholars, is through using it to capture the interdependencies and mutual constitution of nature and society. In science and technology studies (STS) terms, co-production can either be interactional, that is, concerned with epistemic debates around scientific authority and expertise and the interface between science and politics or constitutive. Constitutive co-production raises more profound issues about how knowledge production shapes social order and science–society and politics–nature relations (cf. Jasanoff, 2004b). It could be helpful to distinguish between what Goldman *et al.* term "instrumental co-production" (Goldman *et al.*, 2018: 1) and other forms of co-production. Instrumental co-production basically refers to projects where attempts are made to fit local knowledge into existing schemes of conventional science and draws on the early usages of co-production from the 1970s, which was largely associated with the idea of "co-producing" public services (e.g. Ostrom, Parks, Whitaker, & Percy, 1978).

Some scholars prefer the term joint knowledge production (e.g. Hegger & Dieperink, 2015) to avoid the potential elision of processes that aim to engage in bottom-up collaborative knowledge-making, that is, where there is no attempt to mesh local knowledge with pre-defined sets of categories or typologies. Other terms include hybrid knowledges (e.g. Benessia *et al.*, 2012; Reid, Williams, & Paine, 2011; Thomas & Twyman, 2004), hybrid epistemologies (e.g. Burnham, Ma, & Zhang, 2016) and polysemic epistemologies (Mazel-Cabasse, 2017). While these approaches are promising, there are obvious challenges. How does one assess the salience, validity and legitimacy of coproduced, or hybrid, knowledge? Integrating different types of knowledge is inherently complex, "with no single optimum approach for integrating local and scientific knowledge" (see also Jasanoff, 2004a; Raymond *et al.*, 2010: 1775).

Moving beyond the appreciation of multiple epistemologies, Goldman *et al.* (2018) draw our attention to the notion that people engage in world-making through particular practices and thus there are not only multiple epistemologies – ways of knowing the world – but also multiple ontologies or practices of world-making. Maasai pastoralists might not necessarily experience climate change first and foremost as temperature and precipitation change, but as changes in the ability to predict the weather and changes in vegetation and animal behaviour (Goldman, Daly, & Lovell, 2016). Similarly, in Kutch (Chapter 4), the impacts of climate change are being experienced by the local pastoralists as a cascade of uncertainties that is making their livelihoods increasingly precarious. Appreciating multiple forms of world-making challenges an assumption that "most of us hold dear: that there is one reality out there, about which we can explore different perspectives" (Goldman *et al.*, 2018: 3). But if reality is understood as enacted in practice, then there are multiple ontologies brought into being simultaneously (Mol, 2002: 6), not just multiple epistemologies. Therefore, a comprehensive engagement with knowledge and attempts at bridging knowledge gaps needs to deal with both multiple epistemologies and multiple ontologies.

The project drew on various methodologies of co-production, such as transect walks, participatory mapping and – importantly – photovoice. These methodologies allowed the voices of the local people themselves to be heard and to bring into view often tacit and ignored forms of knowledge. Such co-production efforts formed a necessary basis for building bridges, as they were a means to shed light on marginalised perspectives.

Building bridges: The role of roundtables

Uncertainties in the Indian context – Mumbai, Kutch and the Sundarbans

Other chapters in this volume have provided detailed descriptions of the ways in which uncertainty has been conceptualised by the "above" (Chapters 2 and 3) and the "below" (Chapters 4–6). In the following, we recap some of the main uncertainties of the three research sites, before going on to explore the role of roundtables in bridging divides in understandings and perceptions of uncertainty and climate change.

The coastal megacity of Mumbai is one of the largest and most densely populated urban agglomerations in India, with a population of around 20 million people. It is home to a burgeoning service and manufacturing sector as well as the financial heart of India's economy. It is also a city characterised by deep social inequalities and exclusions. Mumbai has a unique coastal ecological identity, with mangroves, marshlands, salt pans and wetlands that function as potential buffers against floods and extreme weather events but that are increasingly coming under threat from urban development projects and pollution (cf. Chapter 6 on urban flooding in Mumbai).

Islanders in the Sundarbans in West Bengal have had to contend with shocks such as cyclones and floods, sea-level rise, changes in its deltaic ecology and socio-economic marginalisation. Climate change is causing frequent embankment breaching; loss of land, homesteads and other assets and salinity intrusion, leading to the depletion of the traditional agro-fishing economy and straining the islanders' coping capacities (cf. Chapter 5 on the Sundarbans).

The semi-arid district of Kutch in north-western Gujarat faces multiple climate-related challenges, such as more frequent droughts and prolonged periods of high temperatures as well as increasingly erratic rainfall patterns. Such changes are heavily affecting local people's livelihoods, including agriculture, livestock and fishing. Climate change-related challenges are exacerbated by pressures from industrial development in some of the most eco-sensitive zones, leading to a cascade of uncertainties for local people as their livelihoods become increasingly precarious (cf. Chapter 4 on Kutch).

Emerging issues from the roundtables

> Climate change is like an elephant in the story, and while people see different things (ear, tail, trunk), we need to look at it as one whole animal.
> *(January 2018, Gandhinagar Roundtable)*

This quote from an NGO participant nicely summarises the many ways in which climate and its associated uncertainties are characterised by actors from the "above", "middle" and "below".

As part of the project, we organised four roundtables, one in Norway and three in India. Roundtables were organised in Mumbai, Gandhinagar (for Gujarat and Kutch) and Kolkata (for Sundarbans) in January 2018, bringing together perspectives and experiences of government officials, academics, practitioners and activists. These were built on an earlier roundtable organised in Oslo in August 2017. The aim was to understand the way climate change and uncertainty are experienced and understood by diverse stakeholders in order to explore ways to foster transformative, socially just and inclusive development to cope with the challenges of climate-related uncertainty. The three roundtables in India were rooted in their site-specific contexts (the rapidly urbanising coastal metropolis of Mumbai, the deltaic islands of the Indian Sundarbans and the dryland dynamics of Kutch in Gujarat). The roundtables were quite distinct in both orientation and scope, due to the different locations (e.g. whether at a university, government institute or a neutral seminar venue) and the role played by the local partners and co-hosts. In Mumbai, the audience at the Indian Institute of Technology (IIT-Bombay) largely comprised natural and social scientists, with some NGOs and local fisher activists and the discussions revolved around academic discourses on uncertainty. By contrast, the Gujarat meeting, perhaps due to its location in the state capital (Gandhinagar), was dominated by government officials and policymakers from different departments, who welcomed the opportunity to engage with each other's work, alongside many researchers and NGOs. Similarly, in Kolkata, the meeting had a good mix of different scientists, researchers and NGOs as well as government officials. Power differentials were evident in all the roundtables but reflected in different ways (Mehta & Srivastava, 2020).

The roundtables played a key role in highlighting diverse understandings of uncertainty, while simultaneously opening up opportunities for sharing and learning. For some participants, the roundtable was a new experience, and they appreciated the opportunity to engage with and learn from different perspectives. For others, the roundtable rehearsed well-known diverse views and brought to the fore the challenge of reconciling these plural perspectives (Mehta & Srivastava, 2020).

All the roundtables began with a powerful photovoice presentation highlighting the precariousness of ordinary people to climate-related uncertainties (e.g. erosion of lands in the Sundarbans due to sea-level rise or the changing nature of rainfall and droughts and their impacts on livelihoods in Kutch) and how they make sense of, live with and adapt. The photovoice presentations from the three sites helped bring the voices of the communities to the policymakers through capturing their understandings of coping and adapting with livelihood hazards in the remote sites and through showcasing their indigenous understanding and insights related to climate change uncertainties, which are intrinsically geographical and place-based. These alternate views offered policymakers a valuable window into the community's understanding of issues related to mild and extreme uncertainties. These uncertainties are further compounded by wider socio-economic changes, which often destroy key ecological resources such as mangroves (on the Mumbai and Kutchi coast) that both protect the vulnerable coastline and are also key to the livelihoods and well-being of the local communities.

The presentations facilitated roundtable participants' understanding of how people living with climate change make meaning themselves, and construct what matters to them through reflecting on their own community portraits and voices and on what questions can be linked into making inclusive policies and importance of convergence and interrelation between the different state- and private-led adaptation interventions. By bringing in the communities' lived experience, the roundtables advocated for a more integrative process consisting of bottom-up and top-down actions, local and scientific knowledge and a vast array of stakeholders that would help bridge the separation of knowledge and action.

Diverse epistemologies and framings

One characteristic that clearly came out was the diversity of epistemologies and framings. People with different disciplinary backgrounds were framing climate-related uncertainties in distinctly different ways. Yet there appears to be an increasing consensus that interdisciplinary research is important in connecting various dots and bringing together scientific findings and models across fields such as climate/hydrology. A participant with a natural science background describes the trend within meteorological/climate research as follows:

> (…) I have been working as meteorologist for 40 years, and there is significant change in our behaviour (…) when I started, we were the kings (…) we decided what people should know. Now we provide forecasts and projections and people have a lot of sources (…) we need IT people/meteorologists, communication experts and social scientists; now it's a multidisciplinary task. There is scope for cross-learning too, between sociological perspectives and policy action.
>
> *(January 2018, Mumbai roundtable)*

While information sharing is key in mediating such processes, it was pointed out that training exercises for bureaucrats/policymakers can lead to better interpretation of information and more efficient decision-making. This was re-affirmed by participants from "above", "middle" and "below".

Different participants had different entry points in this discussion and looked at climate change through the lens of their sector/departments or epistemological positions. For the scientists in Gujarat, climate change is real and certain and is measured through key variables such as temperature, rainfall, sea-level rise and concentration of GHGs in the atmosphere (see Chapter 4). One scientist referred to a recent study suggesting that there would be drastic changes in the summer and winter temperatures in Gujarat and this would have significant impacts on agriculture, livestock and water resources. He argued that the "most important thing to bridge gaps on climate change and uncertainty is to focus on local scenarios of climate change" (Interview January 2018, Mumbai). Whereas for another scientist (IIT-Bombay) in Mumbai, the most important issue was that "hybrid knowledge is required to solve the problem (…) for example, hydrological as well as climate models should be combined to give overall results."

In the Mumbai roundtable, a civil society representative emphasised the need to understand the city as a fluid space, rather than a static entity. Understanding the city as an integrated urban space, paying attention to its geography and multiple constituents highlights how climate change and climate science are framed. Such an imagining of the city as greater than the sum of its constituent parts is also important for engendering social transformations that are emancipatory in nature. For instance, in imagining cities as fluid spaces, a neighbourhood can be viewed as the basic unit of transformation. In the Mumbai roundtable, the neighbourhood approach came up as an important concept for the fishing community that was dealing with climate-related uncertainties (see Chapter 6). The neighbourhood approach, which begins with empowering neighbourhoods where specific communities (like the fishing community of Mumbai) are concentrated, can then be replicated, contextualised and scaled up to cover entire cities. Such an approach can be an effective pathway to social transformations.

Similarly, vulnerable environments like the Sundarbans require pro-poor adaptation as well as the strengthening and protection of local ecosystems and biodiversity, especially mangroves, in a people-centric way. At the roundtable in Kolkata, it was discussed that various knowledge regimes and experiences, including scientific, technical, administrative and everyday practices, need to come together to plan for alternative solutions to the problems this region faces. In this regard, the state should facilitate spaces to enable sharing between policymakers and local-level policy implementers, NGOs and community-based organisations (CBOs) as well as local communities' own experiences and responses (see Chapter 5). For example, the Sundarbans Affairs Department may need to take leadership in the facilitation of such a platform.

Politics of valuation

Another key theme was the politics of valuation. Several participants emphasised the need to appreciate the importance of ecological elements, such as mangroves. A community leader, from the Koli community in Mumbai, emphasised that port development activities in their area on the outskirts of Mumbai lead to a "loss of livelihoods for future generations" and "mangroves play a highly significant role for fishing and acts as the breeding site for fishing" but that "authorities and policymakers do not have local or indigenous knowledge about seawater pathways, and inter-tidal flows". This, in turn, leads to faulty attributions, wherein the government attributes overfishing as the major reason for decreasing fish catch (January 2018, Mumbai Roundtable). It was also pointed out that comparatively little attention had been given to flood proofing in planning, largely due to a lack of understanding of the importance of ecological elements such as mangroves in flood risk mitigation. An atmospheric and climate scientist substantiated that when it comes to ecosystem services offered by mangroves, continuous evaluation is needed, even though quantitative monitoring remains difficult. The question was raised in response to the emphasis on the need to quantify value, whether one should not find alternatives to monetary valuation? This is not so much a question of economic value, as a question of political priority – it should be the local authorities' primary task to protect and prioritise local livelihoods. It is also a question of culture – cultural values, anchored in livelihood practices, exist, but do not find their way into standardised assessments as pointed out by the Koli community leader. Such assessments, framed as they are by political economy actors (corporate actors, contractors, state), are not geared towards acknowledging uncertainties, diverging valuations, livelihoods or long-term ecosystem dynamics. Traditional and hybrid forms of knowledge can be of importance in efforts to achieve more balanced and sustainable development, yet is usually ignored.

Often, such exercises tend to be opaque and closed and efforts are needed to open these exercises up, to make them more transparent and accountable. Thus, alternative approaches to the monitoring and evaluation of uncertainty and transformation actions are needed. These include standard assessments such as environmental impact assessments (EIAs) and social impact assessments (SIAs) which need to be reframed along more inclusive terms and become more participatory, to broaden up their epistemic base. A participant in Mumbai asked "(...) can EIAs and SIAs be impartial when funded through the project?". The major challenge is bringing in transparency to mandatory exercises like public hearings in EIA, which take place as closed and opaque exercises. Returning to the issue of flood proofing, it is important to look at past disaster response mechanisms with respect to flooding and what scope for learning exists and what opportunities there are for incorporating a wide range of perspectives, including that of the general public. Thus, all the three roundtables had discussions on qualitative approaches to understand the extent of climate-related uncertainties and the scope of transformation. Roundtables with a diversity of actors across different levels can be a way to achieve this.

Attribution, causality and (deflection of) responsibility

Another issue that was frequently discussed was the question of *attribution* and, aligned with this, the question of *responsibility*, or rather, the *deflection* of responsibility. According to a scientist from IIT-Bombay, attribution science (i.e. can the cause of extreme weather events be clearly traced to climate change) is not very advanced and suffers from serious limitations. However, as discussed by Mehta *et al.* (Chapter 2), policymakers are not concerned about whether a phenomenon can be attributable or not to climate change. What matters to them is *response*, not cause. The problem is, however, that limited knowledge on dynamics of various systems, as well as the sensitivity of certain information, prevents the creation of more confident projections and creates uncertainty. Attribution, thus, becomes an important question when seeking to comprehend causality to risk and vulnerability. Policymakers, disaster mitigation officials and politicians tend to blame "outside forces", thereby deflecting responsibility and accountability.

Knowledge and integration of lived experience

The need to integrate knowledge of lived experience of impacts was acknowledged across the roundtables. Translating this acknowledgement into existing research methodologies can prove to be a challenge, especially for modellers, as noted by one of the participants in the Oslo roundtable. In the Gujarat roundtable, policymakers viewed themselves as making up the "middle", as being the ones whose task it was to communicate climate science to local people. Participants acknowledged that climate change impacts are most vigorously felt at the local level, especially in terms of the changes in water supply and resources, health, livelihoods, forests and biodiversity. There was, however, a sense that local people were a form of "black box", policymakers knew very little about how they were affected by climate changes. This reiterated the standard top-down understanding of policymaking and implementation where local people are framed as beneficiaries rather than equal partners.

An example of how to engage local communities and local knowledge was offered by an NGO in Gujarat. In the projects, local community consultations are being organised around water, livelihood and ecosystem restoration, and they pointed out that more efforts are required to work on stakeholder perceptions related to climate change and uncertainty. An academic talked about vernacular architecture to understand ways of dealing with uncertainty (how people live, eat, sleep, experience and recover from trauma). There was also a suggestion that children are also important stakeholders when it comes to uncertainty and projects with a decided focus on children and uncertainty can be very useful (January 2018, Gandhinagar Roundtable).

Another concrete example that came up in the Gujarat workshop focused on health, and how changes in humidity has health impacts. This is not recognised at all by policymakers, demonstrating how more knowledge about the impacts of climate change on local people can be integrated into policymaking to make it more targeted and effective. For instance, it was pointed out by one of the participants at the Gandhinagar roundtable how climate and humidity, as variables for climate change, may not make a lot of sense to policymakers but impacts on health are more tangible and can gain policy traction. Policy practitioners are still trying to understand the impacts of new diseases and how adaptation to climate change requires behaviour change, which is quite complex. This links up to the earlier discussion around the visibility/invisibility of climate change. This insight was surprisingly prescient, given that such problems have come to the fore during the current COVID-19 pandemic.

There was also discussion about factors that exacerbate the lived experiences of climate-related uncertainty. For instance, in the Mumbai roundtable, several participants pointed out how informality reinforces the lived uncertainty, relating how small businesses in the informal sector were hardest hit during flooding. They keep limited stocks of inventory and obstruction in supply chains and production facilities have immediate cascading effects that dent income and employment opportunities. In the absence of baseline data, it is difficult to make accurate assessments of costs, damages and vulnerabilities. Insurance coverage is not available to cover losses for these small enterprises. In the formal sector, on the other hand, losses from natural disasters are often covered – displaying an unequal adaptive capacity and recovery. This demonstrates how informality and uncertainty are closely linked.

Clearly, the lived experiences of the people engaged in the informal sector are not always accounted for in framings of climate-related uncertainties by the "above" and "middle" levels. The disruption to business continuity faced by informal enterprises in the wake of climate stresses and shocks can have a lasting impact on the lives of people employed in such enterprises. This disruption and loss of livelihood opportunities represent the local-level imaginings and understandings of climate-related uncertainty that is often not integrated into policymaking. For instance, India has one of the largest informal workforces in the world. The 2018–2019 Economic Survey of India estimates that almost 93% of the country's total workforce works in the informal sector. This large chunk of the working population does not have access to insurance or other risk pooling mechanism, leaving them extremely vulnerable the adverse impacts of climate change uncertainties (see also Patankar & Patwardhan, 2016). In the Mumbai and Kolkata roundtables, insurance for informal enterprises came up as a potent method for them to deal with uncertainty. Similarly, piloting large-scale insurance and other risk-pooling options can also have large-scale implications on the future of work in a largely informal economy like India. This represents a possible pathway to social transformation.

There was more controversy, however, relating to how people's perceptions of climate change could be integrated more directly into projections and modelling (see Chapter 2). In the Mumbai roundtable, one theme that was explored was the possibility of incorporating social perspectives into modelling practices. According to a citizen scientist, it is a question of "what skills can tolerate other skills" and models require re-examination with respect to incorporating feedback. Some efforts are already emerging, for example, people mark places of local importance/vulnerability (curves, ditches, etc.) not captured in other modelling exercises through smartphone apps or other means, which subsequently feed into models and projections. Several academics and civil society actors in the Gujarat roundtable agreed that communities do have a wealth of information and that there is a need to have a local decentralised information centre, which could act as the connecting point between the "below" and "above". It was suggested that "capacity building" is not just required at the level of the community but also at the level of decision-makers who need to be sensitised to local understandings and lived experiences of climate change and appreciate the multiple interconnections of climate-related uncertainties at the local level. Therefore, policymakers and scientists need to understand the local languages or representations of climate change.

Another issue related to the integration of lived experience is the notion that landscapes are heterogeneous. Policymakers' significant lack of knowledge of the Sundarbans, for instance, is, in part due to the heterogeneity of the Sundarbans. As one researcher pointed out, the Sundarbans is not one place, but many. The "many Sundarbans" refers to various geographical locations, such as the coastal pockets, the deltaic Sundarbans, and the mainland part. Impacts from climate change are, therefore, highly localised and people are responding to the varied manifestations of climate change at the micro-scale, which must be appreciated, acknowledged and accommodated by policymakers.

Institutional complexity and fragmentation

Uncertainty due to heterogeneous landscapes and institutional complexity/ fragmentation was a theme generating much discussion. The case of mangroves and fisheries provided a peculiar case of natural resource management that has fallen between the cracks of various government departments. In Uran, near Mumbai, fishing predominantly takes place in mangrove areas during low tide. However, the land in question is mainly under the purview of the forest/ revenue department. The Fisheries Department has little influence, as its primary responsibility lies beyond the shoreline. This problematic interface between land and sea areas in the inter-tidal zone has created uncertainty that complicates governance efforts and institutional support of traditional fisherfolk. The Mumbai roundtable highlighted the possible benefits of collaboration between researchers and fishers by consistent knowledge generation to back up their legal and other struggles, a process that is not easily amenable to quick decision-making. As one participant expressed, there is a "need to spend time with the community to understand their issues."

Heterogeneity and fragmentation were key issues in the Sundarbans too. The "above" has many conflicting views depending on how they utilise resources and how they understand "development". This is reflected mostly in the divergence between goals and strategies of the line departments. Similarly, the "above" is also constrained by the government's prerogative to control resources and funding sources for the development of the Sundarbans. This acts as an obstacle in efforts to promote collective action on the part of actors in the "middle". For instance, at the Kolkata roundtable, a researcher working in the Sundarbans' health system for several years pointed out:

> When we started working in the Sundarbans, we asked the Department of Sundarbans Affairs about their plans for people's health. They stated that it is the responsibility of health department. Again, when we further probed to the social developmental aspects of health to the State Health department, they said it is not their area of concern.
> *(January 18, Kolkata roundtable also see Chapter 5)*

Such obstacles are also debilitating to the agency of "below" actors to participate in making decisions in situations of uncertainty. As has already been established, the actors from "below" seldom have their voices captured or heeded by "above" actors when it comes to taking decisions regarding uncertainty. This lack of agency is exacerbated by institutional complexity and overlaps. Institutional fragmentation of responsibility can easily lead to a sense of apathy, as is the case in the Sundarbans (see also Parthasarathy's work on the issue of institutional and epistemological "balkanization" (Parthasarathy, 2016)).

One theme that did not directly come from any of the roundtables, but which was indirectly raised in all of them, was the issue of asking the right questions about uncertainty and its concomitant impacts on society, economy and environment. More importantly, there needs to be consideration about *who* asks these questions. The agency of "above", "middle" and "below" actors is skewed in raising questions about uncertainty and ceding some space to actors from "below" in raising such questions would lead to a more integrated and holistic understanding of uncertainty.

Lack of knowledge/insufficient communication

The roundtables also highlighted how uncertainty was grounded in a lack of knowledge and insufficient communication, which was, for instance, the experience in Gujarat. Some argued that decision-makers need to be sensitised to the local understandings and lived experiences of climate change and to the multiple interconnections of climate-related uncertainties at the local level. The participants agreed that "understanding of climate change across the three levels has to improve. Even I do not understand enough about it (…) we need to speak to those who do and understand the limitations. This is why this [bringing people together] is on the dot" (January 2018, Gandhinagar Roundtable). A number of participants agreed that there exists an information gap between the "above" and "below", with poor communication between departments, between local people and the policymakers, and between scientists and policymakers.

Several participants in the Mumbai roundtable also emphasised how there was a need to improve communication, while also conveying problems relating to uncertainty and attribution. Lack of knowledge and communication issues came out as highly salient issues in the Sundarbans case as well. For instance, a climate scientist working in the area noted that Bangladesh has well-researched local-level scientific data on sea-level rise, salinity levels and subsidence or erosion rates. The Indian side does not have the same level of detail. While climate scientists based in West Bengal have worked on climate modelling of the Sundarbans, they agree that data gaps prevent better and more accurate projections. Data gaps also persist in identifying people's coping strategies. An example pertains to whether migration is a seasonal coping or permanent adaptation strategy, as there is scant official data on the actual number of migrants. As discussed in Chapter 4 on Kutch, policymakers usually like to be certain about the course of action that they can work, such as likely scenarios, but not with "something that is highly uncertain" (January 2018, Gandhinagar Roundtable). To a decision-maker, or at least from an economist's viewpoint, the question would be "what can I do to limit losses in case my expectations fail?" so that is the financial risk, that is the risk of poor women in India as well, and there is no correspondence between these two ways of understanding risk. Because, to a decision-maker, you cannot separate risk from decisions, meaning also that risk cannot be expressed in terms of one measure. It is a question of how are you controlling, who are you asking, and what is the objective of that person? For policymakers, the types of uncertainty could be summed up as situations where one can address uncertainty through improving information and communication (epistemological) and where one cannot fix uncertainty (ontological). Policymakers may be able to address the first level of uncertainty. An interesting observation was that many of the policymakers considered themselves as the "middle" in bridging the divide between the scientists and local people. A senior policymaker stated: "We can act as a bridge, we understand below and top and thus can help bridge [the gap]." In the Gujarat roundtable, it was highlighted that there is a tendency towards an elite bias in climate change, with most of the information being in English and there is a need for more vernacular representations of climate change. As a participant highlighted:

> When we work with grassroots (...) they say things, but it is not very well articulated. There is lot of literature in English but not disseminated in Gujarat (...) we need to involve below and also build capacity of local institutions.
>
> *(January 2018, Gandhinagar Roundtable)*

Discussion and concluding reflections

This chapter has focused on the potential of roundtables to bridge the gap between what policymakers do and the experiences and understandings of local people regarding climate change and uncertainty. The roundtables brought together experts in diverse fields, representatives from civil society and other actors, in an attempt to foster dialogue and deepen our understanding of the plurality of perceptions and how one can work towards bridging the gaps in understandings and perspectives.

The brief historical overview at the beginning of this chapter emphasised how knowledge-making practices in environmental realms were once potentially open to being broad and inclusive through incorporating a range of diverse narratives and stories. Subsequently, however, this openness was narrowed down to being more concentrated to a specific or relatively more closed form of knowledge-making. In recent times, there has been a re-opening of ideas and framings around knowledge-making, acknowledging the multiple forms of knowing. This is, in part, reflected through the increasing appreciation of local, indigenous or traditional forms of knowledge in much of the environmental science and governance literature. This is, to some extent, true for climate science as well. However, as discussed by Mehta *et al.* in Chapter 2, there still is a long way to go and part of the reason for this is, as pointed out, the "global" nature of climate science and how it tends towards knowledge-making that is not aligned with on-the-ground understandings, vulnerabilities and realities. Added to this is the often siloed nature of governance which is a barrier to bringing diverse knowledge into conversation Policymakers tend to base their decisions on datasets that draw on the probability of precipitation and temperature changes but have little knowledge of ground-level realities, how people themselves understand and experience climate change and climate-related uncertainties.

While there is an implicit assumption that policymakers are responsible for acting and responding to local-level realities and experiences of climate impacts, questions of attribution, causality and responsibility served to complicate such assumptions. The degree of uncertainty around causal linkages may, in some instances, lead to policy paralysis. Such inertia may be compounded by the heterogeneity of landscapes where impacts are experienced and the fragmentation of institutional ambits of responsibility. This was clearly illustrated in the case of Mumbai's coastal zone, where it is the Forestry Department that has the mandate for mangroves, but the Fisheries Department that claims authority over the coastal zones of which mangroves form an important element. Who should ultimately be responsible and how can such institutional barriers to action be overcome?

We have highlighted the usefulness of bringing together different perspectives and knowledges and exploring the potential role of roundtables, together with visual approaches such as photovoice, in elucidating the challenges and opportunities in doing so. However, there are multiple challenges associated with such efforts. While there was widespread appreciation of the importance of including social science perspectives, there was also concern about how to best incorporate local knowledges. What emerged from the roundtables was a rich set of issues that participants feel need to be addressed in order to foster more constructive dialogue and bridging practices across disciplinary and sectoral divides. Participants across the board agreed that greater awareness is needed around how multiple and diverse epistemologies and framings shape our perceptions of climate science and what counts as "knowledge". While there were useful suggestions as to how "scientific" facts about climate change could be better communicated to local communities – for example, through translating information into local languages – there was less clarity on how local people's knowledges and perceptions could be brought into knowledge-making and policymaking, especially when they are often characterised as anecdotal evidence (see also Chapter 2). While there were several examples of ongoing projects that explore more participatory approaches to knowledge-making and integration of local understandings and perceptions, there was also a prevalent scepticism among some scientists and policymakers about the credibility and validity of drawing on local people's knowledges because such knowledge was perceived as being "less scientific" and more anecdotal. This points to the need to open up understandings of historical practices in knowledge-making, as highlighted in the historical overview section and improving ways to understand and incorporate stories and narratives about change into the wider body of knowledge of climate science. In order words, how to make "invisible" knowledges of climate change visible. Another important issue linked to knowledge and knowledge-making concerned the politics of valuation. Critical valuation exercises of the economic, ecological and social impacts of climate change, extreme events and uncertainty from multiple perspectives are necessary to avoid the pitfalls of simplistic neo-classical models which are often used to justify environment-unfriendly and socially destructive infrastructure projects that dispossess local people and their livelihoods.

Realising that knowledge-making in the past was a broader, more comprehensive endeavour and that much is lost through narrowing down the scope to focus on models could help make policymakers and the "above" realise the value of bringing in more diverse, local perspectives and understandings from the "below". Thus, encouraging more qualitative approaches and reflecting on the challenges of integrating local knowledge can help deepen reflections around what knowledge is and how to think about knowledge in new ways. Key to such efforts is the realisation that spaces must be opened for local people to communicate their knowledge and uncertainties. As Jasanoff (2009) argues, the political and subjective dimensions of uncertainty at the scale of the local have to be recognised in order to achieve more effective bridging of understandings, knowledges and action. Bridging is not simply about translating knowledge, but rather it involves the generating of a vibrant traffic in understanding between the "above", "middle" and "below". In this way the global and abstract as well as local and grounded experiences are brought into meaningful conversations to create appropriate responses to climate change, while simultaneously acknowledging the limitations inherent in existing power relations and hierarchies. Through bridging gaps, we can explore possibilities for producing "hybrid knowledge spheres" in which the "below", "middle" and "above" are reoriented through thick interactions and work collectively towards transformative strategies in response to climate-related uncertainties.

Acknowledgements

We thank all the institutions that facilitated the roundtables, the Gujarat State Disaster Management Authority (GSDMA), Gujarat Institute of Desert Ecology (GUIDE), Indian Institute of Health Management Research (IIHMR), Indian Institute of Technology-Bombay (IIT-B), Norwegian Institute for Water Research (NIVA), and Department of International Environment and Development Studies (Noragric) as well as the participants for their time and active engagement. A special thank you to AIDMI for overall support and co-ordination. We would also like to thank Rohan D'Souza for constructive comments on an earlier draft of this chapter.

Notes

1 The Oslo roundtable brought together researchers, policymakers and funders to discuss uncertainty and climate change. This was the first in the series of roundtables, where the subsequent sessions would focus more on the context and challenges of the specific sites. The first roundtable in the series addressed the overarching notion of 'uncertainty' as it permeates the project work throughout.
2 See https://www.youtube.com/watch?v=MrEIT66oPqU] (accessed 15 March 2020).

References

Agar, J., & Smith, C. (2016). *Making Space for Science: Territorial Themes in the Shaping of Knowledge*. London: Springer.
AIDMI. (2018). Understanding Uncertainty: Views from Kachchh, Mumbai and Sundarbans. In *Special Issue no. 169, May 2018*. Ahmedabad: All India Disaster Mitigation Institute.

Barrett, W., & Wittgenstein, L. (1978). *The Illusion of Technique: A Search for Meaning in a Technological Civilization*. Garden City, NY: Anchor Press.

Benessia, A., Funtowicz, S., Bradshaw, G., Ferri, F., Ráez-Luna, E. F., & Medina, C. P. (2012). Hybridizing Sustainability: Towards a New Praxis for the Present Human Predicament. *Sustainability Science, 7*(1), 75–89.

Bhatt, M., Mehta, L., Bose, S., Adam, H. N., Srivastava, S., Ghosh, U., . . . Pattak, V. (2018). Bridging the Gaps in Understandings of Uncertainty and Climate Change: Roundtable Reports August 2018. In *Experience Learning Series 74*: All India Disaster Mitigation Institute.

Bremer, S., & Meisch, S. (2017). Co-Production in Climate Change Research: Reviewing Different Perspectives. *Wiley Interdisciplinary Reviews: Climate Change, 8*(6), e482.

Burnham, M., Ma, Z., & Zhang, B. (2016). Making Sense of Climate Change: Hybrid Epistemologies, Socio-Natural Assemblages and Smallholder Knowledge. *Area, 48*(1), 18–26.

Carey, M. (2010). *In the Shadow of Melting Glaciers: Climate Change and Andean Society*. Oxford: Oxford University Press.

Coen, D. R. (2012). *The Earthquake Observers: Disaster Science from Lisbon to Richter*. Chicago: University of Chicago Press.

Corburn, J. (2003). Bringing Local Knowledge into Environmental Decision Making: Improving Urban Planning for Communities at Risk. *Journal of Planning Education and Research, 22*(4), 420–433.

Dyson, F. (2015). *Dreams of Earth and Sky*. New York: New York Review of Books.

Edwards, P. N. (2010). *A Vast Machine: Computer Models, Climate Data, and the Politics of Global Warming*. Cambridge, MA: MIT Press.

Eriksen, S. H., Nightingale, A. J., & Eakin, H. (2015). Reframing Adaptation: The Political Nature of Climate Change Adaptation. *Global Environmental Change, 35*, 523–533.

Fairhead, J., & Leach, M. (1996). *Misreading the African Landscape: Society and Ecology in a Forest-Savanna Mosaic* (Vol. 90). Cambridge: Cambridge University Press.

Flohn, H. (1954). *Witterung und Klima in Mitteleuropa: mit regionalen Beitragaegen von Friedrich Lauscher über Oesterrech und von Max Schueepp*. New York: S. Hirzel.

Goldman, M. J., Daly, M., & Lovell, E. J. (2016). Exploring Multiple Ontologies of Drought in Agro-Pastoral Regions of Northern Tanzania: A Topological Approach. *Area, 48*(1), 27–33.

Goldman, M. J., Turner, M. D., & Daly, M. (2018). A Critical Political Ecology of Human Dimensions of Climate Change: Epistemology, Ontology, and Ethics. *Wiley Interdisciplinary Reviews: Climate Change, 9*(4), e526.

Grevsmühl, S. V. (2016). Images, Imagination and the Global Environment: Towards an Interdisciplinary Research Agenda on Global Environmental Images. *Geo: Geography and Environment, 3*(2), e00020.

Hajer, M. A. (1995). *The Politics of Environmental Discourse: Ecological Modernization and Policy Process*. Oxford: Clarendon Press.

Hastrup, K., & Skrydstrup, M. (2012). *The Social Life of Climate Change Models: Anticipating Nature* (Vol. 8). London: Routledge.

Hegger, D., & Dieperink, C. (2015). Joint Knowledge Production for Climate Change Adaptation: what Is in It for Science? *Ecology and Society, 20*(4), 1.

Heymann, M. (2019). The Climate Change Dilemma: Big Science, the Globalizing of Climate and the Loss of the Human Scale. *Regional Environmental Change, 19*(6), 1549–1560.

Hulme, M. (2010). Problems with Making and Governing Global Kinds of Knowledge. *Global Environmental Change, 20*(4), 558–564.
Hulme, M. (2012). How Climate Models Gain and Exercise Authority. In *The Social Life of Climate Change Models* (pp. 40–54). London: Routledge.
Huntington, H. P. (2011). The Local Perspective. *Nature, 478*(7368), 182–183.
Ingold, T. (2003). Globes and Spheres: The Topology of Environmentalism. In *Environmentalism* (pp. 39–50). London: Routledge.
Jasanoff, S. (2004a). *States of Knowledge: The Co-Production of Science and Social Order*. London: Routledge.
Jasanoff, S. (Ed.) (2004b). *States of Knowledge: The Co-Production of Science and Social Order*. London and New York: Routledge.
Jasanoff, S. (2010). A New Climate for Society. *Theory, Culture & Society, 27*(2–3), 233–253.
Lane, S. N., Odoni, N., Landström, C., Whatmore, S. J., Ward, N., & Bradley, S. (2011). Doing Flood Risk Science Differently: An Experiment in Radical Scientific Method. *Transactions of the Institute of British Geographers, 36*(1), 15–36.
Li, T. M. (2007). *The Will to Improve: Governmentality, Development, and the Practice of Politics*. Durham, NC: Duke University Press.
Lidskog, R. (2008). Scientised Citizens and Democratised Science. Re-Assessing the Expert-Lay Divide. *Journal of Risk Research, 11*(1–2), 69–86.
Mahony, M., & Hulme, M. (2016). Modelling and the Nation: Institutionalising Climate Prediction in the UK, 1988–92. *Minerva, 54*(4), 445–470.
Masinde, E. M. (2012). *Bridge between African Indigenous Knowledge and Modern Science on Drought Prediction*. Cape Town: University of Cape Town.
Masinde, M. (2014). *An Effective Drought Early Warning System for Sub-Saharan Africa: Integrating Modern and Indigenous Approaches*. Paper presented at the Proceedings of the Southern African Institute for Computer Scientist and Information Technologists Annual Conference 2014 on SAICSIT 2014 Empowered by Technology.
Mazel-Cabasse, C. (2017). Hybrid Disasters—Hybrid Knowledge. In *Resilience: A New Paradigm of Nuclear Safety. From Accident Mitigation to Resilient Society Facing Extreme Situations* (pp. 337–351). Cham: Springer.
Mehta, L. and Srivastava, S.) 'Uncertainty in Modelling Change: The Possibilities of Coproduction through Knowledge Pluralism', in Scoones, I. and Stirling, A. The Politics of Uncertainty: Challenges of Transformation, Routledge pp 99-113
Mehta, L., Adam, H. N., & Srivastava, S. (2019). Unpacking Uncertainty and Climate Change from 'Above' and 'Below'. *Regional Environment Change, 19*, 1529–1532.
Mol, A. (2002). *The Body Multiple: Ontology in Medical Practice*. Durham, NC: Duke University Press.
Nakashima, D., Krupnik, I., & Rubis, J. T. (2018). *Indigenous Knowledge for Climate Change Assessment and Adaptation*. Cambridge: Cambridge University Press.
Nakashima, D., McLean, K. G., Thulstrup, H. D., Castillo, A. R., & Rubis, J. T. (2012). *Weathering Uncertainty: Traditional Knowledge for Climate Change Assessment and Adaptation*. Paris: United Nations Educational, Scientific and Cultural Organization.
Nightingale, A. J. (2016). Adaptive Scholarship and Situated Knowledges? Hybrid Methodologies and Plural Epistemologies in Climate Change Adaptation Research. *Area, 48*(1), 41–47.
Nyong, A., Adesina, F., & Elasha, B. O. (2007). The Value of Indigenous Knowledge in Climate Change Mitigation and Adaptation Strategies in the African Sahel. *Mitigation and Adaptation Strategies for Global Change, 12*(5), 787–797.

Ophir, A., & Shapin, S. (1991). The Place of Knowledge: A Methodological Survey. *Science in Context, 4*, 3–21.

Ostrom, E., Parks, R. B., Whitaker, G. P., & Percy, S. L. (1978). The Public Service Production Process: A Framework for Analyzing Police Services. *Policy Studies Journal, 7*, 381.

Parthasarathy, D. (2016). Decentralization, Pluralization, Balkanization? Challenges for Disaster Mitigation and Governance in Mumbai. *Habitat International, 52*, 26–34.

Patankar, A., & Patwardhan, A. (2016). Estimating the Uninsured Losses Due to Extreme Weather Events and Implications for Informal Sector Vulnerability: A Case Study of Mumbai, India. *Natural hazards, 80*(1), 285–310.

Raymond, C. M., Fazey, I., Reed, M. S., Stringer, L. C., Robinson, G. M., & Evely, A. C. (2010). Integrating Local and Scientific Knowledge for Environmental Management. *Journal of Environmental Management, 91*(8), 1766–1777.

Reid, K. A., Williams, K. J., & Paine, M. S. (2011). Hybrid Knowledge: Place, Practice, and Knowing in a Volunteer Ecological Restoration Project. *Ecology and Society, 16*(3), 19.

Roe, E. (1994). *Narrative Policy Analysis: Theory and Practice*. Durham, NC: Duke University Press.

Rudiak-Gould, P. (2012). Promiscuous Corroboration and Climate Change Translation: A Case Study from the Marshall Islands. *Global Environmental Change, 22*(1), 46–54.

Rudiak-Gould, P. (2013). "We Have Seen It with Our Own Eyes": Why We Disagree about Climate Change Visibility. *Weather, Climate, and Society, 5*(2), 120–132. doi:10.1175/WCAS-D-12-00034.1

Rudiak-Gould, P. (2014). The Influence of Science Communication on Indigenous Climate Change Perception: Theoretical and Practical Implications. *Human Ecology, 42*(1), 75–86. doi:10.1007/s10745-013-9605-9

Schneider, B., & Walsh, L. (2019). The Politics of Zoom: Problems with Downscaling Climate Visualizations. *Geo: Geography and Environment, 6*(1), e00070.

Shackley, S., & Wynne, B. (1996). Representing Uncertainty in Global Climate Change Science and Policy: Boundary-Ordering Devices and Authority. *Science, Technology & Human Values, 21*(3), 275–302.

Smith, L. A., & Stern, N. (2011). Uncertainty in Science and Its Role in Climate Policy. *Philosophical Transactions of the Royal Society A: Mathematical, Physical and Engineering Sciences, 369*(1956), 4818–4841.

Speranza, C. I., Kiteme, B., Ambenje, P., Wiesmann, U., & Makali, S. (2010). Indigenous Knowledge Related to Climate Variability and Change: Insights from Droughts in Semi-Arid Areas of Former Makueni District, Kenya. *Climatic Change, 100*(2), 295–315.

Stirling, A. (2006). *From Science and Society to Science in Society.* Paper presented at the Towards a Framework for Co-operative Research. Report to the European Commission Workshop Governance and Scientific Advice. Brussels.

Stirling, A. (2010). Keep it Complex. *Nature, 468*(7327), 1029–1031.

Thomas, D., & Twyman, C. (2004). Good or Bad Rangeland? Hybrid Knowledge, Science, and Local Understandings of Vegetation Dynamics in the Kalahari. *Land degradation & Development, 15*(3), 215–231.

Walker, W. E., Harremoës, P., Rotmans, J., van der Sluijs, J. P., van Asselt, M. B., Janssen, P., & Krayer von Krauss, M. P. (2003). Defining Uncertainty: A Conceptual Basis for Uncertainty Management in Model-Based Decision Support. *Integrated Assessment, 4*(1), 5–17.

Walker, W. E., Lempert, R. J., & Kwakkel, J. H. (2012). Deep Uncertainty. *Delft University of Technology, 1*, 2.

Watts, N., Adger, W. N., Ayeb-Karlsson, S., Bai, Y., Byass, P., Campbell-Lendrum, D., ... Depledge, M. (2017). The Lancet Countdown: Tracking Progress on Health and Climate Change. *The Lancet, 389*(10074), 1151–1164.

Williams, T., & Hardison, P. (2013). Culture, Law, Risk and Governance: Contexts of Traditional Knowledge in Climate Change Adaptation. In *Climate Change and Indigenous Peoples in the United States* (pp. 23–36). Cham: Springer.

Wynne, B. (1996). May the Sheep Safely Graze?. In W. S. Lash, B. Szerszynski i B. Wynne (red.). *Risk, Environment and Modernity*. In: London: Sage Publications Ltd.

8
CONCLUSION

Hans Nicolai Adam, Lyla Mehta and Shilpi Srivastava

FIGURE 8.1 Recognising the multiple values of mangroves is important to sustain lives, livelihoods and adaptation pathways (Photo credit: Shibaji Bose).

This volume has explored the different ways in which climate-related uncertainties are understood, conceptualised and mediated by different actors in India, one of the most climatically vulnerable countries in the world. It covered case studies from coastal Mumbai to dryland Kutch and the Sundarbans delta in West Bengal and also studied the perceptions of policymakers and climate scientists, also in historical

DOI: 10.4324/9781003257585-8

perspective. The book introduced the three heuristic categories of the "above", "middle" and "below" to study diverse conceptions and experiences of climate change and uncertainty, with the caveat that this heuristic is fluid and marked by power imbalances between the "above", "middle" and "below" (Figure 8.1).

The importance of embracing uncertainty and its political nature are the key messages of this volume. Attempts to "control" or "tame" uncertainty in the context of climate change remain the primary response strategy, mostly driven by state actors and usually in the form of technocentric and top-down interventions. However, these largely falter on the ground due to dynamic and variable local systems and intersecting uncertainties. These "decontextualised" top-down policies can often hamper efforts to support locally appropriate and socially just adaptation.

Several chapters in this book have shown that predominant deliberations and knowledge production from the powerful "above" have largely failed to acknowledge finer-grained local-level realities. Instead, deterministic tools and approaches have tended to bypass or undervalue the more qualitative lived experience and conceptualisations of uncertainty from the "below". This exclusionary framing by the "above" not only faces epistemic tensions but also sidelines and dilutes valuable "experiential" knowledge and perspectives from the "below" who live at the forefront of climate change, and whose perspectives and realities are key to developing more inclusive and diverse adaptation pathways. In this regard, this volume has highlighted the critical role of the "middle" as translators who play an active role in facilitating plural approaches and act as a mediator between "above" and "below".

Climate-related uncertainties are not new. Climate extremes, variability and seasonality in the Indian subcontinent have been part and parcel of everyday life for generations, and a wide repertoire of knowledge and practices have been developed by the "below" to cope and adapt to them. However, the timing, scale and intensity of climatic patterns have changed, sometimes drastically, signalling the anvil of a new age of radical uncertainty that increasingly falls outside the coping range, which communities have traditionally relied on.

The often devastating impacts of climate change are not the only sources of anxiety and uncertainty for local communities. As we described in this book, dominant concerns for poor and marginalised people relate to daily, existential threats that revolve around livelihoods, access to resources or land that interact with climate-related uncertainties. Uncertainties are being accentuated or re-enforced when people are left disenfranchised and disempowered through forced displacement (Mumbai), state neglect (Indian Sundarbans) and progressive marginalisation of traditional livelihoods (Kutch), leaving them with token livelihood alternatives. For example, the case of chronic flooding and retainer wall construction in Mumbai is an obvious case of maladaptation (Chapter 6). Similar examples are discussed across the volume, which outline the socially differentiated impacts of climate-related uncertainties that often exacerbate the vulnerabilities of the most marginalised communities, especially women. For example, the empirical findings have demonstrated the gendered implications of increasing vulnerabilities linked to climate-related uncertainties and how these add to women's existing daily burdens.

What could be the way forward for concept, policy and praxis? Multi-sectoral and interdisciplinary approaches are required to understand the impacts and manifestations of uncertainty. It is important to challenge the positivist understanding of uncertainty that dominates science and policymaking. Social science aspects concerning socio-political issues, gender dynamics and site-specific vulnerabilities of different social groups and how these interact with climate-related uncertainties also need to be included in mainstream debates (Bhatt *et al.* 2018). It is also important for actors from "above", "middle" and "below" to see different aspects of climate change while recognising the values (and opportunities/limitations) of diverse knowledge regimes. The book has highlighted that a power re-configuration through epistemic and cognitive justice for vulnerable people is a key component to develop transformative pathways.

For this, one needs to recognise and embrace the perspectives from the "below" and bring their voices and concerns to the centre stage of climate action. While policymakers often find it uncomfortable to work with high degrees of uncertainty at the local level, ignoring it is no solution either. There is a need to factor uncertainty into decision-making and scientists also need to effectively communicate the role of uncertainty in their forecasts and models. Instead of paralysing decision-making, effective communication of uncertainty configurations across all heuristic categories can facilitate inclusive change (Bhatt *et al.* 2018). The building of "hybrid alliances" that allow multiple actors (researchers, NGOs, activists, state, ordinary people), disciplines (humanities, natural and social sciences) and perspectives on climate change to come together promises to enable the sharing of knowledge and expertise.

Drawing on creative methodological experiments such as roundtables, we argued that there is a potential to harness this diversity to facilitate practices of engagement and co-production between diverse stakeholders. For example, the use of visual methods such as photovoice and photo stories can effectively capture the lived and tacit experiences of uncertainty. Besides providing agency to the "below", who have often been categorised as "subjects" of research, such approaches provide a voice to vulnerable and marginalised communities, making them active participants in research and the creation of knowledge. Such co-produced research requires sustained engagement but can potentially empower people to shape the conditions of their lives, creating spaces to produce and disseminate knowledge and actively shape development and research processes (see Mehta and Srivastava 2020).

Hence, co-production of climate knowledge will require altering the modernist and homogenising frame of knowledge production and dissemination that has for long colonised practices through target-oriented top-down framings. This means embracing more decentralised and plural ways of knowing with an aim to co-produce both new knowledges and social orders (Mehta and Srivastava 2020).

We have also outlined the challenges in such processes in tackling existing power relations and existing social and gender inequities. We, thus, argue for a more granular, localised, participatory and place-based understanding of climate-related uncertainty to provide entry points to enable a bottom-up transformation that pushes social justice, equity and more inclusive adaptation. This must go hand in hand with a radical re-structing of power relationships that puts the concerns of the most vulnerable people centerstage (O'Brien 2012; Ribot 2014; Taylor 2014; see the Introduction chapter). Climate action and policy will have little meaning or could even be counterproductive unless they are mobilised to question deep-seated inequalities and unjust framings that feed into epistemic closures and deny possibilities of having plural pathways (Scoones *et al.* 2015; Newell *et al.* 2021).

Bottom-up approaches to transformation may, in fact, provide an entry point to challenge precisely such incumbent power structures. In such spaces or "patches",[1] specific processes (alliances, initiatives) are challenging dominant trajectories of development, and where relations of power and knowledge are being reconfigured in more heterogeneous and deliberative ways to challenge dominant framings of nature–society relations and create spaces in which new practice emerge (see Mehta *et al.* 2021). It is also at this "local level" where climate impacts ultimately materialise and complementary responses to market or state directives are formulated. In order to nurture such transformative pathways, new discourses and stories are required to guide our actions. This can be through challenging dominant narratives around what unproductive landscapes are (Kutch) or support different narratives and storylines that emerge from small and incremental changes, experiments and mobilisations and percolate into giving birth to new ideas, values and social norms that are more adept at addressing climate-related uncertainties. However, one needs to remain attentive to structural political economy factors and ensure that the burden of responsibility for adaptation is not shifted "downwards" to the most vulnerable people (Taylor 2014; Blythe *et al.* 2018).

The ongoing pandemic has laid bare problems with local to global inequalities, unequal access to public goods such as health, water and sanitation as well as the unsustainable nature of human–nature relations, all of which underpin the global climate crisis. The pandemic has also intersected with ongoing crises of food, water and climate, thus threatening already fragile livelihoods, especially in marginal environments creating compounded uncertainties and vulnerabilities for marginalised people. In most countries, the responses from "above" have been inadequate, too late, or even failed. In India, the right-wing authoritarian government has used the pandemic to "other" and victimise minorities and marginalised groups, while using the pandemic time to push through controversial and unsustainable projects bypassing social and environmental concerns. Despite inadequate responses from "above", in many cases – even in our research sites – there has been a burst of local forms of mutual aid and solidarity as well as civic action. There are also many examples of resilience at the local level, especially amongst communities that have largely relied on subsistence production (Pickard *et al.* 2020; Mehta *et al.* 2019, 2021).

Lastly, the injustices of the pandemic, especially India's deadly second wave, have called for fairer and more just futures, including the need for investment in public goods and to address issues concerning climate justice. The post-COVID recovery period should, thus, build on reflections, trends and lessons and hopefully bring about the systemic shifts badly needed to address locally appropriate and socially just transformations to sustainability in an increasingly uncertain world.

Note

1 The concept of patches and praxis is investigated in a follow-up project TAPESTRY. For more information, see https://steps-centre.org/project/tapestry/.

References

Bhatt, M.R., Mehta, L., Bose, S., Adam, H.N., Srivastava, S., Ghosh, U., Movik, S., Narayanan, N.C., Naess, L.O., Parthasarathy, D. and Wilson, C. 2018. *Bridging the Gaps in Understandings of Uncertainty and Climate Change: Round Table Reports*. Experience Learning Series 74. Ahmedabad: AIDMI.

Blythe, J., Silver, J., Evans, L., Armitage, D., Bennett, N.J., Moore, M.L., Morrison, T.H. and Brown, K. 2018. 'The Dark Side of Transformation: Latent Risks in Contemporary Sustainability Discourse'. *Antipode*, 50(5): 1206–1223.

Mehta, L. and Srivastava, S. 2020. 'Uncertainty in Modelling Climate Change: The Possibilities of Co-production Through Knowledge Pluralism'. In *The Politics of Uncertainty: Challenges of Transformation*, edited by I. Scoones and A. Stirling, 99–112. London: Routledge.

Mehta, L., Srivastava, S., Adam, H.N., Bose, S., Ghosh, U. and Kumar, V.V. 2019. 'Climate Change and Uncertainty from 'Above' and 'Below': Perspectives from India'. *Regional Environmental Change*, 19(6): 1533–1547. https://doi.org/10.1007/s10113-019-01479-7

Mehta, L., Srivastava, S., Movik, S., Adam, H.N., D'Souza, R., Parthasarathy, D., Naess, L.O. and Ohte, N. 2021. 'Transformation as Praxis: Responding to Climate Change Uncertainties in Marginal Environments in South Asia'. *Current Opinion in Environmental Sustainability*, 49: 110–117.

Newell, P., Srivastava, S., Naess, L.O., Torres Contreras, G.A. and Price, R. 2021. 'Toward Transformative Climate Justice: An Emerging Research Agenda'. *Wiley Interdisciplinary Reviews: Climate Change*, e733. https://doi.org/10.1002/wcc.733

O'Brien, K. 2012. 'Global Environmental Change II: From Adaptation to Deliberate Transformation'. *Progress in Human Geography*, 36(5): 667–676.

Pickard, J., Srivastava, S., Bhatt, M. and Mehta, L. 2020. *In-Focus: COVID-19, Uncertainty, Vulnerability and Recovery in India*. Brighton: Social Science in Humanitarian Action (SSHAP).

Ribot, J. 2014. 'Cause and Response: Vulnerability and Climate in the Anthropocene'. *Journal of Peasant Studies*, 41(5): 667–705.

Scoones, I., Newell, P. and Leach, M. 2015. *The Politics of Green Transformations*. London: Routledge.

Taylor, M. 2014. *The Political Ecology of Climate Change Adaptation: Livelihoods, Agrarian Change and the Conflicts of Development*. London: Routledge.

INDEX

Note: **Bold** page numbers refer to tables; *italic* page numbers refer to figures and page numbers followed by "n" denote endnotes.

AchutaRao, K. 36
activist-oriented groups 99
actors 28, 162, 179, 188
Adam, H. N. 5, 15
adaptation planning 45
adaptation policy 6
adaptive capacity 3, 4
adaptive management practices 7
administrative lexicon 56
aerosols 31–32
African Development Bank 43
aggregate state-level scenario 90
aggressive industrialisation 99, 101
agricultural livelihoods 118
agricultural productivity 116–119
agricultural resources 65
agriculture–climate interface 48
aleatoric uncertainty 13–14, 28, 29
anishchit 95
anti-politics machine 129
apocalypse 16
astronomic signals 143
atmospheric phenomenon 103
attribution 42–44
Automatic Weather Stations (AWS) 37

Berkes, F. 45, 46
Berkes, M. 45, 46
Bhattacharyya, D. 122, 131n3
Bhopas 61

Biodiversity Conservation Act 120
biophysical factors 50
biophysical stressors 102
Blanford, H. F. 74
Border Security Force (BSF) 88
Bose, S. 15
bridging gaps 12; actors 162; bureaucracies and extension services 164; co-producing knowledge 162; emerging dialogues stress 162; global abstraction 162; global/local paradigm 163; hybrid knowledge spheres 181; implications 163; knowledge-making 164–169; measurements 161; practice 163; roundtable engagement *161*; roundtables 169–179; scientific terminology 164
Brihanmumbai Municipal Corporation (BMC) 138, 149
Brihanmumbai Storm Water Drain System 147
Brown, S. 110
BSF *see* Border Security Force (BSF)
Burnes, A. 58
Burnes, J. 58
business as usual development 138

calamities 63
capacity building 176
capitalist economy 84
carbon-centric industrialisation 151

Index

Carey, M. 46, 165
casual labour 103
catastrophic events 130
CCD *see* Climate Change Department (CCD)
Chatterjee, B. 75
chronic flooding 187
citizen science 7, 9, 28, 165
civil society 179
civil society organisations (CSOs) 84, 126, 139
climate adaptation 5, 86, 92, 137
climate change: emissions 2; transformative pathways 150–152; *see also* uncertainty
climate change adaptation 149
Climate Change Department (CCD) 92
climate crisis 151
climate justice 190
climate knowledge 188
climate projections: natural fluctuations/internal variability 28–29; radiative forcing 29; scenario uncertainty 29
climate-sensitive livelihoods 4
climatic shocks 1
climatic threats 113
climatology 45, 166
coastal vulnerability assessment 90
Coen, D. 165
colonial administrative interventions 56
colonial administrative territory 59
colonial interventions 17
colonial officialdom 56
colonial scientific network 74
community-based organisations (CBOs) 111
compounded disasters 17
computer simulations 32
controlling floods 153–155
Conway, D. 108
cooperative system 76
corporate social responsibility (CSR) 99
COVID-19 102
crab catching 12, 120, 121
critical valuation exercises 180
crop diversification 163
crop productivity 117
CSOs *see* civil society organisations (CSOs)
CSR *see* corporate social responsibility (CSR)
cultivation methods 69
culture 19, 46, 77, 140
cyclones: depopulation, Sundarbans 72; devastating 74; devastating impacts 71; force 75; narrowed down uncertainty 44; report 74; storm waves 72, 73

Damodaran, V. 14, 17
deep uncertainty 29, 49, 50
deltaic ecology 18, 109
deltaic ecosystem 6, 170
disaster management 44, 139, 147, 152, 154
disaster response 129
discovering Kutch: barbaric and primitive polity 59; climate 59; climate-related events 63; coarse cereals 60; history 58; infrastructural interventions 60; irregular hill ranges 59; land and people observations 58; pastoralism and weather uncertainties 61–63; political coherence 57; port towns 61; sea customs 60; sea fossils 59; social spectrum 60; state and people 63–66
discursive networks 39
distress 64, 65
distress diversification 18; agricultural productivity 116–119; description 116; female-headed households 108; households 116; livelihood activities 108; livelihood portfolio 130; tiger and deep sea 119–121; wage labour and out-migration 116
donor agencies 126, 128, 129
Dosi, G. 39
Douglass, M. 17
downscaling 34–37, 45
droughts 84
dryland blindness 89
drylands 6, 12, 18
dwindling fishing economy 110
Dyson, F. 31

East India Company (EIC) 66, 71
Eaton, R. 112
ecological harmony 55
ecological knowledge 149
ecological systems 14
eco-sensitive zones 84, 170
Edwards, P. N. 31
Egidi, M. 39
Ellis, F. 116
embankment construction 67–68
emission inventories 32
environmental change: colonial authorities 56; cyclones, uncertainty and devastation 71–76; declensionist 55; discovering Kutch 57–65; epistemic (knowledge-making) 56; forestry against reclamation

68–71; ontological/aleatory dimensions 56; seasonal migration and mobility 57; South Asia 55; stability thesis 55; Sundarbans' migratory rivers and mobile people 66–68
environmental degradations 129
environmental histories *see* environmental change
environmental impact assessments (EIAs) 174
environmental normal 56
environmental politics 86
epistemic contrasts 3
epistemic networks 39
ethnographic exploration: Ghoramara 110–111; historical, political economic and ecological production 112–113; Mousuni 111
exclusionary development projects 155
experiential knowledge 187
expert knowledge 31

Fazl, A. 71, 72
female-headed households 108
Ferguson, J. 129
Few, R. 18, 138
financial networks 39
fishing communities 98
flood forecasting system 46–47
flooding, in Mumbai 27, 134–135
flood mitigation 156
flood-prone city 146–149
flood waters, Indian Sundarbans 1
food security 37
forest demarcation 69
forest resources 68
fragmentation 176–178
fudge factors 31

ganda bawal 95
Ganga–Brahmaputra–Meghna (GBM) 110
general circulation models (GCMs) 30, 31, 91
Ghosh, T. 111
Ghosh, U. 15, 127, 131n5
Girasias 60
globalising instinct 34
globalising reductionism 166
Goldman, M. 169
green economy 5
Greenhouse Gases (GHGs) 4, 30, 33
ground-level realities 111, 129, 179
Gujarat Institute of Desert Ecology (GUIDE) 90

Hallegatte, S. 29
Hamilton, D. 76
hard science gaining authority 31
Harms, A. 126, 129
Hastrup, K. 45
havamaan 93, 94
Hawkins, E. 28
Heisenberg's Uncertainty Principle 13
Henckell, T. 67
Heymann, M. 45
high-yielding varieties (HYV) 118
history, Kutch *58*
Hulme, M. 93
human–environment system 137
human–nature relations 189
human resource development 126
hybrid alliances 188
hybrid knowledges 46, 48
hydrological resource assessments/planning 7
HYV *see* high-yielding varieties (HYV)

Ibrahim, F. 89
imperfect knowledge 39
Inamee 60
Indian context 4–6, 169–170
Indian Meteorological Department (IMD) 34, 38, 91
India's climate diplomacy 6
Indian Sundarbans *1*, 8, 107–131
indigenous knowledge (IK) systems 11, 45–46, 94
industrialisation 11, 151
inequity 3
informal economy 140
information providers 92
iniquitous development approach 148
institutional capacities 56
institutional complexity 176–178
institutional uncertainties 149–150
instrumental co-production 168
Intended Nationally Determined Contributions (INDCs) 5
interdisciplinary research 48, 171
interviewed residents 142
IPCC 32

Jasanoff, S. 6, 56, 181

Khyratee 60
Kjosavik, D. J. 15
knowledge/epistemic uncertainties 28, 29
knowledge-making: constructing bridges 166–167; co-production and bridging

168–169; opening and closing down plural practices 165–166; practices 164; visibility and attribution 167–168
knowledge politics 7, 14–16, 138
Kutch: climate-related events 63; climate variability 85; coastal infrastructure projects 83; disaster reconstruction 99; discovering 57–66; drylands 36; ecological rhythm 84; erratic rainfall 14; fragile eco-system 77; geographical sites 86; history 58; industrial expansion 32; local communities 15; pastoral community 8; pastoralists 57; spatial injustice 5; transition landscape 88–89; *see also* Sundarbans

land fertility 117
land reform process 113
land use change 33
livelihood uncertainties 108; climate shock 115; distress diversification 116–121; ecological vulnerabilities 114–115
livelihoods *see individual entries*
livestock composition 96
livestock rearing 88
local cosmologies: livelihoods 95–98; monsoon patterns 95; resource insecurities 95; social groups 94

Macmurdo, J. 57
macro-level framings 108
Maharashtra Forest Department and Maharashtra Pollution Control Board (MSPCB) 139
maladaptation 11, 18
maldharis 97
male-dominated research 50
Malet, A. 61, 64
mangroves 101, 140, 149–150, 153–155, 173, *186*
marginal environments 6, 56, 57, 76, 130
marginalisation 3, 5
market *vs.* climate change: adaptive capacity 85; aggressive industrialisation 84; business activities 84; coastal infrastructure projects 83; droughts 84; methodology 86–88; politics and perspective 89–102; punishment post for bureaucrats 84; radical uncertainty and transformation 85–86; seasonal cycles 84
Mazel-Cabasse, C. 165
media fraternity 127
megacities 10
Mehta, L. 10, 15, 174, 179
Mehtta, M. 122, 131n3

MGNREGA 5
microclimates 40, 90
Miller, M. A. 17
Ministry of Earth Sciences (MoESs) 43, 48
Mithi River Development and Protection Authority (MRDPA) 138
mitigation policy options 152
mixed methods 8
mobile people 66–68
modelling uncertainty 32–34
MoESs *see* Ministry of Earth Sciences (MoESs)
mono-cropping-based agriculture 110
Movik, S. 10, 15, 18
Mukhopadhyay, A. 110
Mumbai Metropolitan Region Development Authority (MMRDA) 138, 149, 152

National Action Plan on Climate Change (NAPCC) 5
National Centre for Medium Range Forecast (NCMRF) 48
National Disaster Response Force (NDRF) 147
National Environmental Engineering Research Institute (NEERI) 139
natural disasters 73
natural resources 110
natural variability 34
neo-liberal growth paradigms 151
non-governmental organisations (NGOs) 111, 126, 139
non-linear dynamic systems 31
noxious vapours 60

observational data integration 29
Ohdedar, B. 113
organic farming 118
out-migration 124–125

pardes 89
participatory methodologies 162
participatory rural appraisal technique 111
pastoral community 8
pastoralism 18, 61–63, *83*, 85
pastoral system 94
Pelling, M. 86
people-centric approach 128
performative networks 39
photovoice engagement 12
Piddington, H. 74–76
planning development: concretisation 144, 145; disaster preparedness 144; 26/7 event 143; health hazards 143; land

reclamation 146; lived memory 144; respondents 145; state agencies 144; unregulated residential colonies 145; warning systems 144; waterlogging 143
plural knowledge systems 46
policy debates 28
policy discourses 17
policy environments 50
policymaking 27–28, 49, 162
policy planning 92
policy shapers 92
political economy 16–17, 28, 29, 93, 103, 127–129, 149, 156
political exigencies 153
political networks 39
politics of zoom 34
Postans, M. 59
postscript 130–131
poverty alleviation 92
power imbalances 5, 187
power inequity 5
powerlessness 3, 11, 152
precarious fishing, Indian Sundarbans *107*
private–public partnership 155
proletarianisation 108, 118
property rights systems 112
prosopis juliflora 95–97

qualitative assessments 29

radiative forcing 29, 51n1
radical–critical adaptation 130
radical uncertainty 4, 11, 18, 85–86, 102, 136, 143, 156, 187
Raikes, S. N. 59
RCMs *see* regional climate models (RCMs)
RCPs *see* representative concentration pathways (RCPs)
regional climate models (RCMs) 36
regional variation 93
renewable energy 84
re-orient value systems 86
representative concentration pathways (RCPs) 48
resource-dependent communities 93
resource distribution 5
restoring pastoral livelihoods 100–101
retainer wall construction 187
revenue realisation 64
Ribot, J. 85, 137
risk pooling mechanism 176
robust decision-making 28, 45
roundtables: academic discourses 170; attribution, causality and (deflection of) responsibility 174; climate-related uncertainty 170; diverse epistemologies and framings 171–173; ecological resources 171; events 29; Indian context 169–170; institutional complexity and fragmentation 176–178; knowledge and integration, lived experience 174–176; knowledge/insufficient communication 178–179; photovoice presentations 171; politics of valuation 173–174; power differentials 171; sharing and learning 171
Rudiak-Gould, P. 163, 167
Rudra, K. 122
rural communities, Kutch 83

salinity intrusion 120
Sardar Sarovar project 87
Schiller, F. 71, 76
science *see individual entries*
science and technology studies (STS) 9, 168
science–policy communications 10
science–policy interface 38
scientific assessments 30
Scoones, I. 18, 116
sea level rise (SLR) 109
seasonal migration 96, 131, 163
sedentarisation 65
self-help groups (SHGs) 126
semi-structured interviews 86
SEZs *see* Special Economic Zones (SEZs)
shimmering 31
shorter *vs.* longer timescales 29
shrinking development funds 99
Singh, R. 36
site description 87–88
skill/capacity development 126
SLR *see* sea level rise (SLR)
snowballing 138
social activist 150
social differentiation 87
social evolution 127
social exposures 113
social impact assessments (SIAs) 174
social justice 86, 148, 189
social life of models 45
social media 126
social systems 34
social transformation 172, 176
social vulnerability 4
socio-ecological diversity 4
socio-ecological system 109–110
socio-economic dynamics 7
socio-economic marginalisation 170
socio-political disturbances 109

socio-political uncertainties: competitive electoral politics 123; concrete embankments 122; disasters-in-waiting 121; displacement scale 121; embankment failures 121; erosion-prone zones 123; extreme weather events 122; households 124; livelihood inequities 122; local communities 123; sustainable approach 122
spaces of capitalist transition 89
spatial injustice 5
Special Economic Zones (SEZs) 84, 88
Srivastava, S. 5, 15
State Action Plans on Climate Change (SAPCC) 5
state/district-level planning 92
stressors 1, 17, 90
structural change 3
structural inequalities 102
structural interventions 156
Sundarbans: climate policymaking 127–129; climatic and ecological challenges 108; colonial authorities 56; cyclone 71–73; dynamic environments 43; early survey and mapping 66; financial results 69; health system 127; migratory rivers and mobile people 66–68; precarity and livelihood insecurity 12; productive geography 76; tiger deaths 74; wastelands 70; *see also* Kutch
super wicked problem/monster 2, 27
supply chain disruptions 148
sustainability 6, 126, 190
sustainable adaptation 5
sustained engagement 188
Sutton, R. 28

Tata Institute of Social Sciences (TISS) 139
Taylor, M. 130
techno-centric approach 15, 86
techno-management 46
techno-managerial solutions 17
tenancy contracts 113
time horizons 29
transformation 85–86, 99–100
transformative politics/pathways 17–19, 150–152, 188, 189

transformative strategies 7
transition 88–89, 109–110

uncertain models 30–32
uncertainty: definition 2; dimensions 13–17; environmental histories (*see* environmental change); heuristics 9–13; hybrid knowledges and social understandings 44–49; manage and cope 28; policy and public debates 38–42; reducing and mastering 28; understandings 30–37; *see also* climate change
universalist planning modes 157
unscientific grazing patterns 101
urban agglomerations 137, 169
urban development 10, 33
urban environment 6
urban governance 138
urban Mumbai: climate change 140–141; coastal megalopolis 136; conceptual framework 137–138; coping and adaptation strategies 135; ecological uncertainties 138; flooding 134–135; Koli fishers *135*; maximum city 139–140; methodology and study sites 138–139; microcosm 136; Mithi deluge 134; politics and perspectives 141–143; radical uncertainty 136; socio-economic characteristics 135; socio-economic profile 136; structural measures 136
urban precipitation 36

vector-borne diseases 37
Vijay, V. 140
vulnerability *see individual entries*
vulnerable environments 173
vulnerable groups 3

Walker, W. 85
Walker, W. E. 2
warrior castes 87
wastelands 68, 70
water resources 76
water security 37
weather forecasting 37, 38
weather uncertainties 61–63
Wynne, B. 16